CLUB FED

POWER, MONEY, SEX, AND VIOLENCE ON CAPITOL HILL

BILL THOMAS

CHARLES SCRIBNER'S SONS

New York   London   Toronto   Sydney   Tokyo   Singapore

CHARLES SCRIBNER'S SONS
Rockefeller Center
1230 Avenue of the Americas
New York, New York 10020

Manufactured in the United States of America

1 3 5 7 9 10 8 6 4 2

Library of Congress Cataloging-in-Publication Data
Thomas, Bill, 1943– .
Club Fed: Power, money, sex, and violence on Capitol Hill / Bill
Thomas.
p.   cm.
1. United States. Congress. 2. Lobbying—United States. 3. Pressure
groups—United States. 4. Capitol Hill (Washington, D.C.)   I. Title.
JK1118.T35   1994
328.73'078—dc20   94-13516
CIP

ISBN 0-684-19635-2

For Brendan

CONTENTS

ACKNOWLEDGMENTS

Many of those who contributed material assistance to this book must remain more or less nameless. But I would like to thank the following people for their time, tips, and *ad hoc* encouragement: Tim Burger, Graydon Carter, Charles Cook, Clay Felker, Karen Foerstel, Jim Glassman, Jeff Goldberg, Ira Gorbunova, Roy and Jewel Grutman, Christopher Hitchens, Phil Hough, Bret Israel, Mary Jocoby, Bob Kaper, Todd Kliman, Larry Leamer, Jim Link, Dick and Diana McLellan, Dan Moldea, Viktoria Nicoulina, Jayne O'Donnell, Mark Perry, Mark Plotkin, Henry Porter, Peter Range, Alexander and Lena Romanov, Larry Sabato, Glenn Simpson, Sandy Stencel, Volodya and Luba Sterlikov, I. F. Stone (RIP), Frank Sturgis (ibid.), Michael Thomas, Pat Towell, Bill Triplett, Rick Whittle, Nick Williams, Jr., Craig Winneker, Winston, Sid Yudain, the staff of the Washington Historical Society, and the *Congressional Quarterly* politburo.

Special thanks, as always, to *uber*agent Henry Dunow, to Bill Goldstein of Scribners for his timely infusions of insight and capital, and to Belle.

CLUB FED

LOCATION IS EVERYTHING

Lunchtime for Congress was just beginning, but there was already a traffic jam outside the Palm restaurant that had horns honking a block and a half away. In the city that made "influence peddling" a job description, few things bring the talent together like a midday fix of back slapping and cholesterol. Heart attacks, IRS crackdowns—nothing can stop this most basic of all inside-the-Beltway traditions. After a while you get the distinct impression if anything ever came close, the entire legislative branch of government would shut down.

There is a widespread yet misguided belief that the nation's capital is a cold and unfriendly place, when just the opposite is true. With an estimated 149 lobbyists for every single member of Congress, it would be hard to find a more convivial ambiance anywhere, or a better example of the axiom in political science that money and power always seek their own level.

The Palm caters to both. In a ritual unchanged by reforms, the maître d' greets customers at the door and leads them to their favorite tables, which often happen to be right under full-color drawings of their very own faces. The effect is a little like having reservations at the Sistine Chapel. Three feet above the dessert cart is a smiling likeness of ex-Ambassador to Moscow Robert Strauss, the city's most ubiquitous Mr. Fix-it. Not far away is the late Hale Boggs, once the House Majority Leader, now famous for being the father of superlobbyist Tommy Boggs, whose visage is also on display. Boggs's onetime partner Ron Brown, the Secretary of Commerce, is there, and so is a large congressional contingent, including living legends from the Senate like Alfonse D'Amato and Bill Bradley pictured right beside House Speaker Tip O'Neill, who worked the room on a regular basis right up to the time he died.

Throw in a few hundred more honorees from law, finance, and *Larry King Live*, and what you have is a wall-to-wall picture of Washington's deal-making elite, past and present overeaters-in-residence at America's most immovable feast.

This is a book about Capitol Hill, not VIP dining, at least, not VIP dining in the usual sense. It's about the relationship of the Hill to many special interests, and about how those interests are joined at the wallet to 535 congressional profit centers. Just the same, it's no coincidence that feeding plays such a key role in the process. Like the stomach in the digestive system, Congress is where valuable incoming nutrients are separated from outgoing waste. A power lunch is merely lunch until muscles and enzymes convert it into fuel to run the body. The World's Most Deliberative Body works the same way.

Capitol Hill, however, is more than the action of internal organs on the special of the day. It is a whole anatomy of egos and ambitions vying with each other for their share of sustenance. To examine the Hill from inside out is to follow a trail that leads through political back rooms, past favor seekers and shake-down artists into a self-contained community that's part Hollywood, part Peoria, and part someplace you don't want to be after dark.

"Capitol Hill is unique," observed local historian Maryann Overbeck. "It's a wonderful little town right in the heart of a big one."

"Wonderful" may not be the right word to describe any section of a city that regularly tops the charts in annual per-capita homicides. Still, Overbeck is right. The Hill *is* a small town, the most powerful small town in the world.

If location is everything, few places cover more psychic real estate than Capitol Hill. Money, power, sex, and violence come with the territory. Where else could an armed robbery, final passage of a big tax bill, and a front page call-girl or call-boy scandal all happen at the same time—and on the same block?

Books about Congress tend to separate official business from other local activity. In this one I've tried to take a different approach, exploring the multiple cultures of a neighborhood that includes two of the three branches of government as well as dozens of other pursuits, both legal and otherwise, that flourish right next door.

The Hill is where drug dealers can make more money than drug company lobbyists, campaign consultants double as character assassins, and after a hard day of dodging the press and harassing their staffs, lawmakers unwind by indulging their wildest fantasies, as Sen. Ted Kennedy, the chunk-style Massachusetts Democrat, did when he showed up at his 1993 Christmas party dressed as Barney the dinosaur. "They don't call me Tyrannosaurus *sex* for nothing," he said.

Two distinct Washingtons meet on Capitol Hill: one run by and for pampered elected officials and another that would be just like the rest of America, if the rest of America had two lawyers for every five people and an epidemic of violent street crime.

But let's be fair to the criminal element. The Hill gains the biggest part of its bad reputation directly from Congress, which, to angry voters nationwide, is the main source of everything wrong with a country that's $4 trillion in debt.

The House and Senate have become synonymous with getting fleeced—and for good reason. During election campaigns candidates rail against Washington waste and vow to cut spending. Then once they're safely in Congress, they spend more money than ever before, and, to add insult to injury, they do it on coast-to-coast cable TV.

Capitol Hill. Few words in current events cause more uninhibited resentment. Polls indicate disdain for Washington politicians is at an all-time high. Yet the thing that has people so upset isn't only the rampant abuse of power. It's the realization that their duly elected representatives want nothing to do with them.

"There is a tremendous feeling of alienation out there," said pollster Alan F. Kay, who conducted a recent survey in which half of those questioned thought members of Congress should be picked in a random drawing from lists of registered voters. "Politicians only pay lip service to the will of the people. The truth is that the great majority of them have little or no interest in anything the people think."

Except when it comes time to count votes.

Consider, for a moment, the most essential of all congressional concerns: running for reelection. Ever since the Supreme Court ruled that campaign spending, as a form of protected speech, cannot be restricted, the federal government has handed out millions of dollars to political candidates. From 1985 to 1992, Republican Sen. Mitch McConnell spent over $2 million in government funds all by himself, sending promotional junk mail to his Kentucky constituents. And McConnell is considered a reformer. Actually, he's earned the distinction. Many of his colleagues have spent a lot more.

With Congress acting as its own financial cop in these matters, it's easy to see why there's so little sentiment among lawmakers for self-improvement. The fact that nine out of every ten incumbents get reelected obviously has something to do with it. So does the nature of the congressional beast itself, which has mutated into a bicameral Godzilla.

All great horror movies have a scene where some well-meaning scientist tries to reason with the monster. He usually gets treated like snack food, but that's the idea. The monster is bigger than science, and follows no law except its own ravenous need to metabolize everything in sight.

In Washington, the monster is Congress, and the scientist is anyone who thinks he can stop it.

Congress has become the government. Congressional committees, subcommittees, and commissions have taken over most of the duties of the executive branch. Cabinet secretaries report to Congress. Agency heads, bureau directors, and intelligence chiefs all receive their stamp of approval from Congress. And when the president or anyone else does something Congress doesn't like, it sicks a special prosecutor on him.

One way or another, lawmakers always seem to get their man. With Democrats and Republicans on the Hill calling for an investigation of his involvement in the Whitewater scandal, Bill Clinton had his own special prosecutor appointed. But the effort at avoiding a congressional hearing only made matters worse. After the administration admitted the president's staff was regularly briefed on the probe, Clinton was accused of a coverup, his chief White House lawyer resigned, and soon even more members were saying Congress should step in.

Every American schoolchild is taught that the federal government is based on a system of checks and balances. The problem in recent years is that the balance has taken a radical tilt toward Capitol Hill.

Typical of every new president, Clinton likes to talk about reinventing government. But first, he'll have to regain control of it from Congress, and that won't be easy. During the past generation of bitter adversarial dealings with the executive branch, members of Congress have legislated themselves into every aspect of the governing process. The supposed aim is to ensure that money earmarked for constituents gets delivered as intended. The practical effect is an oversight syndrome that puts the entire federal apparatus under congressional control.

Good luck to the cabinet secretary who tries to eliminate federal benefits for jobless sugar workers in Hawaii and has to do battle with Sen. Daniel Inouye, the state's most powerful Democrat. The same goes for anyone questioning the fat subsidies paid to farmers for *not* growing wheat and comes face to face with Senate Minority Leader Robert Dole, the Kansas Republican who's made protecting his state's agricultural economy a personal crusade.

When the Bush administration proposed dropping a few

dozen jobs from Veterans Administration facilities in Texas, former House member Edward Derwinski, who headed the Department of Veterans' Affairs at the time, was immediately summoned to the Hill by angry state lawmakers for a full explanation. Terms like "gridlock" and "bottleneck" take on a whole new meaning to administration officials who spend half their time in Washington trying to placate congressional committees.

To be successful with lawmakers, a chief executive has to be "feared" or "revered," said Kenneth Duberstein, White House congressional liaison under Ronald Reagan. Most presidents, despite elaborate efforts, end up being neither. As a result, those who don't get along with Congress are often punished with probes and indictments. But even those who cooperate may learn to regret it, as they watch their term in office become a four-year opening act for hundreds of House and Senate media hogs.

Maybe Rep. Fred Grandy, a Republican from Iowa, who starred as "Gopher" on the TV series *Loveboat*, best defined the attention-getting clout that goes with his job.

"I'm still 'Gopher,'" Grandy told an interviewer for *Entertainment Tonight*. "Only now, I'm 'Gopher' on the Ways and Means Committee."

In an atmosphere thick with the lust for stardom, Congress has become America's most expensive dramatic vehicle. Members will go to any lengths, pay any price to make news. Costly overseas missions are one favorite method. Making fools of themselves is another. GOP Rep. Jim Nussle, also from Iowa, once gave a speech on the House floor while wearing a paper bag over his head. No one remembers what he said. But everyone remembers the bag and that Nussle was reelected the following year by a comfortable margin.

Because their livelihoods depend on staying in office, rookie lawmakers learn quickly that the only bad publicity is an obituary. During the 1992 freshmen orientation the largest class of House newcomers in nearly fifty years heard one speaker advise them to:

(a) find and/or create an issue, cause, or crisis

(b) condense it into a ten-second sound bite

(c) be on television as often as possible.

The trick to getting reelected, new members soon discover, isn't just raising money. It's raising anxiety. The electorate likes public officials who respond well to emergencies. So what smart lawmakers do is invent their own, then manage them in ways that inspire funding, good press, and support at the polls. On the Hill, appearance isn't just confused with reality, it *is* reality.

The theatrics, though, aren't confined to members of Congress. Over the years, Capitol Hill has become a magnate for irate demonstrators of every type and tendency. Whether it's animal rights marchers pouring blood on the Capitol steps or trans-gender activists parading in leather and chains past the Supreme Court, the Hill mixes politics and performance art in ways that demand air time. Watch a representative from Wisconsin milking a cow for a hometown news crew, and you're seeing a politician in his true element. Watch the whole Senate draining the economy on C-Span, and you're seeing an ensemble company of politicians in their true element.

When Congress rejected his $16 billion "stimulus" package, a proposal that stimulated almost no one, Bill Clinton, then only 100 days on the job, admitted he'd been outsmarted. "I guess I have a lot to learn about Capitol Hill," he lamented.

History is full of useful lessons. Study them, as Clinton eventually did, and one begins to detect the same familiar craving for power, money, and sole possession of first place that have always made political neighborhoods a mystery to new arrivals, especially new arrivals who try to upstage the veterans.

After visiting the Pacific island of Samoa (whose lone congressional delegate not long ago was granted semirestricted voting privileges on the House floor), anthropologist Margaret Mead wrote that life there was an ongoing public drama in which all Samoans played a part. As they do everywhere, politicians took the lead roles, and in her 1928 classic, *Coming of Age in Samoa*, Mead recounted how a typical one spent his time:

"His main preoccupation is the affairs of the village. His main diversion, hours spent in ceremonious argument in some meeting. . . . The less ambitious rest on this achievement. The more ambitious continue to try for higher titles, for greater prestige as craftsmen or orators, for control of more strings in the political game."

And when they achieve seniority status?

They sit with a select few, Mead noted, "and drink kava . . . or stay at home and guard the house while others go inland to the plantations. . . . They braid *cinet* and give advice, or in the final perverse assertion of authority, fail to give it."

Based on her extensive research, Mead concluded that all politics is local—and universally cut-throat. A Samoan power broker "cannot acquire a reputation then let his guard down or another claimant to the same title will take advantage of his indolence and pass him in the race," she wrote. Therefore, the goal of every village politico who wants to stay at the top of his game is "the steady demonstration of increasing . . . superiority over his fellows."

Substitute fund-raisers for kava parties, add nasty campaigns and saturation press coverage, and Mead has provided a perfect description of what takes place every day on Capitol Hill.

In Washington, as in Samoa, politics is inseparable from the daily life of the community. Congress for that matter all but runs the town, having final approval of the city's laws and budget. Congressional control over Washington is so complete that aspirants to the city council regularly campaign against Capitol Hill the same as any shrewd candidate for the House or Senate would.

The Founding Fathers created the District of Columbia as a federal enclave where politics could be conducted in a spirit of thoughtful compromise. Dangerous concentrations of power would be prevented, they believed, by subdividing government into three equal parts, with ambitious men in one part held in check by ambitious men in the other two. It all made perfect sense on paper. What no one had anticipated was that conflicting ambitions might get in the way, or that the eighteenth century's devotion to precise public discourse would be replaced by felonious congressionalese.

Washington, which began as a swamp, has never lost touch with its roots, and lawmakers, when they're not slinging mud, are usually clouding the water with self-serving double talk: A "fact-finding mission" translates into a paid vacation; "constituent communication" is subsidized campaign mail; and a "district service period" means a four-day weekend.

The hard part about being in Congress isn't the actual work. It's figuring out ways to make all the freeloading that goes on *sound* like work.

This book contains no plan for reducing the deficit, raising economic incentives, or solving any of the other problems that assault our sense of national purpose. Which makes it a lot like Congress, where increasing amounts of time and money are spent on things far more entertaining, such as crash-testing pollen, rerouting rivers, and converting the aurora borealis into electricity. The latter undertaking is a pet project of Sen. Ted Stevens, a Republican from Alaska, and it's already cost U.S. taxpayers millions in R&D grants.

But that's Capitol Hill during office hours. Given the many hair-brained schemes and oddball personalities it produces, it's easy to forget this is also a real place with crime, unemployment, and homelessness. Every problem in the country is a problem on the Hill too, in most cases elevated by the prestigious zip code into a far worse version of the same ill elsewhere. Picture members of Congress surrounded by all the wrongs they promised to right the minute they got to Washington, and you begin to appreciate why most learn it's easier to attack one another than the issues.

Congress is under siege, not just by muggers, beggars, and

registered agents of foreign governments, but by constituents all over America. First there were term limits, then campaign reforms. The things that worry lawmakers most are always the ones that directly threaten their earning potential. Lately voters have been producing even more ominous rumbles of discontent, rumbles noticed by career White House adviser David Gergen, who gave this assessment of why everyone's so angry with Washington: "The city is full of too many privileged people. . . . They have a lot of money. They have a lot of power, and they are *not* working together. . . . It's a scandal."

Gergen's other points notwithstanding, the scandal is that they *are* working together, working to keep their privileges, money, and power as long as they can.

It would be tempting to blame this "conspiracy" on the system, and to some extent it would be right. But that would let a principal accomplice off the hook. Namely us.

Members of Congress don't get their jobs through the mail. They win them in open, often honest, elections in which ordinary citizens select somebody they like over somebody they don't like and send him or her to Washington as their representative. For years it was a relatively simple matter. Voters chose the politicians who promised them more for less—more services, more benefits, and *less* taxes. Bad government isn't just the work of a deceitful few. It also requires great multitudes willing to be deceived.

As the recession forced changes in the standard campaign spiel, the election theme became less for more—less services, less benefits, and *more* taxes. Voters not only felt cheated, they wanted revenge. And if many of them are the same ones who still want government to give them more than they're willing or able to pay for . . . well, no one ever said the voting public was motivated by a sense of economic realism.

An astute hack I know once called Congress "America's longest running ego trip." Egos remain the driving force on Capitol Hill, but the signal has gone out to circle the limos.

It would be foolish to underestimate the resolve on the other side of the tinted glass. This is the United States Congress, collectively the most firmly entrenched, fully funded special interest group there is, and members are not going to give up a single golf tournament without a fight.

"If men were angels," wrote the authors of *The Federalist Papers*, "no government would be necessary."

There's something to think about. Suppose for a minute that men *were* angels, that representative government as we know it today *was* unnecessary. That means there would be no Senate Ethics Committee, no House Bank, no Ball-Bearing Caucus, no Dan Rostenkowski indictment, no soft money, no lobbyists, no PACs, no Packwood diaries, no Keating Five, no Gang of Seven, and no ten or twelve guys in Congress, with the fate of the nation in their hands, named "Sonny" and "Bud."

. . . And just think of all the fun we'd be missing.

CHAPTER ONE

CONGRESS 911

Rita Warren has been at it for twelve, maybe thirteen, years. She can't remember exactly how long. What she does know is that God told her to be on Capitol Hill each day Congress is in session, and that's exactly where she's been. Which gives her a better attendance record than most elected officials paid to be there.

Every morning, rain or shine, through snow storms and heat waves, Warren takes her position on the Capitol steps with a life-size mannikin made up to look like Jesus Christ. The figure, dressed in a white toga with a wig and fake beard, is a reminder to members of Congress, Warren said, that they should "try to be good," though she conceded that some will always fall prey to temptation.

"You know what makes them bad?" asked the 70-year-old grandmother. "It's the apathy of the people. If people don't like what politicians are doing, they should come here to see them in action. . . . When they know somebody's watching, that's when they behave."

Warren is right about the need for constant vigilance. But on the Hill, separating good behavior from bad is not always easy.

Every action in the House and Senate is presumably meant to benefit somebody somewhere. Yet what's good for one congressional constituency is often bad for others. Payoffs to this group can mean layoffs for that; giveaways here equal cutbacks there.

Government exists to collect and distribute money, and Congress is where decisions about who gets what are made. Moral questions rarely figure into the equation, and when they do, it's usually for show. After opening a 1993 session of the House with a prayer for the victims of the Mississippi River floods, members of both parties got to work by pledging to send immediate assistance. They ended by attaching and detaching so many amendments to a flood relief bill that it was stalled in debate for weeks before the folks treading water got any help.

The most blatant "gimme" was a $50-million addition to something called the Youth Fair Chance Program stuffed into the flood package by Rep. Maxine Waters, a California Democrat. Waters's proposal redefined a disadvantaged teenager as anybody between the ages of 14 and 30 and authorized paying weekly stipends of $100 to those enrolled in federally funded vocational classes. The plan provided no sandbags, no bulldozers or anything else to hold back the raging Mississippi. But with Congress in a crisis-response mode and preparing to write a big check, linking extraneous amendments to emergency legislation is standard practice.

Lawmakers love when disaster strikes, since relief funds—or supplemental appropriations—never have to be paid for by cutbacks in other spending programs. And best of all, there's no law that says the money even has to be spent on disasters. Since 1990, Congress has appropriated over $13 billion in aid for the victims of floods, fires, and tornados. The Los Angeles earthquake of 1994 could end up costing that much all by itself. But like other supplemental appropriations, the congressional earthquake relief bill contained millions of dollars in non-earthquake spending for highway construction, education, and peacekeeping in Somalia.

Outgoing Senate Majority Leader George Mitchell from Maine got $1.4 million for potato farmers in his state. Sen. Fritz Hollings, a South Carolina Democrat, got another million for a Charleston maritime museum. And Democratic Sen. Daniel Moynihan from New York got over $10 million to renovate

Penn Station. The L.A. earthquake registered big dividends from coast to coast.

The money Waters wanted was needed, she said, to encourage the hard-core unemployed, like gang members in her South Central Los Angeles district, to attend classes where they could learn new job skills, among them, obviously, the art of ripping off the government for a hundred bucks a week. The consequences of not funding her program, she warned, could be an outbreak of rioting and looting all across the country.

For days Congress haggled over spending requests, while Ol' Man River continued claiming everything in his path. In the Midwest whole towns and villages disappeared, but nothing could be done about it until special interests on Capitol Hill were sorted out and satisfied. When the process was finally completed, Waters's amendment and the flood relief measure it became part of both passed.

"Gridlock," the term used to describe why Congress doesn't work, is the result not of inaction, as commonly assumed, but of hyperactive spending frenzies. Liberals and conservatives, moderates and radicals are all pork-barrel pragmatists where federal funding is concerned. If they weren't, they wouldn't stick around long. And once someone's been elected to Congress, sticking around is a full-time job.

Every fiscal year, the House and Senate have to decide how to spend nearly a trillion dollars. The appropriations process, as it's called, goes on from January to October, and the goal of each member is to bring home as much of that trillion dollars as possible. All other congressional chores are secondary to this one crucial activity. Being on the right committees and subcommittees helps, but with allocations based as much on timing and applied dramatic skills as anything else, it's important for lawmakers to surround their pitch for money with an appropriate sense of crisis.

A normal work week in Congress begins on Tuesday morning and ends on Thursday afternoon. Any senator or representative

will tell you that most of those three days is taken up with constituent service, an activity that covers doing all the little things
that being in public office demands, as well as the big things
staying there makes absolutely necessary. A little thing might be
tracking down someone's lost Social Security check. Whereas
big things can range from the semi-large, like Waters's $50 mil-
lion gang rehabilitation program, to the truly enormous, like the
now defunct Superconducting Supercollider, an $11 billion
excuse for sending federal funds to Texas.

Delivering the goods to constituents begins with delivering
speeches, the basic tool for stirring up a crisis and gaining the
all-important network attention needed to transform it into a
fundworthy cause.

It all starts with claiming time on the congressional video
docket and disturbing the monotonous blab of daily business
with something that makes viewers take notice. The Senate,
which resisted cable TV for more than two years after the
House went live, is still too stuffy and self-righteous to be good
television. The main problem is a speaking style so full of professional courtesies that it's hard to sound excited or angry
about anything. Senators refer to each another as *my able
friend from someplace* or *my esteemed and distinguished colleague from someplace else*. Still, on occasion the rhetorical
decorum is forgotten and real theater breaks through. Which is
what happened in 1993, when Sen. Carol Moseley-Braun, a
freshman Democrat from Illinois, seized on an obscure patent
controversy and turned it into an crisis situation of prime-time
proportions.

What got her started was Republican Sen. Jesse Helms of
North Carolina. By a vote of 52 to 48, the Senate had followed
Helms's advice and agreed to extend the patent on a Civil War
flag symbol used by the United Daughters of the Confederacy.
"Most of these 24,000 delightful ladies," Helms said of the
organization, "live in the few remaining rest homes established
decades ago to care for the widows and daughters of Confederate soldiers." The flag patent, he explained, was only intended

to provide them with a few meager earnings in the twilight of their golden years.

Braun, the Senate's first black female member, had nothing against the old ladies, but the idea of the Senate voting to put "its imprimatur" on the Confederate flag set her off on a tirade. There was more at stake here than conflicting impressions of the Civil War. By taking on the Senate's most flaming right-winger, Braun, a newcomer with seven months' experience, wasn't just positioning herself to attract liberal campaign contributions. She was letting her senior colleagues know that if they didn't cut her a bigger piece of funding the next time she asked, they could be in for the same treatment she was about to give Helms.

"I am going to call it like I see it, as I always do," she said. "I was appalled, appalled at a segment of my own Democratic Party that would go take a walk and vote for something like this."

The former Cook County recorder of deeds promised to hold the floor until "this room freezes over." The issue was racism, she said, and even before she started reading from a 130-year-old pro-slavery speech by Alexander Stephens, the vice-president of the Confederacy and a former U.S. senator, many of her colleagues knew they were watching a made-for-TV emergency in the making.

"You know," she told her listeners, "I am really stunned by how often and how much the issue of race, the subject of racism . . . comes up in this body, and I have to . . . constrain myself to be calm, to be laid back, to talk about these issues in very intellectual, nonemotional terms. . . ."

Braun was unloading on Senate white guys, and Democratic lawmakers who had voted to kill the Helms amendment were piling on as fast as they could get in front of a C-Span camera.

"I support my dear friend and colleague," said Sen. Patty Murray from Washington. "I know her sense of frustration. I recognize her outrage. As a woman, I share her same understanding of her situation."

New York Sen. Daniel Moynihan, the Senate's chief left-of-center intellectual, called Braun's speech "an epiphany, a sudden shining through of an internal reality that had not been there."

Sen. Joseph Biden of Delaware, whose Senate Judiciary Committee had been the target of considerable criticism for its grilling of Anita Hill during the Clarence Thomas confirmation hearings, offered a blanket plea of ignorance for all those who had supported Helms. "I think that the vast majority of our colleagues who voted against the position of the senator from Illinois did so without really thinking this through."

Even Republicans knew they'd been beaten by Braun's bold frontal assault. In a matter of minutes, she had converted an ordinary day at the office into a political sensitivity session that had surprised liberals, embarrassed conservatives, and given her career a tactical boost that could yield solid dividends for years to come. The performance also paid off in more immediate terms by putting a stop to Illinois news stories that the state's newest senator was disappointing supporters by taking too many vacations and neglecting her work.

Most senators, it was clear by now, had no idea what they were voting on. Which is the way Congress usually works, only this time members were being forced one by one to admit it, or else be branded white supremacists in a story that was sure to lead every evening newscast in America.

Leave it to Sen. Paul Simon, also from Illinois, to let those who voted for the patent extension know the kind of bad karma they were courting. "When I see a pickup truck driving down the highways of Illinois with a Confederate battle flag on the back . . . I know that is not a symbol of understanding," said Simon, his prominent earlobes flapping with indignation.

At last, the Republicans sent Sen. Robert Bennett from Utah to the floor with their official surrender message. "We did not realize the implications of what had just happened," said Bennett, confessing he had circulated among GOP members, asking, "Do you understand what we have just done? . . . And they said no."

Bennett requested a reconsideration of the measure, and when a new vote was taken, Helms's amendment was defeated by a wide margin. Despite an embarrassing federal probe of her campaign finances, the win earned Braun a promotion to the lucrative status of crisis manager and handed Jesse Helms a humiliating defeat.

Maxine Waters and Carol Moseley-Braun wouldn't have been in Congress a generation ago, and here they were not only members of the club, but using the same techniques as the veterans to leverage money and power. It was too much for good old boys like Helms to take, and when he saw Braun in the Senate elevator the day after her great triumph, he exploded into an angry rendition of "Dixie."

On the surface, the House and Senate have about as much in common as the Rotary Club and the Trilateral Commission. More than one quarter of the Senate is made up of millionaires, and most of its 100 members strut around the Hill like prima donnas, expecting to be not only noticed but held in awe.

The House, on the other hand, is a monument to the belief that every member—no matter how stupid he or she might be— has an opinion worth expressing. The 435 representatives are so average they have to wear special lapel pins to distinguish themselves from tourists. These are men and women with middle-class values, middle-aged spread, and a middle-income talent for running up debt.

But they can also get rowdy.

The House is an ideal place for setting off all sorts of alarms. Despite a decor accented by uplifting Latin prepositions and assorted great seals, function takes precedence over style. Semi-circular rows of tan leather chairs, where members sit, form an amphitheater around "the well," where they rant and rave. In the center of the floor is the Speaker's platform, shaped like a polished mahogany version of Lenin's Tomb, and above it is a four-sided gallery, with separate sections for visitors and the press. The gallery also contains eight remote-controlled television cameras, bolted down at key angles, that cover the place from wall to wall as if it were a convenience store in a high-crime neighborhood. Which, in a way, is what it is.

For more than ten years, C-Span, the cable TV network, has beamed House floor action coast to coast. The constant coverage plays on sets in Hill offices like visual Muzak, and in cable households everywhere has made stars of legislative floor-show artists, such as Republican Congressmen Bob Dornan of California and Robert Walker of Pennsylvania.

From the time the network first went on the air, the outnumbered members of the GOP seemed instinctively to grasp its power to instill political panic, a power they've used ever since as a weapon to infuriate the Democratic majority with ad hoc attack video. During the 1992 presidential campaign, while major candidates were busy shuttling between Phil Donohue and Larry King, Dornan made C-Span his personal idiot box, blasting then-candidate Bill Clinton as a "draft-dodger" and "an adulterer." Every night Dornan harangued, as political junkies nationwide stayed up late to watch his performance.

At a time when Clinton's patriotism headed the Republicans' issues menu, Dornan's after-hours time slot served as a nightly test kitchen to determine what viewers would and would not swallow. While GOP "opposition researchers" were hard at work on rumors that Clinton, during his Oxford days, had written a letter to the State Department renouncing his American citizenship, Dornan's favorite scare story was a student trip that Clinton made to Moscow in 1970. For Dornan, whose TV time has decreased dramatically since the end of the Cold War, Clinton's Kremlin vacation might have been made to order a decade earlier. But the Orange County conservative soon learned a harsh lesson: Nothing in Washington is harder to promote than a new crisis manufactured from the leftover parts of an old one.

Clinton "was massaged [in Russia] by the KGB," Dornan declared to an empty House chamber. "I have to give him the benefit of the doubt—that he didn't have any idea of that— because he was all idealistic. . . . He was there licking their boots, while KGB agents, pretending to be professors and students, are telling him, 'You're great, Bill Clinton.' They probably told him he's going to be president some day."

It wasn't until Dornan started reading from transcripts of the famous telephone tapes made by Gennifer Flowers, Clinton's reputed long-time mistress, that House Speaker Tom Foley stepped in. Decreeing that congressional rules against personal insults aimed at fellow members and the president would extend to presidential candidates, Foley forced Dornan to tone down his rhetoric, effectively pulling the plug on his late show.

Some lawmakers are good at exploiting television's maximum potential for public exposure. However, one tradition that pre-dates live coverage gives every representative the chance to be his or her own personal crisis hotline. Members of Congress work hard at being everything voters want them to be. For many, that means working hard at *appearing* to work, a task taken so seriously in the House that time is reserved at the start of each legislative day for the express purpose of letting members act congressional.

Every morning, approximately a half hour is set aside for representatives to gas for one minute each on any topic they like. Most use the time to test reaction to some newly discovered and/or invented emergency, hoping the networks will notice and put them on the news, with publicity, speaking engagements, and campaign funding to follow.

Rep. Tom Lantos, a Democrat from California, was riding high in 1989. The Hungarian-born Lantos, another anti-communist in danger of losing his crisis constituency in the wake of the Cold War, rebounded with a widely publicized investigation of funding scandals at the Department of Housing and Urban Development during the Reagan administration. But when those hearings ended, the search was on for a replacement emergency. What the congressman and his staff discovered was a little-known medical problem called carpal tunnel syndrome, an acute stiffness in the wrist often associated with repetitive up-and-down motion, such as working at a computer keyboard. It wasn't another HUD scandal, but it did have the potential to be an important health scare in the workplace.

"One of the biggest groups affected was reporters," said Bob King, a spokesman for Lantos. That alone seemed to assure the necessary media coverage, and Lantos went after it full tilt. He made one-minute speeches. He held hearings, one in Washington and another in San Francisco, at which office workers complained dramatically about their aching wrists.

But some body parts don't excite the same emotional response as others, and the wrist, Lantos and his staffers soon learned, was one of them.

"We just didn't get the media push we were looking for," said King, "The issue faded. . . . We're still tracking it, though." Lately, he noted with concern, the problem has spread to grocery store checkout clerks.

Whether the issue is health-care reform or farm supports, the way members of Congress gather public backing or conversely rally opposition is not by engaging in reasonable debate but by throwing controlled tantrums. Staging is important, as is a supporting cast of victims. But even when the only prop is a blank piece of paper, such as New York Republican Sen. Alfonse D'Amato used to illustrate the benefits of Bill Clinton's '94 deficit reduction plan, the point is to excite emotions and keep them excited until no news producer in his right mind can fail to take notice.

A handful of true geniuses can create a critical concern out of anything from germ counts to skid marks. But when real disaster strikes, every amateur in Congress starts pushing and shoving for the chance to announce what he'd do to provide comfort and relief to those hardest hit.

On July 22, 1993, a mother lode of troubles, from floods, corruption, and the threat of higher taxes, transformed the House's normal daily schedule of one-minute speeches into a cable TV talent contest, the object of which was to cram as much outrage and urgency as possible into each sixty seconds of uninterrupted air time.

"Mr. Speaker," said Rep. John T. Doolittle, a Republican from

California, "the stench of corruption is hanging in the air and settling over the Capitol . . . The House bank was just a warmup to criminal activities that have already been uncovered at the House post office, and even after revelations of two decades of wrongdoing, those in charge are still trying to stall and whitewash, to protect themselves, and to prevent another scandal from brewing, at least until after taxes are raised."

Doolittle was referring to a money-laundering scheme involving then-House Ways and Means chairman Dan Rostenkowski, the Illinois Democrat, who was at the time heavily involved in negotiating a compromise version of the Clinton administration's controversial 1994 budget, which, depending on whose one-minute speech you believed, was either a courageous step toward reducing the deficit or the end of the U.S. economy.

"Mr. Speaker," complained Rep. Dan Burton, an Indiana Republican, "my Democrat friends continue to try to turn the facts on their head. They want to raise taxes, the largest tax increase in U.S. history. They want to increase spending more than any time in history. . . . Mr. Speaker [House members always address their remarks to the Speaker of the House, whether he happens to be present or not], we have to bring all the facts to the floor so that everybody knows what's going on."

This was a rousing speech, even though it contained one significant omission of fact. The Clinton budget called for the biggest tax increase in *eleven* years. In 1982, the Republican-controlled Senate passed, and President Ronald Reagan signed into law, a tax plan costing $20 billion more. But accuracy wasn't the key point here. Acting was.

"Mr. Speaker," said Thomas Barlow, a Democrat from Kentucky, "look at our children and grandchildren. Do you want them and their families to respect and cherish the memory of us in a strong America in coming years? . . . To reach our goal of a balanced budget . . . each must pay his fair share. That is our duty as Americans. Let us move now out of the bondage of debt. Let us move to a higher ground."

Barlow's reference to higher ground was particularly apt considering the continuing plight of millions of midwesterners caught in the path of the flooding Mississippi River, which members compared to a biblical plague on Egypt and the Dust Bowl of the Depression. But that hardly meant it was the only catastrophe worth receiving notice or remedial appropriations on this busy day in the House.

There was the departure of the Delco radio division of General Motors from Kokomo, Indiana, a particular embarrassment to supporters of the North American Free Trade Agreement since Delco was headed for Mexico. There was the state of Michigan cruelly snatching over one third of a $300 million highway appropriation, thus depriving forty-nine other states of their fair percentage.

And there was calamity of another sort, the suicide of White House lawyer Vincent Foster, an event that had cast a pall over official Washington, causing many to speculate that maybe the city itself had driven the president's boyhood friend to blow his brains out. Or maybe it was the pressure of having to keep a lid on the Clintons' Little Rock investment portfolio. Either way, the whole town was in a temporary state of shock. "Good-bye, Vincent," said Rep. Jay Dickey, an Arkansas Republican, ending his one-minute eulogy for the first official casualty attributed to Whitewater, which everyone kept inadvertently calling "Watergate."

It didn't take long for the dead lawyer to become a central figure in an executive-branch financial scandal that had Capitol Hill buzzing with questions. What did Foster know about the Clintons' business deals? Were Foster and Hillary Clinton lovers? Did Foster really kill himself, or was he murdered as part of a coverup?

As compelling or crazy as parts of the case may have been, Whitewater was just one more excuse for senators and representatives to make speeches, and every word they said was recorded in the *Congressional Record*. Published each day the House and Senate meet, the *Record* is a verbatim account of floor activity in both bodies, plus a section in the back filled with denunciations, portents, and confessions too embarrassing even by congressional standards to be uttered out loud.

The July 22, 1993, issue of the *Record* contained an attack on TV violence, a member's stark reminder that celebrations like Take Pride in America Week are all that keep us from becoming another Yugoslavia, and a demand by Sen. Herb Kohl, Democrat from Wisconsin, that unpatriotic buyers of foreign footwear recognize that Allen Edmonds Shoe Corporation, headquartered in his home state, "makes quite simply one of the finest shoes in the world."

It was also learned that Alaska Republican Sen. Frank Murkowski was unable to attend an important vote on amendments to the Hatch Act, which prohibits political activity by public employees. This was obviously a big mistake, and Murkowski's absence was surely noticed by his political opponents. So what was his excuse?

"Unfortunately," he apologized in the *Record*'s back pages, "as a consequence of receiving a yellow jacket sting . . . it was impossible for me to travel [from Fairbanks] on Monday night because of my swollen condition. As soon as I was medically able to travel, I returned to Washington."

That and a note from his doctor should keep his foes quiet for a while. But a quick infusion of federal funds could shut them up even longer.

Financial service, not eloquence, is the ultimate measure of success in Congress. But calling for money to be spent is a far cry from actually starting a cash flow. That's why members have long been divided into two basic categories: rainmakers and windbags.

BIG SPENDERS IN THE HOUSE AND SENATE
(Based on projected cost of bills sponsored in 103rd Congress)

SENATE

1.	Daniel Inouye (D-Hawaii)	$530.5 billion
2.	Paul Simon (D-Ill)	511.2 billion
3.	Paul Wellstone (D-Minn)	509.6 billion
4.	Howard Metzenbaum (D-Ohio)	508.9 billion
5.	Kent Conrad (D-ND)	24.9 billion
6.	Conrad Burns (R-Mont)	23.6 billion
7.	William Cohen (R-Maine)	21.9 billion
8.	Nancy Kassebaum (R-Kans)	21.4 billion
9.	Larry Pressler (R-SD)	21.2 billion
10.	Joseph Biden (D-Del)	20.7 billion

HOUSE

1.	Eleanor Holmes Norton (D-DC)	$563.2 billion
2.	Maxine Waters (D-Calif)	556.6 billion
3.	Luis Gutierrez (D-Ill)	554.3 billion
4.	Lucien Blackwell (D-Pa)	553.0 billion
5.	Lucille Roybal-Allard (D-Calif)	552.9 billion
6.	Kweisi Mfume (D-Md)	551.5 billion
7.	Charles Rangel (D-NY)	547.8 billion
8.	Maurice Hinchey (D-NY)	546.6 billion
9.	Bernard Sanders (I-Vt)	545.8 billion
10.	Carolyn Maloney (D-NY)	543.3 billion

Source: National Taxpayers Union

Rainmakers have their hands on the purse strings. They shower money on their supporters and constituents the way God in the Old Testament rained manna down on the Israelites, and the best in the business attain approximately the same reputation for crisis intervention.

The Senate's rainmaker supreme is Sen. Robert Byrd, the

West Virginia Democrat. Byrd, who looks like a geriatric roost-
er, might be just another fiddle-playing hillbilly if he weren't
among the most powerful men in Congress. As head of the Senate Appropriations Committee, Byrd has moved so many federal offices to poverty-stricken West Virginia, the state could pass
for a government in exile.

His technique is simple. Unless he gets the money he wants
for his constituents, nobody else gets any money for theirs.
Trade-offs like this are a part of every committee chairman's
repertoire. It's just that Byrd deals in such big numbers, he
makes all the rest seem like pikers.

Congress has authorizing committees and appropriating committees. Authorizing committees decide *why* money should be
spent and appropriating committees decide *what* it should be
spent on. With almost three quarters of all government programs now authorized as mandatory cash outlays called "entitlements," appropriators, once the Hill's all-powerful fiscal sul-
tans, no longer manage the spending process they way they used
to. With one notable exception:

Robert Byrd.

In 1990, when spending limitations cut off money for projects Byrd wanted, he single-handedly negotiated an end to the
Reagan-era Gramm-Rudman budget restrictions, got President
George Bush to raise taxes, and walked off with $40 billion in
federal funds, a disproportionately large chunk of which would
benefit West Virginia.

Like most members of Congress, Byrd enjoys spending
money. What sets him apart is that he's not afraid to admit it.
"Whatsoever thy hand findeth to do," he likes to say, quoting
from the Book of Ecclesiastes, "do it with thy might." Even in
lean economic times, Byrd is first at the pork barrel. And whenever he's threatened by a home-state rival with designs on taking
away his seat, he isn't shy about retaliating with massive
amounts of federal funding to prove he's still king of the Capitol
Hill rainmakers.

Byrd calls himself West Virginia's "billion-dollar industry," a title he proved he deserved once again in 1988, when Jay Wolfe, a Republican upstart, challenged him for the Senate job he's had since 1959. Wolfe had found what he thought was a Byrd funding failure and tried to convert it into a campaign theme. Byrd, he declared, had been slow on delivering promised federal aid, and to dramatize this, Wolfe decided to walk across the state, a blatant challenge to the vitality of his older rival that Byrd soon made him regret.

Wolfe started his trek on a country road that Byrd had several years before pledged to upgrade to a superhighway. His walk had barely gotten under way when Byrd retaliated with a $5 million grant for road construction. At intervals all along Wolfe's journey, Byrd, who was taking care of business back in Washington, announced new benefits for the state. Before the walk was finished, West Virginia had received an additional $16 million in public works appropriations. The point was made, and Byrd won reelection by a landslide.

Where money is concerned Byrd is not a man to be messed with. When a balanced budget amendment came up for a Senate vote early in 1994, Byrd was against it and the proposal failed. He gave up the Majority Leader's job because it took too much time away from his many pork projects, and if one of those projects is ever attacked by opposing lawmakers (which is rare) or an occasional media exposé, Byrd has been known to go crazy, as he did when ABC News tried to ambush him one morning while he was walking his dog.

Several days later, Byrd, a former member of the Ku Klux Klan, attacked the network from the Senate floor in a speech that quivered with backwoods rage.

"They came to my home," he fumed. "No excess, no savagery, no respect for others, no limits on behavior is too much in the chase for headlines. . . . You and your cameras are not going to intimidate this senator. . . . Even a public person has the right to walk his dog in peace without being attacked by vultures."

If rainmakers get their reputations from speedy "home delivery," windbags get theirs by never shutting up. A few are so good at monopolizing the House and Senate floors, they've achieved the enviable status of living sound bites. Voters get used to hearing them, and keep sending them back to Washington to hear more.

Sen. Alan Simpson, a conservative Republican from Wyoming, who spouts Wild West witticisms every chance he gets, fulfilled the dream of every certified windbag by playing himself in the 1993 movie comedy *Dave*, a film about an ordinary guy who becomes president of the United States, and thanks to a case of mistaken identity gets to make time with First Lady Sigourney Weaver.

But Simpson's habit of reducing world affairs to one-liners has also gotten him into trouble. On a visit to Iraq several months before the Gulf War, he told Saddam Hussein, "I believe your problems lie with the Western media, and not with the U.S. government." The advice, which Simpson denied ever giving, came back to haunt him when he criticized wartime interviews with Hussein by CNN correspondent Peter Arnett as evidence that the reporter was a enemy sympathizer. The media jumped to Arnett's defense. An editorial in the *Washington Post* praised his work and called Simpson's performance with Hussein "bootlicky and obsequious," dealing him the worst blow that can befall a congressional windbag: having it said in public that he'd lost his entertainment value.

If Simpson has made a name for himself as a continuous source of hot air, Sen. Phil Gramm, the Texas Democrat-turned-Republican, elevated windbagism to a science.

Just because Gramm cosponsored a limit on federal spending doesn't mean he's a tightwad about sending money to Texas. Gramm backed the costly Supercollider project outside Dallas, and until its demise in 1993 he was chief shepherd in the Senate for the $190-million-a-year mohair subsidy, 86 percent of which annually went to Texas goat farmers.

These are things Gramm voted *for*. But with his genius for stage managing, he also takes credit for sending benefits to Texas he voted *against*. His opponents call the practice

"Gramm-standing," a knack for announcing federal payments to the state in a way that gives the impression Gramm himself was responsible for every one of them.

"If we have a project providing money and I think it is a bad investment, I'm going to vote against it," Gramm told the *Dallas Morning News*. "But once the money is being provided, I'm going to fight like hell to see Texas gets its fair share and more."

Typical was Gramm's 1989 announcement of a $1.2 million grant to Southwest Texas State University for the development of a drug prevention program. Although Gramm opposed the measure that provided the money, that didn't stop him from being there when the check arrived. Using political contacts in government agencies and departments, his Senate staff makes sure their boss knows the status of each federal dollar on its way to Texas so he can be the first member of the state delegation to herald its coming whether he supported the legislation to send it there or not.

Playing both sides of an issue is an old political stunt, but Gramm has added a whole new twist to the game of claiming credit where *no* credit is due. His office dubbed the practice a "funding scare."

In 1990, Gramm spent a record $166,700 in reimbursed home-state travel expenses. Coming in second that year, with $64,337 in free trips, was Senate fellow-windbag Alan Simpson. Reimbursed travel is defined as travel unrelated to politics. But in 1990, Gramm was running hard for reelection, and every move he made was political. His personal goal was to win back his Senate seat with 60 percent of the vote, a figure that he believed would position him to be the Republican nominee for president in 1996. Gramm was all over the state, and funding-scare strategy was a major element in his victory plan.

A kind of now-you-see-it-now-you-don't routine, the funding scare is a high-concept spinoff of Gramm's credit-taking scam, only the impact makes him seem even more powerful.

Here's how it works: Once assured that a federal project was in absolutely no danger of having its funding cut, a member of

Gramm's staff would leak word to the Texas media that the opposite was true, that the project was in serious trouble, and only swift and decisive action by Gramm could save it. The announcement would put people into shock. Then Gramm would pretend to throw his weight around in Washington, and like magic the funding would be "restored" and a community rescued from the brink of disaster.

Gramm made the funding scare a key element in his 1990 reelection bid. The target was Brooke Army Medical Hospital Center in San Antonio, and before a visit to the site to check progress on new construction, he was reminded by a staff memo of the shady politics involved.

"We have tried to create a BAMC 'funding scare' while feeling comfortable that BAMC is safe from the budget knife," the memo read. It went on to caution that if anyone found out what Gramm's office had done to freak out citizens in San Antonio, "the situation could change to our detriment."

That's what happened when the *Dallas Morning News* broke the story. Luckily for Gramm, it was three years after Texas voters reelected him with the 60 percent margin he said he needed to keep alive his '96 presidential hopes.

A funding scare operates on the same principles of crisis management that have worked on Capitol Hill for years. But members of Congress aren't the only ones who have learned to get what they want by using scare tactics. During the battle over his 1994 budget, Bill Clinton, with the help of then-White House adviser David Gergen, fashioned a "damaged leader scare" that not only helped pass his budget package, but it gave Clinton the chance to appear presidential even as he begged members of his own divided party in Congress to have mercy on him.

With Republicans closing ranks and scores of Democrats defecting, passage of the budget would depend on a handful of undecided senators and representatives. Many of the latter were House freshmen from GOP districts and clearly reluctant to endanger their careers by approving the called-for tax increase. Clinton was like a college fraternity president who had become president of the United States, and right in the middle of Greek Week he was losing his pledge class.

Gergen knew the administration would have little luck in persuading holdouts to vote "yes" without generating the right atmospherics. For that he needed to create a sense of crisis that went far beyond any alarm the Clinton White House had previously sounded for government reform, national service, or family leave.

Rarely had the House and Senate made a chief executive crawl the way they'd done with Clinton during his first year in office, but Gergen had a plan for using the situation to the administration's advantage. With polls showing that Congress had a higher negative rating than the president, Gergen let it be known through friendly communicators on the Hill and in the press that a vote against Clinton on the budget wouldn't just be another of many setbacks, it would Bring Down the Presidency.

The *New York Times* said Clinton "desperately" needed a win. The *Wall Street Journal* wondered if the administration could "recover" from another failed initiative. Who knew what might happen if the president lost again? He might even pull a Vince Foster!

The White House hadn't raised the stakes this high since special prosecutors were closing in on Richard Nixon during Watergate. And then, the presidency really *was* in trouble.

It was a risky move but Gergen, who had helped manage communications for three previous Republican presidents, was confident it would pay off. In 1986, at the height of the Iran-contra scandal, Gergen used a similar ploy to shield Ronald Reagan from Congress. As lawmakers called for a full-scale investigation of the administration's arms-for-hostages deal, Gergen went on national television to portray any congressional inquiry as a direct attack on the presidency.

"The first ramification," Gergen told CBS News, "is that [Reagan] may well have such a damaged presidency that it's going to be more difficult to govern. We could have two years of drift and deadlock, not only here in Washington, but in our foreign relations. I think that's a very real danger for the president."

The warning bought the president several months to get his story straight, and the Congress never touched him. Later, Gergen explained that such strategic exaggerations about the presidency were "parables." He told the *New York Times* in 1993 that no one cares if they're not literally true, "so long as the symbolic truth is defensible."

Washington politics is the art of mixing images and numbers to create the appearance of reality. Since the only values are production values, what is important isn't truth but perception. As crunch time on the budget drew near, the press was already reporting a marked improvement in the administration's prospects. "After months of terrifying near-death experiences things have settled down," pronounced the *Washington Post*. The plan was working.

"I don't think the Senate will let this plan go down," Clinton said at a Capitol Hill pep rally the day before the House passed the measure by two votes. "I don't think they'd do that to the country."

The White House needed two Democratic votes in the Senate to reach a fifty–fifty draw and give Vice-President Al Gore a chance to break the tie. But to get those votes, Sen. Dennis DeConcini of Arizona and Bob Kerrey of Nebraska would have to be "bought" into the fold.

Holdout No. 1, DeConcini, was easy. As a member of the famed Keating Five, the group of senators that had tried to convince federal bank regulators to stop bothering savings-and-loan swindler Charles Keating, he was ipso facto damaged goods. Facing a tough reelection bid in 1994, DeConcini wanted something to show voters back home as proof he'd put up a good fight before agreeing to a $240 billion tax hike. What he got was an executive order creating a special "bank account" to protect the budget's $496 billion in deficit reduction money from being appropriated and spent by Congress. But since the president has no authority to make Congress apply new tax revenues to deficit reduction, the order was strictly cosmetic.

And so was DeConcini's attempt at playing hard-to-get. A month later, saying he was fed up with Congress "and all the B.S." that goes with it, he announced his decision to retire from politics.

Holdout No. 2, Bob Kerrey, would be harder. Kerrey had run against Clinton in the '92 primaries, and in the event things got bad enough, he might challenge Clinton again in 1996. Given his first opportunity to reenter the serious limelight, Kerrey seemed eager to take full advantage. If the media-savvy former governor and onetime live-in boyfriend of movie star Debra Winger wanted a little extra attention, Gergen and his White House scare squad would be glad to accommodate.

Gergen, former Clinton Chief of Staff Thomas "Mac" McLarty, and the administration's head congressional lobbyist Howard Pastor met Kerrey for lunch on Capitol Hill. The working theme, laid out by Gergen, was that Kerrey and Clinton were political soul mates. According to that scenario, if Kerrey chose to destroy the president, he would really be destroying himself.

Kerrey was up for reelection before Clinton, and therefore would be the first to test voter response no matter which way he decided to cast his ballot on the budget. He may have been a Medal of Honor winner, but would he have the courage to face a Nebraska electorate that held him personally responsible for bringing down a president?

Not hardly. What Kerrey really craved was some quality time in the eye of a crisis, and that's what he got, plus an agreement from Clinton to set up a Commission on Entitlements and Tax Reform. After a last-minute phone call to the president, he formally announced his support for the budget in a dramatic floor speech timed to make the nightly newscasts.

Sen. Bob Kerrey, policy wonk, had become Sen. Bob Kerrey . . . *Disaster Master.*

"Mr. Clinton," he said, looking straight into a C-Span camera, "if you're watching now, as I suspect you are, I tell you this:

I could not and should not cast a vote that brings down your presidency."

The scheme had worked. Within forty-five minutes, Clinton was on the air himself, calling the two-vote win in the House and the tiebreaker victory in the Senate a landslide.

"The margin was close," he said, "but the mandate is clear."

The presidency was saved, the government preserved, and Congress, having averted another catastrophe, could leave town for summer vacation.

CHAPTER TWO

THE MR. SMITH SYNDROME

It was 7:00 A.M. on a muggy morning in mid-July, and the Democrats were taking batting practice. Dick Swett (pronounced "sweat"), an aptly named congressman from New Hampshire, lined a pitch into left field. Another swing sent a hard grounder skipping between short and third. In 1991, Swett was his party's secret weapon, and judging by his killer instinct at the plate three weeks before anything counts, he was ready to give the GOP problems all over again.

Swett and two dozen of his Democratic colleagues were getting ready to play a team of Republicans in the annual congressional baseball game. The legislative year doesn't end with the budget vote. The real conclusion takes place on the ball field, where the two parties forget about crossover votes and defections, and fight it out in a real game of hardball. If the snarling on both sides seems a little exaggerated, it's not, at least not to those who appreciate the longstanding Capitol Hill tradition of rubbing your opponent's nose in the dirt.

It's only a baseball game, but such rituals have the force of gravity on the Hill. How members address one another in floor debates, where they sit in committee hearings, and, if need be, how they're banished from the ranks of the duly elected are all prescribed by time-honored customs. Take those away, and the whole United States Congress would turn into the same sort of disorganized melee that passes for government in 95 percent of the world's other countries.

That doesn't mean Democrats and Republicans don't hate each other as much as opposing political factions anywhere. They just express their feelings in a different context.

Not long ago, a group of congressional jocks started getting together for a yearly basketball game. The occasion gives bigger and taller members a chance to elbow each other for fun instead of political gain. But basketball favors physical size over the subtler skills and strategies useful in baseball: trick pitches, stealing, playing the percentages. These are the things that win ball games—and elections—and they're also what make America's national pastime the ideal demonstration sport for Congress.

It's easy to see why politics and baseball go together. No two pursuits are more preoccupied with regulations, records, and statistics. "The Greeks took their games very seriously," declared talk-show pundit and newspaper columnist George Will. "Why shouldn't we?"

It all makes perfect sense in a place where parliamentary procedure is a passion. No wonder the nation's capital can't get a real team to replace the one that moved away more than twenty years ago. What major league owner in his right mind would relocate to a city where nobody can discuss a pop fly without referring to *Robert's Rules of Order*?

A slugfest between House Democrats and Republicans is an entirely different matter. It's not *about* congressional rules and customs. It's about the power those rules and customs are supposed to contain. Everything that goes on in Congress, from crushing victory to humiliating defeat, is squeezed into this once-a-year athletic contest that pits the two parties against each other in the kind of winner-take-all matchup the public seldom gets to see.

The only thing most congressional Democrats and Republicans have in common is their government paychecks. Except for a brief period when the GOP was on top in the Senate during the

Reagan administration, the Democrats have controlled Congress for the past 40 years. That's longer than Stalin ran Russia, Mao ran China, and Fidel Castro has been running Cuba, and to many Republicans, life under Democratic majority rule has been just about as pleasant.

The casual observer may assume that party labels are as interchangeable as blank name tags. Not true. Parties exist to round up campaign contributions and keep alive a sense of mutual animosity during the physical act of making laws. The majority party in Congress has always treated the minority as if it hardly existed. "Republicans would do the same thing to us," said ex-Rep. Tony Coelho.

If the parties are mad at each other the rest of the year, they're positively foaming at the mouth for the Big Game.

"Sure, each side wanted to win in the old days," said Sid Yudain, the founder of *Roll Call* newspaper, which sponsors the event. "These guys are politicians. They went to Florida for spring training. Some of them even stopped drinking. . . . But they basically played the game for fun. That aspect is gone now. Like everything else on the Hill it's gotten very serious and mean. . . ."

From the time it began more than thirty years ago as a opportunity for congressmen to strut around in old Washington Senators uniforms, the game has been exclusively male. Over the decades, there have been dozens of women elected to Congress, but none ever broke with Hill custom and took the field until Rep. Ileana Ros-Lehtinen from Florida announced that she wanted to play for the GOP.

"I realize the game is very important," she said. "I just hope I don't embarrass the Republicans."

It didn't seem to matter that Ros-Lehtinen, a Cuban American from Miami, barely knew a bat from a glove. The GOP manager, Colorado Rep. Dan Schaefer, said the team "would regard her as any other rookie." But with the Democrats talking about adding a woman player too, others complained that the presence of females would affect everyone's will to win. By a kind of testosterone telepathy, male members in both parties communicated a sense of displeasure that was hard to put into words without sounding politically incorrect.

"If you treat them like men and play hard, people will accuse you of being sexist," griped a close observer. "If you slow everything down, what does that do to competition?"

It was a familiar situation. One of the last bastions of partisan rivalry, like so many other things in Congress, was being threatened not just with alteration—but with virtual emasculation.

Campaign restrictions, staff cuts, term limits. All over Capitol Hill the old rules of the game were up for revision. Almost every incumbent running for reelection in 1992 pledged to throw out influence peddlers, interest groups, and special privileges. Now the call for reform had even reached the ball diamond! But the difference between "safe" and "out" in politics, as in baseball, is largely a matter of perception, and nowhere is the perception of change more error prone than it is on the Hill.

Recent studies report a "growing . . . hostility" toward Congress and a "dismally low level of confidence . . . in the national legislature." In a joint analysis of this discontent by the American Enterprise Institute and the Brookings Institution, two of Washington's most respected think tanks, authors Norman Ornstein and Thomas E. Mann write:

"For many critics of Congress, including a large segment of the public, the agenda for congressional reform is obvious. . . . The task is to cut Congress and its entrenched incumbents back to size by depriving them of the institutional and individual resources they need to pursue their parochial interests. Since Congress is populated by self-serving career politicians out of touch with Americans and inattentive to the public interest, only radical surgery can contain the cancer of political ambition and restore the health of our democratic experiment. This profoundly cynical view of the contemporary Congress would undoubtedly shock the framers of the constitutional system, who carefully fashioned an independent and powerful legislature as the bedrock of a responsive democracy. But today, Congress bashing is a sport enjoyed . . . by one and all."

While not exactly giving the House and Senate a AAA rating for trust and integrity, Ornstein and Mann make it sound as though it's misguided outsiders who are doing all the harm. Let's not forget that the biggest bashers are often members themselves who have made attacks on Congress a standard feature in their campaign repertoire.

Nevertheless, the two authors go on to make note of an interesting phenomenon. While voters may take a dim view of Congress as a whole, most think their own senators and representatives do a pretty good job. This, no doubt, is one of benefits of keeping the folks back home happily employed building highways, airports, and other assorted public works projects. But it also shows how the pursuit of "parochial interests" that Ornstein and Mann refer to has undermined the effectiveness of the institution.

In 1992, when voter sentiment against Capitol Hill was the worst it's been in two decades, only twenty-four House incumbents lost their seats in the general election. Before the election, Rep. Ronald Coleman, a Democrat from Texas, was one member picked by the experts to lose big. After being cited by the Ethics Committee for having bounced 673 checks in the House banking scandal, Coleman, a bespectacled porker from El Paso, was written off as a guaranteed goner. But the power of incumbency—not to mention the $650,000 he spent to convince voters he was good for the local economy—paid off. When the ballots were counted, Coleman was back in Congress.

If voters think Capitol Hill is a place of rampant greed, they're also convinced it's no place to send someone who might take two or three terms just to get the hang of things. No member of Congress ever made a name for himself by *not* spending money. Most people would like to see government cleaned up. But until that happens, they'd just as soon have somebody working for them who's willing to get his hands dirty sending home loot.

Still, the lack of heavy incumbent casualties in the 1992 general election is misleading. Of the 110 nonreturnees, 67 of the most endangered members retired after the banking scandal and never even faced voters. The remaining 43 members who lost in primary and general elections dropped the actual reelection rate for the 102nd Congress to 88 percent, the lowest since the post-Watergate housecleaning of 1974.

Americans have always been suspicious of concentrated power, and polls indicate that suspicion is now focused squarely on Congress. Some surveys suggest that veterans may soon feel even greater pressure from voters. A poll by Public Opinion Strategies in 1993 found that 78 percent of those questioned agreed with the following statement: "Congress isn't doing the job we elected it to do, and it's time for a change, even if it means voting against my incumbent congressman." That represented an 8 percent increase from two years earlier. In the same survey, those saying they "strongly" agreed with the statement increased over two years from 38 percent to 54 percent.

Although the impact of such findings is sometimes hard to measure, higher disapproval ratings combined with lower reelection margins could have the effect of improving Congress by making lawmakers nervous about losing their jobs, and therefore more responsive to the people they're supposed to be serving. Or it may just make them more inclined to serve themselves while they still can.

Other polls reveal similar anticongressional feelings, especially among those who cast their 1992 presidential ballots for independent H. Ross Perot, the last election's none-of-the-above candidate.

Perot followers, if not Perot, could be the deciding factor in every major election for the rest of the century, and both major parties have been busy studying their particular brand of anger for clues that could help woo them away. Less than a year into the Clinton administration, the Democratic Leadership Council, a liberal policy planning organization that Bill Clinton himself once headed, commissioned a study that told the new president everything he needed to do to win over Perot's people. The

DLC found that 72 percent of those who voted for the tiny Texas billionaire in '92 might be tempted to switch their support to another candidate, but only one who pushed for bold changes in government.

Perot supporters, the study determined, were looking for someone willing to take a get-tough approach to federal spending. So luring them to the Democratic ticket in 1996 wouldn't be easy. DLC leaders advised Clinton to demonstrate "a more assertive approach toward Congress [and to] push Congress harder to enact a program of radical change." Under no circumstances, they cautioned, "should President Clinton permit himself to be captured by the Washington establishment."

Ever since the collapse of the Soviet Union, Congress and the White House have both been searching for some larger-than-life evil to take its place. Saddam Hussein, Bosnian Serbs, health insurance companies, and North Korea have all been tried out with varying degrees of effectiveness. For presidents, the need for a Soviet substitute is particularly noticeable. With the U.S.S.R. no longer around to test their strength in a crisis, the new measure of leadership ability is how bravely they stand up to Congress and all the special interests that cluster around it like a thousand satellite states.

It would be convenient if chief executives could avoid Congress completely. A few, like Jimmy Carter, have tried without much success. But unless they want to spend the entire four years of their term meeting with sports teams in the Rose Garden, they not only have to deal with Capitol Hill, they have do business with the same Washington Establishment the DLC warned Clinton against.

After a disastrous first six months in office spent avoiding any association with Congress or the power lunch crowd, it was obvious that Bill Clinton couldn't afford to hide anymore. On the eve of his first meeting with the leaders of the world's industrialized nations in Tokyo, he showed up at Duke Zeibert's restaurant for peace talks with Senate Minority Leader Robert Dole and Washington's facilitator-emeritus Robert Strauss.

America's moderator-in-chief, Larry King, even stopped by. You don't get much farther inside the Beltway than that.

It used to be said that Washington's ground zero in the event of a Russian nuclear attack wasn't the Pentagon or State Department, but Duke's, whose lunchtime and dinner clientele included the best minds and fattest stomachs in Washington. During the 1987 Washington summit conference, Soviet Premier Mikhail Gorbachev ordered his ZIL limousine to stop outside the restaurant for a photo op. Six years later, Gorbachev, then on a U.S. speaking tour, came inside for pickles and tea.

While other D.C. eateries, like the Palm, have lured away some of its high-level customers, the symbolism of the president's dinner date at Duke Zeibert's was as anthropologically significant as a night in an Indian sweat lodge. Clinton was being publicly initiated into Old Washington's culture of meals 'n' deals, although judging by his chronic spare tire, he had the meals part down pat before he came to town.

That his mentor should be Robert Strauss wasn't surprising. What *was* surprising was that it took six months for them to finally sit down at the table.

The last time Strauss had tried to broker a peace treaty between Congress and the White House, he invited Carter, House Speaker Tip O'Neill, and Democratic Sen. Robert Byrd of West Virginia to dinner. The intraparty powwow was intended to patch up Carter's poor relationship with the Hill. But the rift was too big even for Strauss to repair. Tip O'Neill failed to show, and by dessert Carter and Byrd hated each other. The Dole–Clinton meeting went much better.

In bringing powerful politicians together to iron out their differences over a couple of steaks, Strauss was right in his element. Which explains why he soon got tired of being ambassador to Moscow, a city with a long tradition of powerful leaders, but a shortage of food and restaurants. No such problems in Washington.

After the Whitewater scandal forced the president's stumblebum counsel Bernard Nussbaum to resign, Clinton turned to

Lloyd Cutler, another member of the first-team Establishment, to take Nussbaum's place. The appointment of Cutler, known as "Cool Hand" Lloyd for his grace under pressure in the same job for Jimmy Carter, sent a signal to Congress that White House legal problems were being dealt with by a major Washington player. Never mind the fact that he would only be in the game for 130 business days to avoid having to resign from his law firm.

Even Cutler made it sound as if he had more important service to perform. "I'm married fairly recently to a very young and very peppy wife, and I want to spend some time with her," he said.

As for Clinton and Dole, the dinner didn't help. After repeated White House problems in Bosnia, Somalia, and Haiti, Senate Republicans challenged Clinton's ability to deal independently with any overseas crisis. "I don't want to micromanage foreign policy," said Dole. "But we have some role to play." The question, as always in politics, was how big it would be.

To understand what Bill Clinton or any president is up against in trying to develop a productive relationship with Congress, it's helpful to remember that the House and Senate operate on 535 separate agendas, all functioning more or less independent of one another and usually in opposition to the executive branch, something the Clinton administration learned when it introduced its ambitious plan to "reinvent" government.

The Washington bureaucracy didn't get big and unwieldy all by itself. Much of what government does, it does because Congress wants it to. Having a large number of federal programs gives lawmakers more things to fund and therefore more things to control. Thus reinventing anything in government first requires getting the approval of legislators who often like things just the way they are.

Take the Department of Agriculture, a bureaucracy rife with duplication, inefficiency, and political oversight. One of Clinton's proposals called for consolidating the USDA's meat and poultry inspection programs under the Food and Drug Administration, which is part of the Department of Health and Human Services. The idea might make all the sense in the world, but that's not the point. Each inspection program has its supporters in Congress, who may be all for reinventing some things in government as long as one of *their* things isn't among them.

House Speaker Tom Foley thought the USDA should keep meat and poultry inspection, and that fish inspection, now the responsibility of the FDA, should be moved there as well. But Rep. John Dingell, a Democrat from Michigan, whose Energy and Commerce Committee oversees the FDA, disagreed. Dingell let it be known that he wouldn't oppose moving meat and poultry inspection to the FDA, but he would certainly put up a fight to keep fish inspection right where it was.

When he heard the administration's plan, House Agriculture Committee Chairman Rep. E. "Kika" De La Garza, a Texas Democrat, announced that the USDA should supervise all food inspection programs from "the farm to the fork." The most accommodating of all was Sen. Dale Bumpers, chairman of the Senate Appropriations subcommittee on agriculture. Bumpers, a Democrat from Clinton's home state of Arkansas, said he might back an inspection shift to FDA, but only if it didn't result in the proposed closing of 10 percent of the USDA's 10,000-plus field offices where legislative mandates specify personnel levels.

Other than that, congressional Democrats were all for the president's plan.

Until C-Span brought video vérité coverage of congressional action to living rooms across the country, all most Americans knew—or wanted to know—about the institution was what they remembered from *Mr. Smith Goes to Washington*, an inspirational Hollywood study of graft and individual endurance. In the movie, Jimmy Stewart plays a good-hearted average Joe named Jefferson Smith, who gets plucked from obscurity to fill out the term of a recently deceased senator. The plot develops from there into the kind of us-against-them melodrama director

Frank Capra made famous, except in this case "them" happens to be a cast of characters right out of the *Congressional Record*.

When the story opens, Mr. Smith has no idea that he's been chosen for his new job by the political machine that runs his home state, or that he's expected to take orders from Claude Rains, playing a senior senator, who had sold out a long time ago.

As a member of the Senate, Mr. Smith's only legislative concern is upgrading the quality of America's youth, an important cause in the late 1930s when film studios and the government joined forces to show that patriotic draft-age males were the nation's most important product. Smith introduces a bill to create a national boys' camp, and FDR would have surely signed it into law if the proposed camp site hadn't been on land the machine back home was reserving for a big dam. And that's when things begin to heat up on the Senate floor.

As soon as he figures out he's been duped, Mr. Smith, under the guidance of his one-woman staff played by Jean Arthur, uses the rule book to flush out the wrongdoers. He filibusters against the dam until he collapses into a stack of constituent mail, at which point the opposition cracks and the scandal is exposed.

The moral of the story: The system works, as long as there are guys around like Jimmy Stewart to keep guys like Claude Rains from stealing the country blind.

Like most movies about Congress, Mr. Smith's party affiliation is left purposely vague. But it hardly matters whether he's a Democrat or Republican. His was a party of one. No whips, floor managers, or anyone else could tell him what to do. In the end, he didn't get what he wanted by being the heroic figure of myth and legend. He got it by being a pain in the ass.

If he were on Capitol Hill today, Mr. Smith would have plenty of company.

Not much has changed in Congress since Jefferson Smith came to town. It doesn't take long for newcomers to realize the fix it is in. Leadership sets the agenda. Committees and subcommittees, by deciding which bills get to the floor, all but dictate the vote on every issue. Despite occasional talk about reform, Congress is still a closed shop, and members who don't like the way things are done have little recourse except to go along or get out.

If Rep. Tim Penny, conservative Democrat from Minnesota, wasn't an exact Mr. Smith clone, he came close. A stubborn young midwesterner in 1982 when he ran against the kind of insider trading that keeps incumbents in office and influence in the hands of a few senior members, Penny soon learned that the same issues that got him elected also made him a man without a power base.

Congress is a hierarchy that rewards acolytes, not apostates. So Penny, blocked from choice committee posts, became a troublemaker in the Mr. Smith mold. He held court with the Hill press corps and spoke his mind on the issues—the most controversial being Congress itself.

When Penny told a reporter, "This place doesn't operate on the level," it could have been Jimmy Stewart talking. Which seemed to make him the ideal congressional counterpart to Bill Clinton, another "outsider" who got elected president by promising to change the system. Clinton had also given the cold shoulder to Congress during the campaign, and Penny saw that as a good sign the two would work well together.

He was wrong. Once in office, Clinton showed no inclination to do the things Penny thought he would. To reduce the cost of government meant reducing the role of government. Clinton's plan called for increasing both. The new president wasn't reinventing government. He was reinventing *spending*.

After watching Democratic operatives strongarm the administration's budget through the House, Penny had seen enough, and in one last anti-Washington gesture, he announced his retirement, effective 1994. Ten years in Congress was all he could stand, he said at a press conference. "It's evident that far too many politicians end up staying far too long."

Considering the fact that the president's budget package had yet to pass the Senate, Penny's statement amounted to a pre-emptive strike at Congress *and* the White House. The surprise retirement triggered a flood of newspaper and TV profiles that treated him like the most righteous lawmaker in town. Here was someone who didn't need to be told to get out of office. He *term limited* himself.

"I'm not doing it with any ambition for higher elective office," Penny told the *Minneapolis Tribune*. But being retired didn't mean he was unavailable for admiration.

In fact, quitting Congress, the ultimate act of reform, positioned him to be the moral spokesman of the House, at least until the spotlight was stolen a month later by four other congressmen who announced they were quitting too.

"I've already stayed here longer than I planned," said departing Rep. Jim Slattery, a Kansas Democrat, in a slight variation on Penny's statement. "I believe in citizen legislature. I think it's important to move in and out of government service."

Call this movie *Mr. Smith Goes Back and Forth to Washington*.

Americans believe in teamwork, individuals pulling together to get the job done. Alexis de Tocqueville noticed the impulse on his trip to the United States 150 years ago, observing that people "of all ages, all conditions and dispositions constantly form associations . . . religious, moral, serious, futile, general or restricted, enormous or diminutive. . . ." Such societies, he wrote, "unite into one channel the efforts of diverging minds, and urge them vigorously toward one end. . . ."

Congress is supposed to work that way. But with party unity threatened by constant fighting, and traditional legislative alliances downsizing into ever more highly specialized interest groups, a Congress of diverging minds vigorously moving toward one end has become a Congress of diverging minds moving all over the map.

Jefferson Smith was a single-issue idealist in a Senate full of team-playing con men. Bad government, the movie says, doesn't come from individuals but from conspiracies to keep individuals quiet. One senator wanted a boys' camp, and the rest of the Senate did not. So what did he do? He asserted his individuality. He started talking and didn't shut up until both he and his colleagues caved in. The man was way ahead of his time.

Mr. Smith, the patron saint of special-interest tantrums, may not have sold out to the National Latex Council or the Home Siding Institute, but the same can't be said for those who followed in his footsteps.

Lobbyists and other message bearers assault the Hill every day with requests for specialized legislation. Often these requests are preceded by generous campaign contributions designed to get a lawmaker's attention, and frequently followed by invitations to join a member's "steering committee" as a favored supporter/adviser by making donations on a regular basis. Money doesn't buy votes. It buys access, and if the giving continues, a useful friend in Congress. No one would call this bribery, but nobody calls it charity either.

In *The Lobbying Handbook*, by John Zorack, Washington lobbyist Tommy Boggs remarks on the importance of maintaining such one-on-one contacts. "If you expect a member of Congress to give you a few extra minutes, spend time raising money for him. Members keep track of contributors."

The real competition in Washington, as Boggs suggests, is for time, a particularly precious commodity on Capitol Hill, since congressmen and senators normally only work three days a week. Time constraints are so strict that elected officials are forced to become instant experts, and it's far more profitable to be an expert on something that pays campaign dividends than something that doesn't.

Special interests have become so specialized that every conceivable concern and emotional pulsation not only has its own lobbyists, but its own congressional caucus. A caucus is like a lobbying firm managed by dues-paying members of Congress, who hype their pet issues every chance they get. If there's a cause—economic, social, or socio-economic—that doesn't have a caucus, then some group of lawmakers is probably starting one right now. But it will have to battle for floor space with a roster that already includes the . . .

Alcohol Fuels Caucus
Animal Welfare Caucus
Army Caucus
Arts Caucus
Ball-Bearing Caucus
Boating Caucus
Caucus for Ethiopian Jews
Coal Caucus
Copper Caucus
Fire Services Caucus
Footwear Caucus
Hispanic Caucus
Insurance Caucus
Mining Caucus
Mushroom Caucus
Olympic Caucus
Soybean Caucus
Space Caucus
Sportsmen's Caucus
Steel Caucus
Sweetener Caucus
Textile Caucus
Truck Caucus
Wine Caucus

There are ninety-seven caucuses in all, though the number is subject to constant change as new ones form.

The essence of congressional deliberation is supposed to be compromise, giving up something to get something. Caucuses are designed around the higher principle of special-interest politics that says: *Never give up a thing!* Most caucuses, as the above list illustrates, are little more than chamber of commerce offices. Yet threaten any one of them, and members fight back with everything they've got.

The largest and most powerful of the congressional support groups, the Black Caucus, operates like a mini-political machine, using tough talk and a highly disciplined voting bloc to intimidate House leaders. Once, after Black Caucus members teamed with conservative Republicans to help defeat a Clinton administration attempt to broaden presidential veto power, Speaker Tom Foley was so flustered he promised to seek the group's input on all future legislation.

But the Black Caucus isn't completely unified. The only Republican in the forty-member organization, Rep. Gary Franks from Connecticut, has been repeatedly threatened with dismissal for not voting the party line with other members. Franks, a conservative, has been attacked for not siding with the liberal majority on entitlement issues and for endorsing the nomination of Clarence Thomas to the Supreme Court. When Franks criticized the creation of special minority congressional districts as unconstitutional gerrymandering, several caucus members demanded that he quit the group entirely. If he wants to participate in the conclave, said Rep. Cleo Fields, whose own district in Louisiana is under legal review, "he can join the Democratic Party."

Franks has also angered Rev. Jesse Jackson, who often uses the Black Caucus as a backup group for his important televised statements. Calling himself "the highest elected black Republican official in the United States," Franks likes to point out that Jackson has never held a political office and, unless Washington, D.C., becomes a state—an idea the Black Caucus favors and Franks opposes—never will.

When Lani Guinier, the black lawyer picked to head the Justice Department's Civil Rights Division, had her nomination withdrawn, the Black Caucus turned on the Clinton White House with threats to stall the budget and other key pieces of legislation. It also embarked on a media campaign designed to let the president know he was dealing with professionals.

On Jewish New Year, 1993, a congressional day off and therefore a golden opportunity to monopolize Capitol Hill news coverage, the rival Hispanic Caucus invited Clinton to its annual dinner where he gave a boring speech on the North American Free Trade Agreement. Media attention: light to moderate.

The same day, the Black Caucus opened its "Legislative Weekend" with a fiery harangue against the government by guest speaker Minister Louis Farrakhan, leader of the Nation of Islam. Afterward, the two groups announced they were joining forces to pressure the administration for housing, jobs, and money. Media attention: heavy.

The high-profile event made two important points: that the Black Caucus was the most show-business savvy of all the Hill's grievance groups and, following its surprise alliance with the militant Black Muslims, the only one with its own Ministry of Defense.

Implied muscle is always a useful commodity in special-interest politics, but only as long as it enhances leverage. Maybe Black Caucus chairman Rep. Kweisi Mfume from Maryland stated the working philosophy of his group—and of all congressional caucuses—best when he told members: "We have no permanent friends, no permanent enemies, just permanent interests."

Mfume proved that point a few months later. After a Muslim spokesman was widely criticized for making a speech in which he accused Jews of being "bloodsuckers" and called the Pope a "cracker," he announced that the relationship between the caucus and the Nation of Islam had been seriously "jeopardized."

This kind of strategic realignment is normal and takes place on the Hill all the time. Only now, with parties no longer in full control of their troops, marching orders come from a whole host of subgroups that spend more time fighting each other for influence and federal funding than they do solving the nation's problems, one of which happens to be them.

Congressionally supported "select committees" were another by-product of a micromanaged legislative branch. The Select Committee on Hunger is a good example. The committee was started in the 1980s as a response to what was then called

"America's new awareness of the hunger problem." Of the four original select committees, one on aging, one on families, and one on drugs, the hunger committee invariably got the most publicity.

Hollywood was into hunger and so was the music industry. Werner Erhardt, the guru-founder of est, was involved too, with an organization called the Hunger Project. There were hunger rock concerts, celebrity relief missions to "hunger hot spots," and perhaps the biggest publicity stunt ever attempted on behalf of any cause, "Hands Across America," a coast-to-coast demonstration of unity on the hunger issue by hundreds of thousands of people holding hands. In the rest of the world, hunger was the grim reaper's calling card. In America, it was Kenny Rogers, Diana Ross, and Michael Jackson singing "We Are the World. We Are the Children."

Hunger was an issue that needed something more than a caucus, so Congress created a select committee. The first chairman was Rep. Mickey Leland, an outspoken Texas Democrat, who used the position to make hunger a major concern on the Hill and in Hollywood, where the entertainment industry represented an increasing source of congressional campaign contributions.

No member of Congress would ever use starvation as a fundraising device, but trips to Ethiopia *were* important stops on many a lawmaker's reelection itinerary. On one such trip Leland, who was black, was killed in an airplane crash, an event that further enhanced the political status of hunger as well as the job of heading the select committee.

Leland's successor as chairman was Democratic Rep. Tony Hall from Ohio, a man who bears a remarkable resemblance to TV evangelist Jim Bakker. Hall's timing couldn't have been worse. The recession struck, and select committees became expendable luxury items. The first slated to go was the hunger panel. *Washington Post* columnist Coleman McCarthy, a militant vegetarian who once urged readers to give kids fruit and vegetables for Halloween, came to Hall's defense. So did other hunger enthusiasts. But when all efforts at stopping the budget ax failed, Hall, in admitted desperation, decided to do something no other member of Congress had ever done before.

After the House voted to drop the committee, Hall announced he was going on a fast until funding was restored and hunger given back its rightful place on the list of congressional concerns.

People magazine did a story on his fast. All the network news programs covered it. *Roll Call* even ran a weekly weight loss watch. Hall got more publicity than he ever had in his life, and after three weeks his liquid diet paid off.

Speaker Tom Foley, in carefully worded language, promised to make hunger an important priority and hinted that Hall, who shed twenty-two pounds to get his attention, would play a significant role in the effort.

Hall went back on solid food and not long afterward formed the Congressional Hunger Caucus, which would, as a press release stated, "sustain the momentum" generated by his fast, and "push hard to place hunger in the top echelon of importance."

Hunger is an issue Congress should study, and Hall has made sure there's an ample supply of information. But with most members having no time to devote to any special interests but their own, who knows how many are paying attention, let alone willing to shed some of their own personal pork the next time Hall called a hunger strike.

CHAPTER THREE

SEX, LIES, AND CABLE TV

The hallway outside the Senate Rules Committee hearing room looked like backstage at a rock concert. Television crews had been setting up all morning, and with less than an hour to go before curtain time the place was such a mess Capitol Hill cops were called in to clear a path to the door.

Most congressional hearings are so boring only the stenographers stay awake. But when one comes along that involves sex, lies, and possible election fraud, it not only draws a big crowd, people actually pay attention.

As always, the first to appear on the scene were members of the media, who filled two tables behind the spectators' section. The *Washington Post* and *New York Times* were represented, naturally; so were the major TV networks, wire services, and a half dozen policy-wonk weeklies that analyze every minute aspect of the legislative process. The Hill press corps tends to be deadly serious, even when they're trying to be funny. "Another opening, another show," smirked one reporter just before his briefcase hit the floor with a business-like thud.

Next came the committee staffers. They check the microphones, fill water pitchers, then, once testimony gets under way, wait in the background, ready to look up facts and figures or run little errands. Staffers are the grunts of Congress whose tireless dedication to duty and nonstop groveling are what make the whole system work.

Finally, there were the committee members themselves. They entered one at a time through a rear door, chatting amiably as they took their assigned places (Democrats on the left, Republicans on the right) behind a long judicial-style bench. They may look casual and unrehearsed, but they're not. Each witness has been thoroughly interviewed in advance by committee experts, who then brief their bosses on everything they're going say. The main rule at sessions like these is always the same: *No Surprises.*

Here it should be pointed out that a hearing is not so much an inquiry into the unknown as it is a carefully planned presentation of the *known*, or at least that portion of the known that committee members think they have something to gain by making public. Politics is the art of revealing and concealing information in premeasured doses, and a congressional hearing is a medium designed to do both.

The arrival of Committee Chairman Wendell Ford signaled that work was about to begin. Ford, an affable old-timer from Kentucky, had assembled his colleagues on the panel to consider a most delicate matter, one that could ultimately affect the welfare of each and every member of Congress, maybe even change the future of American politics.

The problem was the behavior of Sen. Robert Packwood, a fifth-term liberal Republican from Oregon, who for more than twenty years had been living a double life as a kissing bandit. During his 1992 reelection campaign, Packwood was the subject of an exposé then being prepared for the *Washington Post.* When the article was published three weeks after the election, which Packwood won, it contained allegations by twenty-six female aides, lobbyists, and campaign workers that the senator had made "unwanted sexual advances," grabbing, feeling, and kissing them in a sustained demonstration of unrequited horniness dating all the way back to 1969.

One woman said that during an interview for a position on his campaign staff, Packwood without asking permission had chased her around his desk and kissed her "sensuously." Another reported that Packwood had attempted to massage her leg.

And another said that Packwood told her: "If I ever run for president, I want you by my side as my vice-presidential running mate." The senator then "laid a juicy kiss on my lips," the woman said. "I could feel his tongue coming."

The *Post* article, written by Florence Graves, a former editor of *Common Cause* magazine, portrays Packwood as a man so chronically unlucky at consensual romance that he was reduced to standing on women's feet to keep them from running away or else cornering them in his Senate office, where he kept a wine-in-a-box dispenser to ply his would-be dates with economy vino. No one admitted being forced to have sex with Packwood, married for most of the period in question, but now divorced. Nor does it seem that the Oregon lawmaker ever met anyone in all his many attempts to score who succumbed to his ardor. If power is "the ultimate aphrodisiac," as Henry Kissinger once said, it sure didn't work for Packwood.

On paper, he was committed to a strict policy of hands off. In the spring of 1991, Packwood was one of fifty-eight Senate signers of a petition circulated by the Capitol Hill Women's Caucus calling for members of Congress to refrain from "unwelcome flirtations," "ill-received dirty jokes," and other forms of male behavior defined as sexual harassment.

Democratic Sen. Brock Adams from Washington, another signatory of the document, was later accused of molesting eight different women, one of whom he allegedly drugged into unconsciousness before having his way with her. Adams denied the accusations, but decided not to seek reelection. In Packwood's case, charges were made public only after the election, a fact that angered many Oregon voters.

At one time, all of this would have been a standard tale from the Capitol Hill casting couch, more deserving of a slap on the back in the cloakroom than a full-scale investigation. In fact, compared to other Hill sex scandals of recent years, Packwood's French-kissing fetish was strictly Little League. Yet in the present era of political correctness, it had career-ending implications.

A button-down moderate with his back to the wall, Packwood

had become the focus of a feminist frenzy. Without being charged or convicted of any crime, he was nonetheless guilty of the worst male offense in the 1990s—*not getting it*—not knowing that the rules for picking up women have changed. To many, Packwood had become the quintessential predator. And while no one could deny his persistence, there were those who thought his persecution was a little extreme.

"He's really a very nice man," said a female photographer who works on the Hill. But gender-war correspondents had already demonized him into "Pack the Ripper."

Packwood was unable to appear in Oregon or anywhere else without being attacked by angry protesters, demanding his immediate resignation. However, it was not Packwood's sex drive that concerned the Senate Rules Committee. That was the subject of an Ethics Committee hearing. The senators on the rules panel had a far more difficult task to contend with.

Oregon voters were unaware when they went to the polls that Packwood was about to have his multiple tongue thrusts make headline news. When rumors leaked out prior to election day that the *Post* article was in the works, Packwood did what any smart politician would do when reporters in his home state began to ask embarrassing questions. He lied. He knew of no such story, he told the Portland media. He also denied engaging in sexual misconduct or using his staff to intimidate his female accusers.

Packwood beat his Democratic challenger, Rep. Les AuCoin, by 78,000 votes in a particularly mean campaign. Calling himself the "Senator from Clout," Packwood characterized his rival as "a study in hypocrisy." AuCoin had been a House Bank customer, but was exonerated of any wrongdoing. Still, Packwood pounded away on the issue of AuCoin's honesty, while artfully sidestepping all questions about his own.

Was Packwood's win the product of false and misleading statements? Even Packwood couldn't deny it. A good argument could be made that every election is the result of false and misleading statements; however, this case was different. Two hundred and fifty irate Oregonians had signed a petition, officially asking the Senate of the United States to throw out a win by one of its most senior members because he didn't tell the truth.

Normally, something like that would be round filed and forgotten. But Packwood's indiscretions and the public's negative response had forced senators to stage a one-day show trial. The Constitution gives both houses of Congress the power to judge the elections of its members. It also empowers them to expel anyone found guilty of bribery or vote fraud. The latter category covers such offenses as stuffing ballot boxes and coercing voters with threats of physical violence. The Oregon petitioners argued that by concealing his personal history—details of which could have cost him the election—Packwood had in effect defrauded the citizens of his state.

Just before heading off for the standard alcohol treatment program, Packwood admitted in a post-reelection press conference that he may not have been Capitol Hill's smoothest make-out artist; still it was never his intention to harm or harass anybody. "If any of my comments or actions have indeed been unwelcome or if I have conducted myself in any way that has caused any individual discomfort . . . for that I am sincerely sorry. My intentions were never to pressure, to offend, nor to make anyone feel uncomfortable, and I truly regret if that has occurred with anyone either on or off my staff."

Democrats would have liked to get rid of him, to have another election, and hopefully increase their Senate majority. But it didn't take a genius to see what peril they were courting. Every politician tells people what they want to hear, regardless of whether it's true or not. Campaign rhetoric exaggerates, bends, and distorts reality. That's what it's supposed to do. Political speeches aren't meant to be analyzed for their veracity. The same goes for politicians. Bounce one elected official for telling lies to win votes and nobody's job is secure.

Roll Call, which rarely finds fault with Congress, wondered if the Rules Committee hadn't gotten slightly carried away. The claim that Packwood had deceived the people of Oregon, editorialized *Roll Call*, "is so lame, so downright weird, that we can't believe a committee that has better things to do is wasting more than eight seconds on it."

Oregon is one of a handful of so-called "good government" states known for practicing clean, responsible politics, a place big on movements and causes. During the late 1960s, hippies, Jesus freaks, and back-to-the-earth types flocked there, and over the years helped turn it into a haven for activists of every persuasion. Oregon was the first state to decriminalize marijuana possession. The first state to fight litter by instituting a mandatory deposit on glass bottles. And now it wanted to be the first state to apply the truth test to a Senate election.

In a way there was legal precedent. Oregon has a anti-corrupt political practices law that local courts take very seriously. In one case a few years ago, a state senator who was defeated in a primary got himself declared the winner by claiming his opponent, who once held the office, had used the slogan "reelect" when in reality the man had been out of the job for two years. So it made sense that Oregonians might be upset when it came to light that their very own Senator Bob had hoodwinked them.

Nevertheless, their tradition of goodness, admirable as it is, may have given Oregonians an unrealistic view of how politics is practiced in other places. The contention that Packwood should be unseated because he was *not* duly elected—that was taking good government to a whole new level. Never before had the Senate been called upon to throw out one of its members on charges that he had lied about his personal history. What Oregon voters were asking the Rules Committee to do was broaden the concept of fraud beyond simply buying votes and other similar infractions to making misleading statements—or making no statements at all when a candidate knows that omitting information could change the outcome of an election.

The anti-Packwood forces were every elected official's worst nightmare, and by giving them a forum the Democrats were entertaining a theory of accountability that could change the most basic rule in politics.

The petitioners wanted the Senate to adopt a special interpretation of the law that would force candidates to tell the truth about all "personal information." Have they ever used illegal drugs? Have they ever committed adultery? Have they ever rented an XXX movie? Precisely the kinds of questions that can decide who wins and who loses in a major election.

From the Oregonians' viewpoint the logic of their position was simple.

"Imagine you owned a pizza restaurant and you had recently hired somebody to run deliveries," wrote David Schuman, a University of Oregon law professor and a supporter of the Packwood petition drive. "After sifting through applications and interviewing finalists, your choice had come down to two almost equally qualified applicants, and you had hired the one you believed to be marginally better for the position. But a week later . . . you discovered that he lied on the application and in the interview. In response to your direct question, 'Have you ever been convicted of drunk driving?', he replied 'No.' But your routine inquiry to the Department of Motor Vehicles had revealed a series of driving-under-the-influence cases going back over a decade.

"No court in the land would make you put that candidate to work," concluded Schuman. "But what happens if the job you're hiring for is U.S. senator?"

Does a professional lawmaker occupy the same moral plane as a pizza delivery boy? Or put another way: Should politicians be held to the same standard of truth as everyone else? A significant number of Americans would probably say "Yes," and now the Senate was going to take up the question.

It was against this background that the senators on the Rules Committee settled into their leather chairs and prepared to hear both sides of the argument. Knowing the gathering would get full media coverage, big-name members from both parties were camera ready. Jesse Helms, Robert Dole, Daniel Moynihan, Claiborne Pell. All were veterans of campaigns in which things said and unsaid might never stand up to the kind of scrutiny about to be applied to Packwood, who, though not present, was certainly watching on cable TV.

The Rules Committee hearing room in the Russell Senate

Office Building resembled a richly appointed gentlemen's club, which is what it would have been except for the presence of freshman Sen. Dianne Feinstein, a Democrat from California and the only female member of the panel. The walls were lined with bookcases, and in one corner there were handsomely framed pictures of past Rules Committee chairmen, going back to the invention of photography when they all wore Horace Greeley beards. High above the members' bench at one end of the room was a scale model of *Old Ironsides* and the inscription "1812." At the opposite end was a model of Christopher Columbus's ship the *Santa Maria*, with "1492" written underneath. The symbolic motif said: "We're all in the same boat," and on this particular day shipmates were out to protect one another.

The case went right to the heart of the way political races have worked in America for two centuries. In the heat of a campaign there's no such thing as truth. Adopt the sort of civic-minded lie-detection plan the people from Oregon were proposing, and who knows what you'll end up with? It may be more honest. It may be more open. But it *won't* be politics.

"We must proceed carefully in considering the question of rendering an electorate's decision invalid," warned moderate Republican Sen. Mark Hatfield, also from Oregon. "Even though the framers of the Constitution bestowed upon the Congress the power to nullify that decision, it should be exercised with great care."

So great would be the care that Republican Sen. Ted Stevens, of Alaska stipulated in opening remarks that it would be inappropriate for the committee to consider the facts of the case, since most of those were still in dispute.

Senators solemnly nodded in agreement, and with that, Chairman Ford told Katherine Meyer, the lawyer for the petitioners, to begin her presentation.

"Mr. Packwood *stole* the November 3, 1992, election," she declared, sounding like a prosecuting attorney out to put away a repeat offender. Packwood should be unseated, she said, because his denial of allegations against him and subsequent attempts to pressure his female accusers to keep quiet constituted an "impermissible interference with the integrity of the electoral process."

Sen. John Warner, a Virginia Republican, who was once married to actress Elizabeth Taylor, furrowed his brows and called a young female staffer to his side. The two whispered in one another's ears for a few seconds, then Warner, whose flowing gray hair and steely eyes make him look like the senator from central casting, resumed his previous pose of deep contemplation.

Meyer's strategy was to show that a sense of decency and fair play required the Senate to cancel Packwood's election win. But that approach assumed that the senators *had* a sense of decency and fair play to begin with. Meyer was taking a big risk. "Mr. Packwood," she told the committee, "knew that disclosing evidence of his sexual misconduct would have cost him the election, and he went to extraordinary lengths to ensure that the public did not find out about that conduct."

Clearly, he had good cause. For years Packwood, one of the most liberal Republicans on Capitol Hill, had the strong support of women's groups. "They would have been gravely offended to learn of his twenty-year pattern of sexual harassment," Meyer rightly pointed out. She referred to a poll taken after the election that showed only 34 percent of those who had cast their ballots for Packwood would have done the same after the *Washington Post* story appeared. In the general election, Packwood won 52 percent of the vote. Polls, several senators interrupted, can't be trusted. The only poll that counts is an election, and Packwood had won that.

When his turn to speak came, Packwood's attorney, James Fitzpatrick, a lawyer from the trusted and expensive Washington firm of Arnold & Porter, wasted no time getting down to the central issue. "This proposal would turn elections into a giant game of 'gotcha,'" he said. "A losing candidate would comb the record for any snippet of personal information that the winning candidate may allegedly have misrepresented, shaded, or fudged."

And why limit the test to sex? Isn't lying about policy issues just as much a violation of the public's right to know the truth? Fitzpatrick demonstrated the point by proposing "a hypothetical situation" in which someone running for office "repeatedly and eloquently promises that he will support a middle-class tax cut. Just after the election, he reverses his position and says that he will *not* support a middle-class tax increase."

Wasn't that precisely what Bill Clinton had done? Of course, there was also suspicion that Clinton too had lied about sex and drugs. By wanting to appear fair and give the Oregonians their day in court, Democrats had started a debate on telling the truth that could make every politician in Washington look bad, including the president, who at the time could hardly look worse.

Suddenly, not being honest was the hottest topic in town. Robert Samuelson of *Newsweek* was the first to come right out and accuse Bill Clinton himself of being a leading offender. "Clinton lies," Samuelson wrote in a column that had the whole city talking. "I could put it more delicately but that would miss the point. Sometimes they are blatant untruths. Sometimes they are artful distortions, technically true but misleading in their overall spirit and impression. Sometimes they amount to willful ignorance and self deception. But the effect is the same. They destroy public trust."

White House adviser George Stephanopoulos, without specifically denying charges that Clinton had lied, blamed the negative public response on reporters who had used Nexis, the on-line computer research service, to compare Clinton's campaign pledges to his actions as president. Stephanopoulos's defense of his boss was an electronic-age variation of "kill the messenger," or in this instance, the printout.

"The problem," Stephanopoulos complained, "is an excess of literalism." It wasn't that Clinton had lied. Voters had made the

mistake of confusing rhetorical devices with actual commitment. Take away the capacity for electronic data retrieval and
no one would have remembered what candidate Clinton had
said about tax breaks for the middle class, lifting the ban against
gays in the military, or any of his other broken promises.

After being suspended by the press during the presidential
campaign, character questions were back in vogue. But Packwood's lawyer had found a loophole.

"Consider the number of people and their state of mind that
would have to be investigated in a Senate fraud trial to determine whether there was a misrepresentation," he said, raising
the complicated matter of enforcement, thus giving each senator
the out he would need eventually to vote "No."

"One would have to reconstruct what the candidate said to
the press, what the candidate intended to say. Was the candidate
dissembling, attempting to avoid an unpleasant issue, or just
putting forth an answer he wanted to have a television audience
hear? . . . In the free-for-all debate of an election contest, statements are made, promises are set forth and positions are
espoused that ever since the beginning of the Republic were
thought to be no more than what they claimed—campaign
promises."

Politicians, Fitzpatrick concluded, are *supposed* to lie. A campaign promise wasn't a promise in the ethical sense. It was more
like a wish, something people hoped for but never expected to
get. Besides, everybody knows elections aren't based on morality. They're based on expediency. To assume otherwise isn't just
unrealistic—it's un-American!

Congressional politics only appears complicated. Take away the
posturing over issues and pleas for party loyalty, and what
you're left with is a single principle that governs almost everything that happens on Capitol Hill. *Fear.*

All 535 members of Congress have one thing in common, a
deep-down dread that one day they will run for reelection, lose,
and no longer *be* members of Congress. To the man on the street

who has never been a senator or congressman, that may not seem like a big deal, but to anyone who has ever experienced the power and glory of high office, losing an election is the equivalent of being taken out and shot.

This is why fear is the most effective organizing tool in either house of Congress. Fear motivates members and makes even those who hate each other stand together in defense of whatever common enemy might threaten their continued employment. Some senators may have had problems with Packwood's technique, even so they weren't going to desert one of their own on an issue so vitally important as job security. This was something liberals and conservatives could both agree on. It would take more than a few campaign lies to deprive a senatorial colleague of his rightful place in Congress.

The problem was giving the Oregon voters an audience without letting them steal the show. True, lying is wrong. But when a politician tells a lie, does anybody really believe it? And if some people do, whose fault is that? Voters are adults, and if they don't know how the political game is played, they have no business voting.

That's what the senators on the Rules Committee *wanted* to say. What came out was a little less direct.

"Mr. Chairman," said Jesse Helms. "I am reminded of Lewis Carroll's *Through the Looking Glass* when Humpty Dumpty said, 'When I use a word, it means exactly what I intend for it to mean, nothing more, nothing less.'

"There is a lot about this area that bothers me," Helms went on. "Am I correct, Ma'am, that the petitioners have told this committee that the fundamental guarantee of innocent until *proven* guilty is merely an intellectual snare?"

"An intellectual what?" Meyer asked.

"*Snare*," repeated Helms, whose beady eyes magnified through a thick pair of glasses were zeroed in on the witness table. "S-N-A-R-E . . . snare," he repeated.

"I don't know," said Meyer. "I am not as familiar with it as you are. But I don't agree, if that is your question. . . . We are saying that this committee should investigate the charges that Senator Packwood tainted the outcome of the election by lying to the public about an important issue."

This last comment drew the perpetually pink-faced Daniel Moynihan into the fray.

"Wouldn't that be the qualification of 'Thou Shalt Not Taint,'" snickered the prissy New York Democrat, smiling at his fellow-senators to suggest even an ultra-liberal could see the humor in pretending that any election can ever be 100 percent free of falsehood and fabrication.

One of the committee's newest members, Dianne Feinstein, hastened to concur. Feinstein had just won an election in California in which both sides were accused of grossly distorting the truth. Feinstein may have run as a feminist, but she's a politician first.

This wasn't a women's issue, even if it did involve two decades' worth of sexual harassment. Or a fairness issue, even if Packwood himself admitted he had misled voters. No, this was a matter of basic political survival. And Feinstein wasn't about to desert her new coworkers.

At first, members of the Rules Committee weren't sure they wanted to hear the case against Packwood. They changed their minds when Meyer, in an earlier lobbying effort, had reminded them that the Senate Judiciary Committee didn't want to hear from Anita Hill during the Clarence Thomas confirmation hearings either.

"When they finally agreed, it was just so they could say they didn't deny the petitioners due process," said Meyer several weeks after the hearing. "But some senators still refused to see me. Dianne Feinstein probably got elected because of the way the Senate treated Anita Hill, and she *wouldn't* see me. She wouldn't even let her staff meet with me. I was amazed at how she treated the whole issue."

In the controlled environment of the hearing room and in front of her fellow committee members, Feinstein, however, was eager to talk.

"I am concerned," she said to Meyer. "I see your request

opening a Pandora's box for this body. . . . How do you see this thing as different from the case where an individual candidate does a television spot which is false, maligning, even what some people might consider to be libelous, and wins with it. Why doesn't that taint an election?

"Well . . . it may," said Meyer.

Just to make sure they knew what kinds of things might come out of the Pandora's box Feinstein was talking about, Packwood, who had kept a diary that was reportedly full of juicy data, sent memos to every panel member that mentioned drinking, womanizing, and other "personal problems" not unfamiliar to several of his Senate colleagues. One Rules Committee member, Sen. Daniel Inouye, had recently made tabloid-type headlines of his own for sexually harassing a Honolulu hairdresser. In effect, Packwood was saying, "He who's without sin cast the first *vote.*" The message got through.

"Mr. Fitzgerald, would you care to comment?" said Sen. Hatfield.

Sensing the momentum that was building for his side, Packwood's attorney indicated that he would indeed welcome the opportunity to comment.

"Built into the concept of a lie is an intentional misstatement, so I think one can't dodge the fact that the process would have to get into the speaker's mind, and as was said earlier, that is one of the snares that's contained in this proposal."

Since no accurate test for intention exists, how can the Senate reasonably be expected to sit in judgment of what is or is not an honest statement in any election? What all this was leading up to was obvious. Telling lies is so much a part of what politicians do, the act itself can't even be positively identified.

But Robert Dole, the Senate Minority Leader and its most sarcastic source of good quotes, had a compromise solution.

Dole: "I wonder if Senator Packwood or anybody else had just said, 'No comment.' We have all been through campaigns. . . ."

Meyer: "That would be fine."

Dole: "That would be fine?"

Meyer: "Absolutely fine. We have no problem with that. That would not be grounds for investigating an election contest."

Dole: "So that would be an escape hatch, from here on for all candidates. Any time they are asked any question. Just say, 'No comment.'"

Meyer: "You can either say 'No comment.' You can say 'That would invade my personal privacy.' Or you can give the truth? There are all kinds of answers. . . ."

Dole: "But you may not be able to answer the question. You may not be able to tell people the truth. Sometimes, you can't answer some of the questions."

In coming up with a possible solution, Dole had isolated the problem in all of its fundamental simplicity. A wounded World War II veteran who carries a ballpoint pen in his paralyzed right fist to make it look functional, Dole understood the practical value of keeping up appearances. Sometimes—actually many times—politicians *don't* tell people the truth, because they can't afford the consequences. And by now it was obvious that none of the assembled public officials was about to disturb the tradition.

A few reporters, like Nina Totenberg of National Public Radio, left early. Totenberg, one of the recipients of leaks that eventually turned the Clarence Thomas hearings into a national debate on talking dirty at work, had heard enough. Journalists, who for months had been following Packwood around like a posse, weren't going to see their man handed over to them today. Halfway through the hearing, you could sense their disappointment. Maybe Packwood's protection would hold up, maybe it wouldn't. But what began as a sexual harassment case was changed by the Rules Committee into something much more revealing, though far less newsworthy.

After two hours, many spectators were also starting to leave. A group of a dozen high school students came into the hearing room, sat down for five minutes, then departed. That didn't give them much opportunity to hear the senators defending political deception, but as one of their teachers explained, "We just wanted to give them a taste of what goes on."

When Wendell Ford finally brought down his gavel closing the session, reporters who stayed till the end rushed to the front of the room. By the time they got there, though, most committee members were already out the back door. Only Feinstein stuck around long enough to perform her Pandora's Box theory for a TV crew.

Two weeks later the panel, stating that it had no jurisdiction in the matter, voted 16 to 0 not to send the Packwood case to the full Senate for further investigation. The decision, as it turned out, had more to do with administration than morality. If senators had to investigate every lie told in every campaign they'd never have time for their other work. Packwood's attorney called the outcome justified.

Katherine Meyer, who represented the anti-Packwood forces, had a different opinion. Lawyers who testify before congressional committees and lose may have little that's nice to say about the other side, but they generally don't attack the system. Meyer was an exception.

The senators, she told a reporter, are not going to do anything to one of their colleagues for lying "because they want to be able to engage in the same kind of behavior to win elections."

In one respect, Meyer's clients had learned a valuable civics lesson. It was as if somebody dropped sodium pentothal in the Senate bean soup. Rarely have lawmakers been so honest in public about how campaigning works.

"We can't get into this or we'll never stop," said political analyst Norman Ornstein, appearing on *The MacNeil/Lehrer Newshour*. "Lies and distortions and exaggerations are part of the process."

While Packwood still had the Senate Ethics Committee to contend with, he'd won an important victory. His colleagues had unanimously confirmed his right to be where he was, and as long as he stayed there, he would be the direct beneficiary of thousands of dollars in corporate donations to help pay his mounting legal bills.

"The people from Oregon were completely stunned," said

Meyer, after a few months to reflect. "They thought because their charges were just, the Senate would automatically see things their way. I guess they found out Washington doesn't work like that."

But the effects of too much reality soon wear off. Americans want to believe politicians, even when they know they're lying, and especially when the lies are told in such a convincing setting as Congress has arranged for the purpose.

In a clump of trees in front of the Capitol there's a place where microphone outlets seem to be growing up out of the grass. Congress has given the spot to TV networks for broadcasting outdoor interviews with members. The angle is perfect. Stand a senator or representative there, with all that white marble architecture in the background, and whatever he or she says doesn't just look better, it sounds *true*.

All of Washington was designed that way. Few capitals of the world have more false heights and illusory depths. This is a city made for covering up shortcomings with mesmerizing vistas, putting the most deliberate falsehoods into proper political perspective. The Oregonians may have gone home emptyhanded, but they had to be impressed.

CHAPTER FOUR

A 200-YEAR MISUNDERSTANDING

Historians disagree over the exact date that Washington began. Some say it was 1751, when the "Town of George" (now Georgetown) was founded. Others argue it was thirty-nine years later, when a French engineer by the name of Pierre L'Enfant drew up his master plan for the city. Still others insist on 1800, the year Congress came to town, making official the city's status as the new nation's capital.

When the first congressional contingent arrived, Washington had a total of 3,210 residents: 2,464 whites, 123 free blacks, and 623 slaves. No favor seekers, no influence peddlers, and no special-interest groups. Relocating the federal government to the middle of nowhere did have some positive benefits.

In the quarter century since the Declaration of Independence was signed, the capital had been moved to eight different locations, including York, Pennsylvania, and Trenton, New Jersey. In Philadelphia, their last stop before Washington, federal lawmakers suffered the indignity of being hounded by Revolutionary War veterans demanding several years' worth of back pay. Pennsylvania officials offered little protection, and while no harm was done, the experience made members of Congress realize the time had come to find a permanent job site unconnected to any of the thirteen states.

This was a period, remember, when the states were stronger

than Congress. What those in favor of a powerful central government wanted was a national capital that stood alone and, just as important, had enough grandeur to impress everyone.

In 1790, President George Washington, who happened to own riverfront property in the area, picked out what he thought was a nice piece of real estate on the banks of the Potomac River. The area, made up mostly of cattail marshes and mud flats along the Maryland-Virginia border, came with unusually high recommendations. English explorer Henry Fleete, when he dropped anchor there in 1632, called it "without all question the most pleasant land . . . in all the country & the most convenient for habitation."

Since few members of Congress had ever laid eyes on the place, they deferred to Washington's judgment, endorsing his choice by a vote of 32 to 20. But starting a city from scratch would be hard work. As things turned out, building the sort of place America's first president had in mind would take the better part of the next century.

Jenkins Hill, the spot selected for the Capitol building, was a sparsely populated clay plateau that rose 100 feet or so above a huge swamp. Dividing the more habitable West End of town from the malarial dogpatch where the House and Senate would meet, the swamp, and the smell it emitted, according to one early arrival, gave everything around it a "wild, desolate air."

To another newcomer the lack of local development presented a rare opportunity. Pierre Charles L'Enfant, a French civil engineer who came to America with the Marquis de Lafayette, besieged Washington with letters, begging for a chance to design the new capital. City planning was big business in the colonies, but most efforts tended to follow the same checkerboard pattern popular from Williamsburg to Boston. Washington was impressed by L'Enfant's intention to depart from the norm and create a capital city "magnificent enough to grace a great nation." So in January 1790, he gave him the job.

As later events would prove, L'Enfant was a true visionary. Unlike other American cities, he predicted, the capital's suste-

nance would be derived from "its public buildings rather than
. . . its trade centers." Washington, which had no name at the
time, "would grow out of itself, and spread as the branches of a
tree does toward where they meet the most nourishment."

If L'Enfant understood that the natural tendency of government is to expand in the direction of available revenue, he also
had definite ideas about how the unique facilities of the new
democracy should be put on display. Of the 6,111 acres of land
inside the city's original federal boundary, his plan called for
devoting over half the total area to Parisian-style thoroughfares
and boulevards. Ordinary streets would be 110 feet wide, major
avenues 160 feet, and one grand concourse connecting the
White House and the Congress would be a mile long and 400
feet from one curb to the other.

L'Enfant had also decided that streets should be interrupted at
regular intervals by multiple-access circles designed to eliminate
traffic tie-ups and hasten vehicles to their destinations, although
the destinations, like the streets, had yet to be built. Members of
a congressional oversight committee in Philadelphia were
understandably concerned. L'Enfant wanted to turn the city into
an eighteenth-century version of Los Angeles. But Washington
shared his French friend's think-big approach and declined to
interfere.

L'Enfant's plans for Capitol Hill were just as elaborate. The
look he was after was something between ancient Rome and
pre-revolutionary Versailles, with the "cathedrals of government" surrounded by lush gardens, fountains, and an intricate
system of man-made canals. "The mode of . . . improving the
whole district," L'Enfant wrote, "must leave to posterity a grand
idea of the patriotic interest which prompted it."

L'Enfant's devotion to the project soon became an obsession.
Convinced that nothing must stand in the way of his overall
design, he assumed almost dictatorial powers. Washington has
that effect on people. After only a year's work, however, his
quest for elegance did him in.

Daniel Carroll, the wealthiest landowner in the region, decided to build a mansion right in the middle of land set aside by L'Enfant for one of his most splendid boulevards. After Carroll dismissed an order to tear the house down, L'Enfant stepped in and supervised the destruction himself.

The fiery Frenchman was called to Philadelphia to explain, and when he refused to submit all future plans to a special board of commissioners for preapproval, there was nothing Washington could do but fire him. As a parting gift, he offered his architectural alter ego a choice plot of property in what would eventually be the heart of the city. L'Enfant was too proud to accept it. Which was just as well with most members of Congress, who wanted him out of town.

Broken-spirited, L'Enfant moved to Maryland and died in obscurity, leaving behind blueprints for a nation's capital that nearly everyone except the city's namesake would have been happy to burn.

The War of 1812 achieved approximately the same result, when fires set by invading British soldiers left many of Washington's federal buildings, including the Capitol, in ruins. A reconstruction effort began soon afterward, when the steady influx of government workers and the accompanying demand for everything from saloons and brothels to suitable housing kept the city in a perpetual state of urban renewal. In one year alone, some 300 new dwellings were built on and around Capitol Hill. Just the same, Washington was a long way from becoming the elegant world capital L'Enfant had conceived. By European standards it hardly even qualified as a city.

Nevertheless, one thing was clear. The District of Columbia was under the complete control of Congress. The language of the founding fathers on the subject of the federal city, unlike their language on other matters, was direct and to the point. Article I, Section 8 of the Constitution states: "The Congress shall have power . . . to exercise legislation in all classes whatsoever over such a District."

James Madison, one of the top brains of his time, explained in *The Federalist Papers* (No. 43) what the drafters had in mind:

The indispensable necessity of complete authority at the seat of the government carries its own evidence with it. It is a power exercised by every legislature of the Union, I might say of the world, by virtue of its general supremacy. Without it . . . the public authority might be insulted and its proceedings interrupted with impunity.

Under the Constitution, Washington was conceived as a combination federal headquarters/theme park, someplace the states could look to for guidance and inspiration. At the same time it would be purified by law of all local political activity that might impede, hinder, or otherwise complicate the work of the central government. At any rate, that was the plan.

The city may have begun as a preserve for high-minded public servants, but that didn't stop it from attracting more weird characters than a Nathaniel Hawthorne novel. An account of the social scene written in 1835 noted that Washington's population was "compounded from the largest variety of elements: foreign ambassadors . . . members of Congress, from Clay and Webster to Davy Crockett . . . flippant young belles, pious wives dutifully attending their husbands . . . grave judges, saucy travellers . . . melancholy Indian chiefs, and timid New England ladies . . . All of these are mixed up together in daily intercourse . . . because there is nothing else."

And there *was* nothing else! More like an outpost than a nation's capital—actually, more like an improved mudhole than an outpost—Washington was not much to look at and less to call home.

After he paid a visit to the city in 1842, author Charles Dickens described it as a place of "spacious avenues that begin in nothing and lead nowhere; streets a mile long that only want houses . . . and inhabitants; public buildings that need but a public to be complete; and ornaments of great thoroughfares which only need great thoroughfares to ornament." Dickens called Washington "a monument to a deceased project" and complained he had never seen a more uncivilized city.

What made it that way wasn't merely the pronounced absence of culture, but the presence of Congress. Capitol Hill was also largely responsible for Washington's growing reputation for violence and mayhem. With democracy still in its formative stages, elected officials literally fought each other for power on a daily basis. Get caught in the middle of a dispute over tariffs, land rights, or Indian removal, and the result could be serious, if not fatal, injury.

From the earliest days of the Republic, whenever Washington politicians couldn't end their disputes on friendly terms, there was always a final option. Until Congress passed a bill in 1839 prohibiting the practice, dueling was the city's ultimate means of conflict resolution. While the practice may seem a little uncivilized, historian Robert Kyle thinks it may have served to promote law and order. "Gentlemen welcomed the custom," he wrote, "believing the constant threat of a duel improved conduct, prevented informal brawls and gave personal encounters an atmosphere of gentility."

Two hundred years ago, if prominent public figures got on each others' nerves, they didn't debate on Sunday talk shows, or write opposing think pieces in the *New York Times*. Settling scores in the old days was basically a do-it-yourself project. When someone harmed you, you harmed him back, and if you both happened to be gentlemen, you did it with dueling pistols.

Being a Southern city, Washington soon became a place where antebellum codes of honor meant that any insult, no matter how slight, might be reason enough for rivals to kill each other. People would fight duels in defense of virtue and they fought duels over a misdirected wad of tobacco spit.

Duels originating in Congress often began with a political difference of opinion, and by the time they were over, there was an excellent chance that one or both participants might never be heard from again.

Washington's most popular dueling field was located in the nearby Maryland town of Bladensburg, where a grove of trees just off the main road to Baltimore created a natural shooting range. Today gas stations and auto-body shops surround the area, but a nearby plaque suggests why this may be the capital's most appropriate historical landmark. "On this site," it reads, "more than 50 duels were fought. Here, on what became known as 'The Dark and Bloody Grounds,' gentlemen of Washington settled their political and personal differences. . . ."

The first Bladensburg duel, according to Kyle, was fought on March 2, 1808, between two congressmen: George Washington Campbell of Kentucky and Barent Gardenier of New York. The trouble started when Campbell accused Gardenier of "falsehood" and "baseness," complaining in a speech that he was part of a French plot to take over the government. Gardenier was wounded in the fight but continued to serve in the House for three more years. Campbell, who walked away unharmed, proved that a successful duel could also be a valuable career boost. He was later elected to the Senate.

The most famous duel between Washington notables took place in New Jersey in 1804, when former Treasury Secretary Alexander Hamilton was shot and killed by then Vice-President Aaron Burr, whose election Hamilton had called a "disgrace [to] our country."

Washington, however, was a favorite dueling venue, and the city hosted dozens of political shootouts. Commander Stephen Decatur was killed in a duel fought in 1820. In 1826, Secretary of State Henry Clay fought a duel with Virginia Sen. John Randolph. Both missed and returned to work with their egos intact. In 1835, four years before the congressional ban took effect, Naval Academy midshipman Daniel Key, the son of Francis Scott Key, who wrote "The Star-Spangled Banner," was killed in a duel with a classmate.

Twenty-five years later, a member of Congress shot and killed another of the famed composer's sons. The victim this time was Philip Barton Key, who was having an affair with the wife of New York Rep. Daniel S. Sickles. An ambitious Democrat in the Tammany Hall tradition, Sickles had cultivated a friendship with Key in hopes of gaining admission into Washington high society, but the plan backfired when Key and Sickles's young wife fell madly in love.

After a friend told Sickles what was going on, he forced his wife to write out a full confession. "I did what is usual for wicked women to do," she said, describing in explicit detail for the time, how the two lovers shared "intimacy of an improper kind. . . . I undressed myself. Mr. Key undressed himself also. . . . [We] went to bed together."

A few days later Sickles spotted Key walking across the street from the White House and shot him dead. Not strictly speaking a duel, the incident nonetheless made news around the country. Sickles's trial got even more attention when he was acquitted of murder following the first successful temporary insanity plea in American history. The public was outraged. Two politicians aiming pistols at one another was one thing, but the fact that a U.S. representative could walk out of court scot free after killing someone in cold blood only added to the general feeling that members of Congress could get away with anything.

The Civil War divided America over the question of slavery. But hostilities began on Capitol Hill long before the first shots were fired on the battlefield.

The Hill for years had been a refuge for runaway slaves, some 400 of whom, known as "contrabands," lived in shacks on Duff's Green across the street from the Capitol. In 1856, the issue wasn't ex-slaves in Washington. It was extending the institution of slavery into the new Western states, and debate centered on Kansas, where a bloody guerilla war was taking place. At the height of the conflict, Sen. Charles Sumner of Massachusetts, an upright Republican abolitionist, made a two-day speech, denouncing Southern intentions in rhetoric heavy with sexual innuendo.

Southerners, he declared, had participated in the "rape of a virgin territory, compelling it to the hateful embrace of slavery." He singled out Democratic Sen. Andrew Butler from Carolina for special contempt, comparing him to a "Don Quixote who had chosen a mistress to whom he has made his vows, and who . . . though polluted in the sight of the world, is chaste in his sight—I mean the harlot, Slavery."

Several Southern members of Congress considered challenging Sumner to a duel right there on the spot, but they knew the self-righteous New Englander would refuse. Even so, the South's honor demanded that he pay for his insult.

Preston Brooks, a congressman from South Carolina and a cousin of Butler, confronted Sumner in the Senate chamber. His speech, Brooks informed Sumner, was "a libel on South Carolina and Mr. Butler, who is a relative of mine."

The hot-tempered Brooks then attacked Sumner, hitting him over the head more than twenty-five times with a wooden cane. The near-fatal beating incensed Northern opponents of slavery, whose anger quickly turned to outrage when Brooks, who became a hero in the South, was fined $300 by the district court. The mild rebuke seemed to give legal sanction to barroom brawling inside the Capitol.

Sympathizers sent Brooks dozens of replacement canes, many inscribed with encouraging phases like "Hit Him Again!" and "Use Knock-Down Arguments!" As for Sumner, his injuries, and what some historians call the "posttraumatic stress disorder" that followed, kept him from returning to the Senate for the next four years.

The War Between the States was really the war on Capitol Hill between Republicans and Democrats, with several hundred thousand constituents added to the fray. The country had never seen so much death and destruction, and by the time the smoke cleared, Washington was a much different place. The Reconstruction period that followed changed the role of government from organizer to provider. Overrun by lawyers, government bureaucrats, and social reformers, what the nation's capital would become a hundred years later was already taking shape before the last century was barely half over.

But the Civil War had another side effect. Hardly was the fighting over before American entrepreneurs with their habitual

clairvoyance seized control of the postwar economy. Washington became a magnet for economic "fixers" from everywhere.
When the war ended, so did any pretense that the government
was run by selfless idealists. Many lawmakers became the virtual
hired hands of robber barons, and those who hadn't been hired
yet were eager to get on the payroll.

Graft and corruption made elective office profitable. The
most notorious disgrace of the time, the Credit Mobilier scandal, involved scores of senators and congressmen, and eventually set the standard by which congressional financial misdeeds
would be judged for years to come. A scheme designed to
defraud the government by skimming money from federally
supported western railroad projects, Credit Mobilier worked
like a bogus consulting firm, charging inflated fees, falsifying
expense claims, and generally treating the U.S. Treasury like an
automatic teller machine.

The enterprise was managed by Oliver Ames and his brother
Rep. Oakes Ames, a Massachusetts Republican for whom conflict of interest was just another economic opportunity. With
one Ames handling the take and the other preventing bothersome inquiries by distributing company stock to important
members of Congress, the two brothers managed to net more
than $20 million dollars over the life of the scam. When the
deception was finally uncovered, it destroyed several long-run-
ning careers on Capitol Hill and forced President Ulysses Grant
to drop Schuyler Colfax as his running mate in the 1872 election. Like many others in Congress, Colfax was a Credit Mobilier stockholder, receiving his shares when he served as Speaker
of the House.

The demise of Credit Mobilier didn't put an end to shady fiscal affairs in the nation's capital. If anything, it seemed to give
aspiring swindlers added incentive. By the beginning of Grant's
second term, Washington was synonymous with corruption, and
no one personified the connection better than the city's first and
last true political "boss," Alexander R. Shepherd. Appointed
governor of the District of Columbia by Grant in 1873, Shep-

herd, who owned a plumbing company, a newspaper, and other businesses, had been active for years lining his pockets and those of his friends, among them Grant himself, whom Shepherd advised to invest in a Maryland paving-stone company.

The Civil War had left Washington in such a shambles, an effort was started in Congress to move the capital to another part of the country. Judging by the condition the city was in, it was hard to tell the North had been victorious. The muddy streets contained so many prostitutes, robbers, and homeless ex-slaves that the chief of police wrote in 1867: "Crime, filth and poverty seem to vie with each other in a career of degradation and death."

Calling Washington the ugliest city in the whole country, Sen. William Stewart, a Republican from Nevada, said, "The idea of inviting the world to see this town . . . seems to me altogether out of the question."

Shepherd and a local citizens' group lobbied to keep the capital where it was, urging Congress to pass legislation to make Washington a territory. Just below statehood, territorial standing would afford the city a greater degree of autonomy in conducting its own affairs while it continued to receive federal money to help pay for expenses. It was the perfect setup for someone with Shepherd's ambitions, and when the measure passed, he knew what to do.

As head of the city's Board of Public Works, which included such notables as Civil War General Montgomery Meigs and landscape architect Frederick Law Olmsted, Shepherd asked the new territorial legislature to give him $4 million to cover the cost of urban improvements. When he only got $500,000, he brought all city building projects to a halt until a special election was held on a bond issue to make up the difference. The vote, which appears to have been rigged, gave him the money he wanted.

Shepherd used his position to award city contracts to members of his so-called "Washington Ring," who then resold them again at a profit. In the meantime, he continued to acquire more businesses of his own. He bought a gravel quarry, a bank, a streetcar line, and each new company became the recipient of new city contracts. By 1872, Shepherd's spending spree had produced parks, sewers, and downtown buildings—many of them designed by his favorite architect, Adolph Cluss, who moonlighted as Karl Marx's American literary agent—but it also put the city $20 million in debt.

Two congressional investigations concluded that Washington's public works projects had been badly mismanaged, although neither panel blamed Boss Shepherd. His ties to the Republican Party and the Grant administration got him off the hook, and it didn't hurt that he had also helped scores of congressmen and senators buy luxury homes at discount prices.

Shepherd's influence, while it lasted, was extraordinary. "Cronyism," as a critic put it, "was his modus operandi." On one occasion, Grant, his whole cabinet, and a sizable portion of the diplomatic corps attended a housewarming party at Shepherd's suburban estate. Commenting on the event, the *New York Sun* wrote:

> The president not only gave this fellow the countenance of his official presence, but he took his whole family with him and sat down on a level with the thieves, contractors, fraudulent measurers, notorious jobbers, and colluding clerks, who made up a large part of this "distinguished company."

After years of making deals behind the scenes, Shepherd only lasted nine months in the governor's office. Despite Grant's efforts to keep him there, congressional leaders, responding to popular muckraking crusades, decided that Shepherd's shenanigans had gone on long enough.

They didn't just take back the governor's title, they abolished the post altogether. Territorial status and the right to vote were revoked—and a commission was formed to run the city. Because of Boss Shepherd, it would be more than 100 years before Congress granted Washingtonians anything that even resembled home rule.

In one last attempt to strike it rich while Grant was still in the White House, Shepherd claimed the government owed him $200,000 for services his companies had provided the city during its three years as a territory. When payment was denied, the Boss declared bankruptcy, but he was far from finished.

With his political power base taken away and his business conglomerate dissolved, Shepherd embarked on a new career. In 1880, he left Washington to take over a struggling silver mine near Chihuahua, Mexico, and in a few years he built another fortune. He reported earnings back to his family in Washington by telegram, using fake football scores as a secret code: "Sewannee twenty-eight, Vanderbilt fourteen. Hard game. Nobody hurt." On his return to the nation's capital for a visit in 1887, Shepherd's misdeeds were forgotten and he was hailed by the city as a hometown hero.

While in Mexico, according to one newspaper story celebrating his return to Washington: "Boss Shepherd blossomed out as a bonanza king. He devoted all his masterful genius and tireless energy to developing the property he had and acquiring more, and pretty soon he had charge by absolute ownership of a kingdom greater in extent and far richer in revenues than many an hereditary monarchy famous in the world's history."

In an age that admired men of action, some Washingtonians worshiped Shepherd. Another local paper predicted: "The day will surely come when a grateful people will erect in honor to Alexander R. Shepherd the finest monument in a city where fine monuments are not rare."

A statue *was* erected after Shepherd's death in 1902, and for decades it stood in front of the District Building, Washington's city hall. In recent years, officials decided the Boss might look better somewhere else, and moved his likeness to its present site outside the city's main sewage treatment plant.

Washington has always been a convenient proving ground for political experiments by lawmakers in Congress. During Boss

Shepherd's time, the city went from municipality, to territory, to congressional protectorate—all in the space of five years. But it's voting rights, not political status, that have been the source of the city's longest running political controversy.

Soon after the Civil War, enthusiasm for freeing the slaves produced the inevitable problem of what to do with them. The influx of blacks into Washington was so great that army barracks and storage depots had to be converted into emergency housing. A bill passed over President Andrew Johnson's veto in 1867 gave the vote to all males in the city over 21 years old, regardless of color. But when a local election was held later that year, whites stayed away from the polls in large numbers, many complaining, as historian Constance McLaughlin Green wrote, that Congress was trying to make the District a "Negro paradise." The near sweep by radical Republican candidates sparked anti-black violence throughout the city.

Under Reconstruction, the government's first large-scale venture into the entitlement business, Congress assumed the responsibility for "uplifting the Negro race." In the beginning many lawmakers pursued the task with a religious zeal. Freed black voters were registered, training schools and hospitals were built. While some Washington blacks moved ahead, the majority of new arrivals, most of whom had never lived anywhere but farms or plantations, were unprepared for life in a city where the main occupation was paperwork.

As Congress gradually lost interest in its crusade, blacks were left to fend for themselves. Poverty and sickness were rampant in overcrowded black communities and, as one Washington settlement worker observed, so were "all the vices which slavery inevitably fosters."

Given the District's strong ties to the South—the local slave trade was only officially abolished in 1862—the city was an unlikely place for any experiment in racial harmony to succeed, and predictably it didn't. Instead the nation's capital developed dual racial cultures. The 1880 census reported that Washington's 60,000 blacks represented nearly one-third of the city's population.

Black Washingtonians became as class conscious in their part of town as whites were in theirs. At the top of the nonwhite social ladder was the "black bourgeoisie," called "the most distinguished and brilliant assemblage of Negroes in the world." There was a flourishing black professional class of business owners, doctors, and clergymen. But in the separate-but-equal America of the late nineteenth century, they still lived in a city as racially segregated as any backwoods town in Dixie.

By 1900, Washington, in fact, had become two different cities, one white, one black. One with exclusive neighborhoods and the picturesque Mall; the other made up mostly of slums and shanty towns with names like Swampoodle, Foggy Bottom, and Bloodfield.

When it ended Washington's days as a territory and removed the right to vote, Congress disenfranchised the entire population. Afraid of what might happen if black voters gained too much power, legislators turned the nation's capital into a two-tier congressional colony. On Capitol Hill the effects were obvious.

In no other part of Washington did whites and blacks live so close together yet so far apart. At the turn of the century, as the white areas of the Hill were transformed into pockets of wealth and high Victorian architecture, black sections became a national disgrace. Thousands of Capitol Hill blacks lived in overcrowded alleys. Addressing Congress in 1904, President Theodore Roosevelt called such places "a breeding ground of vice and disease" and challenged lawmakers to come up with a comprehensive plan for improving the lot of the poor in the nation's capital.

Congress was characteristically uninterested. President Woodrow Wilson's first wife pleaded on her deathbed for the passage of measures to clean up Washington's slums. But again little was done. One reason for the lack of congressional enthusiasm was her husband.

Wilson, who regarded himself as a "southern man," favored strict segregation in the government and throughout the city. During his second term in office, Washington's race problem reached the crisis stage. Triggered by rumors that a white woman had been raped by a gang of blacks, tensions erupted in four days of rioting in the summer of 1919, as returning World War I veterans rampaged through black neighborhoods burning homes and beating residents. The riots unleashed Washington's resurgent Southern heritage, and in 1925 a Ku Klux Klan parade down Pennsylvania Avenue put it on full public view.

The Klan had the blessing of many members of Congress from the South who praised the group as if it were a community service organization. Some lawmakers, while stopping short of endorsing the march, nevertheless took the opportunity to point out that Washington should remain a "white" city under the firm control of the House and Senate.

"Have we the right to continue to do things that will inevitably make our Capital City more and more a Mecca for a great influx of Negro population?" asked Rep. Thomas L. Blanton, a Texas Democrat. "We are doing our Nation a wrong, we are doing our Capital City a wrong and we are doing the Negro race itself a wrong every time we pass legislation that tends . . . to place our National Capital under the domination of the Negro race, if they should be given the franchise. We are perilously near that now, because there are enough today to hold the balance of power in almost any election, if not enough to make a majority in any election."

Having no power at the polls, since they couldn't vote, many District residents, white and black, came to see full representation in Congress—and along with it freedom from congressional oversight—as the only way to improve their status. Yet any form of increased self-rule for the city would mean a brand-new set of concerns for lawmakers, not the least of which was being surrounded by an unfriendly local government, exactly the sort of situation the Founding Fathers had hoped to avoid by moving the nation's capital to Washington.

In the 1950s, after white migration to the suburbs left the District's population three-quarters black, the city's political plight became a civil rights issue. For years powerful members of Congress, mainly from the South, had prevented any home rule bill from getting out of committee. All that changed in 1961, when the city was given the right to vote in presidential elections. Six years later, President Lyndon Johnson appointed Walter Washington the first D.C. mayor in over a hundred years. And in 1973, congressional legislation allowed the District to elect its own mayor and city council.

That may sound like local self-government, but it isn't, since Congress still retains final approval over every local law. If history is any indication, there's an excellent chance Washingtonians may never know what it's like to live in a democracy, though that could change if advocates of statehood get their way.

At present, Washington, with a population of 570,000, has more residents than Vermont, Alaska, and Wyoming. But is the rest of the country ready for a fifty-first state with no visible means of support other than a cozy relationship with the federal treasury? And is Washington ready to say good-bye to the hundreds of millions of dollars in government payments it could lose and start supporting itself on revenue from parking tickets? Actually, giving out tickets already is a major industry, adding over $30 million a year to the city's treasury, about $10 million more than the D.C. lottery contributes.

The city has no farms, no factories, and is so short on usable space, its prison facility is located twenty miles out of town in Virginia—an arrangement many nearby residents are hoping will end if the District becomes a state.

They could have a very long wait. The last time full congressional representation for D.C. was put to the ratification test in the late 1970s, it went down to resounding defeat. Not even a do-your-own-thing place like California could find good cause for admitting a new state to the Union whose sole function would be making life more expensive for the other fifty states.

"There is a fundamental conflict of interest between Washington and the fifty states," wrote former Republican Sen. S. I. Hayakawa in opposing the amendment. "Washington produces no wealth. Its primary mission as the seat of government is to spend money. What is good for Washington is, therefore, not good for the states."

When it wants to ignore certain problems, Congress simply funds them, then looks the other way. That's how the District of Columbia has been run for 200 years. Official Washington operates from crisis to crisis, but senators and representatives have never seen the city as a critical concern, except when they're up for reelection and they all pretend they've never been there.

The last four presidential elections and thousands of congressional races have revolved around anti-Washington themes. President Jimmy Carter started the trend in 1976. Watergate was on everyone's mind, and Carter pledged to de-Nixonize the bureaucracy and change Washington's reputation for self-indulgence.

"Too many have had to suffer at the hands of a political and economic elite who have shaped the decisions and never had to account for mistakes," Carter said in a speech on the subject. "When unemployment prevails, they never stand in line looking for a job. When deprivation results from a confused welfare system, they never do without food or clothing or a place to sleep. When the public schools are inferior or torn by strife, their children go to exclusive private schools. And when the bureaucracy is bloated . . . the powerful always manage to discover and occupy niches of special privilege."

Although Carter's campaign made it almost impossible for him to work with Congress once he was elected, the born-again former Georgia governor showed other candidates how to get voters' attention. Ronald Reagan, George Bush, and Bill Clinton all campaigned against Washington and won. In his campaign Clinton also favored statehood for the District, so it was sometimes hard to tell which part of Washington he was running *against*.

The problem, as Carter had discovered, is having it both ways, making the transition from an outsider promising to reform the system to an insider trying to keep his job.

During his campaign Clinton specifically pledged to clean up Congress. After a succession of scandals, culminating in a notorious check-kiting scam at the House Bank, the legislative branch of government had its worst public approval rating in years. Clinton promised to take government away from "the powerful" who "worry endlessly about who is in and who is out, who is up and who is down," and give it back to the people in the form of spending cuts and tax reforms. But once he went to work, it didn't take long for Congress to begin treating the new chief executive like Jimmy Carter, Jr.

Members of the House and Senate have their own anti-Washington script, and acting it out requires consummate performance skills.

"The strategy is ubiquitous, addictive, cost-free and foolproof," explained political scientist Richard Fenno. "In the short run nearly everybody wins, [but] in the long run somebody has to lose." And to avoid that, lawmakers spend millions of dollars every election cycle on corrective image adjustment. It's not easy—or cheap—to convince voters that while they may be members of Congress, they have nothing to do with anything that happens there.

George Washington was right. The nation's capital would command attention. What might surprise him if he were alive today is the kind of attention it gets. The city was supposed to inspire respect. Not suspicion. Confidence. Not the creeps. But there's one big difference between then and now. When Washington was president, there wasn't any *Washington*.

CHAPTER FIVE

WELCOME TO THE CLUB

When it comes to handling the press, Hill staffer Katie Cullen favors the direct approach.

"Get back!" she barked at a gang of reporters and photographers awaiting the arrival of four busloads of newly elected members of Congress. "Let's go . . . Move it!"

Huddled together in the subfreezing dawn, the media mob obediently retreated across the parking lot. Cullen, assistant superintendent of the House Radio and Television Gallery, was in charge of posing freshmen for their biannual class picture—and shooting would begin when she said it did.

The 1992 elections produced so many new representatives—110 in all—they had to be arranged seven rows deep on the Capitol steps. With the great white dome looming in the background like a giant postage stamp, this was the moment of glory all of them had been waiting for.

"Wow," said a voice from somewhere in the middle of the crowd. "We must have won!"

These were people used to positive thinking. But it would be a long time before most of them were that sure of anything else. Life in Congress is based on self-doubt and uncertainty, and even happy occasions like this one are full of painful reminders that permission to play lawmaker only lasts from one election to the next.

To get where they were, the Class of '92 campaigned against government gridlock, special privileges, and all the other things Washington is famous for. But that was back home. Now they were part of the franchise and subject to every job-threatening nuisance that goes along with it, one of which was unleashed when Cullen gave the signal and several dozen cameramen, sound technicians, and assorted pencil jockeys took off in a mad dash for the smiling newcomers.

While incoming lawmakers posed for their portrait, reporters yelled questions at anyone who made eye contact. What were they going to do about the deficit? How about term limits and campaign spending?

Florida Democrat Carrie Meek, the daughter of black share-croppers, said she was ready to start reforming immediately. "I may look like a sweet grandmother," she warned, "but I'm capable of impaling." The combative reference was to plans for challenging the all-male power structure that Meek and twenty-three other female freshmen promised to dismantle during their first 100 days in office.

Michael Huffington, owner of a film production company, declared he too was anxious to get down to work. He should have been. The California Republican spent an all-time House record of $5.4 million of his own money to win a seat. "I'm an athlete and runner," he said in a voice that reeked of financial security. "I put everything I had into the race." Huffington's top priority was to eliminate perks—every single one of them. The fact that he could afford to pay for his own had nothing to do with it. In the 1992 election it was principle that mattered.

Freshmen accounted for over one quarter of the new Congress, making this the biggest turnover since 1948. They came to Washington, said the *New York Times*, with a "mandate for change," and every new member arrived with his or her own special formula for fixing the government.

Unfortunately, the morning's media blitz had its cruel side. In the celebrity-conscious news environment of Capitol Hill, this would be the last national press attention many of these eager frosh would receive. Statistics show that over the last fifty years freshmen have lost their seats at twice the rate of other members. So the smart ones were making the exposure count.

"In the retail business we believe the customer is always right, and in politics the customer is the people," said Howard P. "Buck" McKeon, proprietor of a Western clothing store and a new Republican congressman from the Los Angeles area.

Ted Strickland, an Ohio Democrat, who once was an occupational psychologist, used his few seconds in the limelight to be a bit more introspective.

"I've worked in a prison. I've seen the results of stress, and I think that will help me be a better decision maker," he said. Then again, maybe it wouldn't. "I've only been here for four hours," he added. "I really don't know what's going on. I'm telling you what I think."

There's a bad habit that could get him in trouble.

It isn't easy to hold a smile for five minutes, make meaningful hand gestures, and dispense broadcast-quality chatter, all at the same time. Yet for anyone who planned on making a career out of Congress, those were just some of the skills that would have to be mastered before the next election.

As if to drive that point home, who should suddenly appear as the picture session was breaking up but Rep. Newt Gingrich. The House Minority Whip and head of the in-your-face wing of the GOP just happened to be jogging past the Capitol at 8:00 A.M.

"Hi, fellas," beamed the chubby, gray-haired Georgian, trotting by the press herd with a pretty blond assistant. Gingrich was running hard for the minority leader's job, and his morning workout seemed to impress the new Republican members whose votes he would need when push came to shove.

Gingrich was wise to get an early read on this bunch. The new class of freshmen, one of the most diverse in years, had been typecast as a wrecking crew, and House veterans were anxiously assessing their destructive potential.

There were sixty-five Democrats and forty-five Republicans, with sixty-nine of them from the baby-boomer generation born after World War II. Sixteen were black, seven were Hispanics, with four immigrants from Cuba, Kenya, the Netherlands, and Korea.

The class included a direct descendent of a signer of the Declaration of Independence, and a cofounder of the Illinois Black Panther Party. One freshman was drawing unemployment while he ran for office. One was an impeached federal judge from Florida, and one was a former governor of Delaware. There was an optometrist, a shrink, and two public relations consultants. Two were Rhodes scholars, four were television anchor people, and forty-eight were lawyers. Seventeen came from California, two had served on the New York City Council, and only ten had no previous political experience.

They looked competent enough, but the problem for party leaders was training them to act like they were in Congress, an undertaking filled with more political implications than normal since the 1992 Freshmen Class comprised a potential voting bloc that could easily mess up the leadership's game plan.

"They're not a lot of revolutionaries. Everybody knew that," said Washington political analyst Charles Cook. "They got elected on a changed agenda. I wouldn't call this group of freshmen anti-establishment, but that doesn't mean they're business-as-usual types."

With that in mind, House Speaker Tom Foley, Majority Leader Richard Gephardt, and the rest of the Democratic hierarchy set out on a cross-country victory tour two weeks after the November elections to scope out the new talent and see what it would cost to bring them into the fold. Congress works best when everybody gets along—or at least gets what he wants—and Foley's trip, part fact-finding mission, part peace feeler, was aimed at making sure all the uproar about changing government was merely colorful campaign rhetoric. But following stops in Atlanta, Chicago, and Los Angeles, the tough talk from newcomers showed no sign of letting up.

"We'll be a force to be reckoned with. Watch out!" announced Maria Cantwell, a Democrat from Foley's home state of Washington, after the Speaker made his rounds.

Foley, known for his crash diets and a briefcase full of spray-on salad dressings, had good reason to be nervous. So did his GOP opposition. Republican freshmen at a special post-election summit meeting in Omaha, Nebraska, issued a shock-therapy manifesto, calling for a ban on all campaign contributions from political action committees, an end to the seniority system, and the immediate abolition of free parking for members of Congress at Washington's National Airport.

Incumbents were understandably concerned. This new group seemed to have more in mind than a little House cleaning. It was as if a chain saw of reform was about to tear into Washington and turn the entire legislative branch of government into one big pile of wood chips.

These kinds of threats hadn't been heard since the Watergate Class of 1974 came to town determined to remove every last trace of Richard Nixon and the Imperial Presidency. In the process, what that group of reformers helped to create was an Imperial Congress whose power far exceeds anything Nixon ever dreamed of, and its present leaders weren't about to see it destroyed from within by any first-term do-gooders.

The freshmen of '92 were no pushovers, but the fact that so many had law degrees and backgrounds in state government said they weren't out to break the rules either. They were trained consensus builders, hyper-ambitious pragmatists, ready to bargain for things they wanted. Only two Democrats bore watching as would-be radicals: Dan Hamburg, a Zen teacher from California, who refused to wear a necktie; and Bobby Rush of Chicago, an ex-Black Panther turned insurance man. The apprehension didn't last long.

Hamburg was picked by *People* magazine as one of its "50 beautiful" celebrities of the year, and Rush, the first freshman to let the leadership know he wanted an assistant whip's job, was soon impressing everyone with his networking skills.

In Washington, the deepest political concerns are always disguised as praise, and soon accolades for the freshmen began pouring in from fearful old timers. "I look forward to working with them," said House Majority Leader Bob Michel. Steny

Hoyer, chairman of the House Democratic Caucus, assured the *Washington Post,* "These freshmen are coming here to make changes that people back home can feel in their lives."

But it was the folks back home—the same ones who had cast over 20 million ballots nationwide in favor of mandatory term limitations—that wanted members of Congress to feel changes in *their* lives. And the Class of '92 was supposed to deliver the message.

First, they'd have to get past a formidable prevent defense. To defuse the looming menace, party bosses activated a mechanism already in place—Freshmen Orientation—an elaborate incumbency-protection plan designed to bury newcomers in almost three weeks of collegial bonding and heavily scripted mind games. The initial phase on Capitol Hill would teach them about the duties and privileges that come with serving in Congress. Then would come trips to Harvard or Annapolis for total-immersion issue briefings.

It's during this crucial period that even the most diehard anti-Congress outsiders are encouraged to confront the awesome task before them, as well as the stark reality that the same institution they had attacked in the campaign was now their main source of clout, and the only reason they'll ever be invited to appear on *Nightline,* assuming they could first land a choice committee assignment.

Everyone blasts Congress during the campaign. That's normal. Once you're elected the rules change. For Democrats, most of whom made congressional misconduct, like check bouncing and sexual harassment, a major issue, their first official trip to Washington was a time for discussing cooperation, especially economic cooperation, with the Bill Clinton White House. Clinton had campaigned against Congress too. But most House Democrats knew right from the start that their political futures were directly tied to the dollar value of the president's programs back in their districts.

"I'm heavily invested in the success of Congress and President Clinton," Democrat Leslie Byrne, a new House member from Virginia, admitted in a *Post* interview.

Other freshmen Democrats expressed similar sentiments. This wasn't how reformers talked. "Heavily invested"? The new people were sounding just like seasoned cash grabbers, even though withdrawals wouldn't begin until after an official swearing-in ceremony, still more than a month away.

When it's open for business, Congress runs like a big bank, with branch managers hard at work collecting deposits from contributors and handing out giveaways to their constituents. After each election, the most successful managers are sent back to Washington to accumulate more deposits and deliver more freebies. But from the majority point of view, having a Democrat in the White House doesn't necessarily represent an improvement to the system.

That's why a president who campaigns against Congress is always suspect.

"I believe most, if not all, of us campaigned against Congress," said Oklahoma Republican Ernest Jim Istook not long after the cold truth hit him. "It was us against them. Now, we find we're about to be one of them."

On Day One of Freshmen Orientation, the new arrivals looked right at home as they entered their first party caucuses, hugging each other and eyeballing the hallways for anybody who could help them land a key committee slot.

Congressional committees are conduits for big-buck appropriations. Freshmen who get picked for one with the power to dispense money to their districts are well on their way to long and productive careers. That's why nearly half the class wanted seats on the Public Works Committee, a funding pipeline for pork-barrel projects, such as the airport in the Ozarks one congressman-to-be was hoping for or the superhighway to Disney World another one wanted. In 1992, the huge exodus of House veterans left dozens of empty seats on top committees, vacancies the freshmen were after and the leadership could use to keep them in line.

The main concern of every Washington politician is job security. In that respect, new members were no different. Since

almost three-quarters of them came directly from state legislatures and city councils, for most, being elected to serve in the
House of Representatives wasn't so much a new career as it was
the next logical career move.

"My brother Dan, who was in Congress for ten years, warned
me never to announce what committees I wanted," said John
Mica, a Florida Republican.

If you don't get the ones you're after, you could look like a
jerk.

Then too, there's mixed opinion on how much obvious ambition is *too* much? Even before orientation began, some freshmen
were in Washington lobbying hard for committee assignments.
Another beginner from Florida, Democrat Karen Thurman, let
it be known that she wanted a seat on the powerful House Ways
and Means Committee. The problem was that former Ways and
Means Chairman Dan Rostenkowski, who had to approve,
hated the sight of freshmen. But "Rosty," as his friends call him,
may have had his resistance lowered after being linked to a
stamps-for-cash scam at the House Post Office. Thurman figured the only way to find out for sure was to ask.

"I went in and talked to him for an hour," she reported. "It
was a very nice meeting . . . When we were finished, he said he
didn't like freshmen and that was that."

What she learned from the experience is basic to every political transaction.

"You gotta know when to hold 'em and know when to fold
'em," Thurman said. "You have to be persistent to succeed in
this business. I'll just try again next time."

One freshman for whom a campaign of kissing up to top
senior members paid off was Sherrod Brown, a Democrat from
Ohio. Brown, whose last government job was a stint as Ohio's
Secretary of State, visited nearly everyone on the thirty-five-per-
son Democratic Steering and Policy Committee, the panel
responsible for making committee assignments. He followed up
his visits with letters, stressing his work habits, loyalty, and will-
ingness to take orders. These are qualities much in demand on
the Hill, but particularly appealing to Energy and Commerce

Chairman John Dingell, one of the most powerful men in Congress and someone always on the lookout for lieutenants. Dingell not only tapped Brown for a spot on Energy and Commerce, he made him vice-chairman of its high-visibility Oversight and Investigations Subcommittee, which Dingell himself heads.

Brown knew that after getting elected, the next step was getting ahead. Which means telling congressional leaders everything they want to hear. And when Brown isn't available to say the right things, he makes sure his staff is. Asked what his boss's subcommittee duties were, Brown's press secretary said, "sitting next to Dingell."

After lunch with Foley, Democratic freshmen, most lugging around thick folders full of information, were already complaining about the heavy workload. Having only a mail drop in the Rayburn Building for an address, they were up to their necks in job-seeking resumés.

Every new Congress means a relocation of staffers, and the 110-seat turnover in 1992 meant some members were getting as many as 50 employment applications a day. Democrat Cynthia McKinney of Georgia estimated receiving over 500 in one week alone, so many she had to store the overflow in shopping bags at her parents' house in North Carolina.

"I'm going to spend the next few weeks prioritizing," said Karan English, a Democrat from Arizona. But thanks to a yearly budget of $557,000 per member to cover staff pay and expenses, $122,500 more for office supplies, a personal salary of $133,644, plus cost-free mail and a generous travel allowance, finding enough money to do everything most new members had in mind would soon be no problem.

"When you're talking about budgets of billions and billions of dollars, the money spent on each member of Congress doesn't seem like much," said retired Sen. William Proxmire, who made a career out of publicizing the government's wasteful spending habits. But to a lot of first-time representatives, the take-home pay alone qualified as a windfall.

For freshmen—many of whom made high legislative salaries a campaign issue—getting elected to Congress meant the biggest raises of their lives. The average pay increase was 70 percent per new member, but in the case of three House Democrats the boost was bigger than that.

The year before her election, Eva Clayton, president of her party's freshmen class, earned an annual $8,000, working in North Carolina county government. Elizabeth Furse from Oregon received under $5,000 selling grapes. And California's Dan Hamburg made $2,262 in unemployment compensation. Few among the new lawmakers had grossed even half their congressional income in former careers. Being a member of Congress was nice work.

On the Republican side, where Gingrich and last-term Minority Leader Bob Michel greeted freshmen by telling them Congress is a place for teamwork, the theme *du jour* wasn't reform but peace and goodwill. Crusading against the seniority system and other congressional traditions may have impressed voters, but that's not the way to win influential friends and useful committee appointments, Gingrich said. Down by eighty-two bodies to the Democratic majority in the House, the GOP's opening day good-neighbor policy clearly disappointed many who came to town looking for a fight.

"My biggest surprise was hearing Newt Gingrich say he thought he could work with Bill Clinton," said Alabama Republican Spencer Bachus. "That's not the Newt Gingrich I've been seeing on television."

Bachus was right. Gingrich and other officials in both parties were hovering over new representatives to the point where some, after just a few days on the Hill, said they felt controlled and manipulated by leaders conspiring to preserve the status quo. But given all the attractive extras that went with it, none of them seemed too upset.

"I'm really disappointed by the way most of these new guys became socialized into the system," said former *Roll Call* editor

James Glassman. "The freshmen were supposed to be agents of change, but they have pretty much gone along with the program."

In the first three days of orientation there was a fancy reception at the Library of Congress, sit-down dinners in the Capitol Rotunda, and a Union Station champagne buffet for new women members, with *Vogue* magazine there to take pictures. The seduction was in full swing. Who wants to overthrow a system that treats you like a minor Greek deity even before you have a permanent phone number?

"Change" may have been the mandate delivered in the election. But that wasn't the message Democrats sent when they voted to retain the party's full slate of standing committee chairmen. The most coveted job title on the Hill, a "chairman" is the congressional equivalent of a South American strongman, "ruler for life," or until old age, defeat at the polls, or a party coup dictate otherwise. The one exception to a clean sweep by incumbents was an ailing 82-year-old Rep. Jamie Whitten of Mississippi, the longest-serving House member in history, who was ousted as head of the Appropriations Committee, only to be replaced by 83-year-old Rep. William Natcher from Kentucky, who died a year later.

The new people weren't being held hostage. They were just being initiated into the familiar folkways of Capitol Hill. The official orientation program for the twelve Senate freshmen lasted only two days. By contrast, the weeks of intense schooling for new House members left little time for anything but briefings and occasional trips to the bathroom.

There were seminars on stimulating the economy, panels on rebuilding America's infrastructure, and, for spouses—there were a half dozen new House husbands—some you're-not-in-Kansas-anymore advice on moving to Washington, with specific emphasis on avoiding high-crime areas east of the Capitol, the scene of frequent murders.

"We were told not to look for houses past Eighth Street, wherever that is," said Betsy Mann, whose husband David is a Democrat from Ohio. "Frankly, I'm a little afraid."

All sessions were officially closed to the press, but House Administration Committee Chairman Charlie Rose brought a few of his favorite reporters in through the back door to witness an ethics lecture. Rose, the kind of guy you might run into clocking speeders at a radar trap, wanted to show off his updated audiovisual approach to teaching freshmen the do's and don'ts of dealing with people who may try to buy their votes.

This is the time, they were informed, when many among them will first encounter Washington lobbyists, who, for instructional purposes, are made to sound like people to be avoided, when in reality it's the continuing financial assistance of lobbyists and their political action committees that keep most members solvent.

Some freshmen already knew that. Eva Clayton, a North Carolina Democrat, had collected more than $281,000 in PAC money for her campaign.

After promising as a group to fight against special interests, the freshmen of '92 took in almost twice as much money from PACs during their first six months in office as the previous class of freshmen did during the same period two years before. According to Common Cause, which compiled the statistics, only 10 of the 110 new House members reported having received no funds from PACs.

PACage Deal

Top 20 House Freshmen Recipients of PAC Money
(January 1, 1993–June 30, 1993)

Name	PAC Receipts	Percentage of Total Receipts
1. Peter Deutsch (D-Fla)	$120,650	58%
2. Marjorie Margolies-Mezvinsky (D-Pa)	105,300	61
3. Mike Kreidler (D-Wash)	104,850	75
4. Gene Green (D-Texas)	96,000	84
5. Ron Klink (D-Pa)	93,791	85

6.	Jane Harman (D-Calif)	93,207	62
7.	Carolyn Mahoney (D-NY)	85,449	66
8.	Eric Fingerhut (D-Ohio)	76,841	55
9.	Mel Reynolds (D-Ill)	73,750	67
10.	Earl Pomeroy (D-ND)	72,220	73
11.	Michael Crapo (R-Idaho)	71,221	90
12.	Earl Hilliard (D-Ala)	66,350	83
13.	Melvin Watt (D-NC)	66,164	83
14.	Melvin Minge (D-Mich)	65,631	73
15.	Lynn Wollsey (D-Calif)	64,400	81
16.	John Linder (R-Ga)	63,611	55
17.	Leslie Byrne (D-Va)	61,400	69
18.	Pat Danner (D-Mo)	59,600	74
19.	Maria Cantwell (D-Wash)	59,275	76
20.	Rod Grams (R-Minn)	56,500	34

SOURCE: Common Cause

As freshmen were studiously taking notes, a message flashed in huge letters on the movie screen in front of them: "DON'T ACCEPT PAYMENT FOR ANY SERVICE WHERE THE FEDERAL GOVERNMENT IS INVOLVED."

"You *can't* use your office to enhance your personal gain," explained a serious-sounding former Ethics Committee Chairman Louis Stokes (551 bounced checks in the House banking scandal). "But you *can* vote for things to enhance your financial wellbeing."

On Capitol Hill there is often a dotted line between right and wrong.

With so many congressional freshmen already experienced in holding elective office, most knew the routine by heart. In politics, dues must be paid at every level, and part of the price of moving up the ladder is treating each rung with proper respect. However, in the time-honored tradition of letting numbers speak for themselves, the freshmen Democrats as a group finally asked for and got a piece of the action commensurate with their class size: five seats on Energy and Commerce, three on Appropriations, and one on Ways and Means, where Rostenkowski broke with tradition and picked freshman Mel Reynolds, a Democrat from Illinois, for a coveted seat on his panel.

It didn't hurt Reynolds's case that he happened to be a black Rhodes scholar from Chicago, Rosty's hometown, or that he beat former Rep. Gus Savage, one of the most loathsome members ever to serve in the House. Savage, also black, used to address white male reporters as "faggots," and once got in trouble for propositioning a female Peace Corps volunteer during a fact-finding mission to Africa.

Republican freshmen, who made their presence felt by voting to impose term limits on all ranking GOP committee members, got two of the seats on Appropriations and two on Energy and Commerce.

In the most obvious booby-prize committee assignment, newly elected Florida Democrat, Alcee Hastings, a former federal judge impeached by Congress in 1989 on bribery charges, received another comeuppance from the same people who took his old job away. Hastings, whose name was conspicuously missing from the list of freshmen selections for the House Judiciary Committee, instead got selected for Merchant Marine and Fisheries.

But these days members who get tossed into backwater committees aren't always doomed to automatic obscurity, no matter how much they deserve it. As more and more lawmakers become issue entrepreneurs, pushing their own causes and attracting media attention outside the normal channels, getting on a powerful committee isn't the absolute requirement it used to be.

Take the case of three-term Rep. Bernie Sanders, a self-described "Democratic Socialist" from Vermont. Not being a member of either major party guaranteed Sanders the worst committee assignments on the Hill. Rather than languishing in neglect, the disheveled left-winger became his own talent agent and a regular fixture on cable talk shows, like CNN's *Crossfire*.

The leadership on both sides of the aisle may think Sanders is a flake, but voters in Vermont like seeing him on television. If the goal is getting reelected, that's what counts.

Publicity cuts both ways, though, and what may look like a golden opportunity one minute can easily turn into a PR nightmare the next. That's what happened when *Spy* magazine decided to call members of the Class of '92 and find out what they would do to stop ethnic cleansing in the nation of "Freedonia," the fictional country made famous in a Marx Brothers movie. The question was asked during a bogus radio interview, and a high number of newcomers, trying to sound statesmanlike, came off making total . . . *congressmen* of themselves.

"I think anything we can do to use the good offices of the U.S. government to assist stopping the killing over there, we should do," said James Talent, a GOP congressional trainee from Missouri.

"We need to take action to assist those people," advised Corrine Brown, a Florida Democrat.

"Yeah," said Indiana Republican Steve Buyer. "It's a lot different situation than the Middle East."

Later, indignant cries of media entrapment only made things worse. "Most of these people don't have any idea what a den of vipers this place really is," said freshman John Mica. The one possible benefit, he speculated, is that looking stupid in politics sometimes builds character.

On Wednesday of Week Two, as the Washington phase of orientation was coming to an end, so were all pretenses of peaceful bipartisanship. Gingrich and Michel were threatening to go to court over a proposed rules change that would give delegates from Guam, Samoa, the Virgin Islands, Puerto Rico, and Washington, D.C., added voting privileges on the House floor, thus increasing the current Democratic majority by five.

Foley retaliated by laying down the law. According to several freshmen, under pain of having their committee assignments reviewed, new Democratic members were forbidden to attend the conservative issues conference in Annapolis. None did.

When the freshmen first arrived in Washington, they seemed to share a genuine sense of common purpose, or else they did a good job of pretending whenever they were on television. By the time they went their separate ways to Annapolis and Harvard, party leaders had stirred up so much unrest that people who had been total strangers less than a month before were treating each other as if they'd been feuding for years, which, if they were lucky enough to get reelected a few times, they would be.

Freshman Orientation functions like Marine boot camp, replacing the natural political desire to make friends with a hate-the-enemy dedication to party objectives. Here's where the dividing and conquering begins. If the goal was to Gringrich*ize* and Gephardt*ify* new people through vindictiveness training, the plan worked. Not only did the sessions leave most Democratic freshmen thoroughly despising their Republican counterparts and vice versa, it kept them from doing anything that threatened the established chain of command.

Freshman caucuses later produced a list of proposed changes in congressional operations, and the only things new members could agree on was asking that Congress stop exempting itself from the laws it imposes on the rest of the country and suggesting that former House speakers should be given smaller paid staffs when they retire. So much for radical reforms.

The three-day Annapolis get-together, sponsored by the Heritage Foundation, Free Congress, and the Family Research Council, was purposely scheduled to conflict with the gathering at Harvard, and organizers in Cambridge were not pleased.

"We wanted to break up Harvard's monopoly," stated Kate O'Beirne, chain-smoking vice-president of the Heritage Foundation. It was about time somebody offered an alternative, she said. "We're free-market types, so let's compete."

Former Education Secretary William Bennett told thirty GOP freshmen who made the trip to read Thomas Jefferson. Outgoing HUD Secretary Jack Kemp urged them to embrace cultural diversity, fiscal restraint, and not to forget the importance of family togetherness.

"One night, I saw Gerald Ford moping around the Capitol, and I asked him what was wrong. He said he had to work late and was going to miss seeing his son's football game. Jack, he said, never miss seeing your son play football."

Another speaker, Dan Oliver, a former Federal Trade Commissioner during the Reagan Administration who gave off lethal hate vibes, conceded that some regulation, like the yellow line down the middle of the road, serves a useful purpose.

"But the *reg-u-la-tors*," he sneered, stressing his disgust with every syllable in the word, "they want to turn America into an intensive-care hospital ward!"

Many in the audience solemnly agreed, among them Ken Calvert, a representative-to-be from California, who got a big laugh when he told everyone he had sent away to Washington for a copy of the Federal Paper Reduction Act, and they sent him back *three*.

Attendees in Annapolis received all sorts of useful information. Between sessions with titles like "Dethroning the Imperial Congress" and "How to Deal With Lobbyists and Preserve Your Integrity" (one suggestion was to pray for guidance), new members compared committee assignments and probed each other for pointers.

Michael Crapo from Idaho, who was picked for Energy and Commerce, wondered if anyone knew of a course he could take to help him remember names. Tim Hutchinson, a former state legislator in Arkansas, filled colleagues in on Bill Clinton's political style, which, he said, includes lots of late-night phone calls. Don Manzullo of Illinois, who said he would hang up if Clinton ever called him, proudly stated that he never even considered joining the liberals at Harvard.

"I'm not interested in that kind of stuff," he said, invoking the party line on federal spending. "You have to listen to people explaining why we *should* have a deficit. As far as I'm concerned, that place ought to be called the Kennedy School of *Big Government.*"

If there had been accurate polling techniques a hundred years ago, public opinion probably would have rated politics, as a profession, somewhere between horse theft and circus performing. It's still far from being a respectable profession, but thanks in large part to Harvard's John F. Kennedy School, politics today is considered a legitimate field of academic study in the same category with criminology, statistics, and casino management.

The JFK School, a modern glass-and-brick complex on John F. Kennedy Street—no wonder conservatives feel funny being there—is a monument to the New Frontier conviction that public service is a noble calling. In keeping with that idea, the school has been adding an Ivy League polish to new congressmen since 1972.

The Institute of Politics, which does the actual polishing, is well known for turning out Washington insiders. Robert Reich, secretary of labor in the Clinton cabinet, is a past faculty member. David Gergen, Ron Brown, and others in the administration have also been affiliated with the school, which provides employment opportunities for out-of-work politicians, like former presidential candidate Michael Dukakis, who taught there between terms as governor of Massachusetts.

"We put new members of Congress together with the best people we can find," said Director Charles Royer, a former mayor of Seattle. "The Heritage Foundation can call it tax-and-spend training if they want, but we try to give a balanced program that can serve as a bridge between academia and the real world of politics."

Activities are funded by the Pew Charitable Trust and the John D. *and* Catherine MacArthur Foundation, the genius-award people, with a congressional stipend tossed in by the House Administration Committee. Transportation and baggage handling are provided by the U.S. Air Force.

A few Republicans skipped the Annapolis conference and came straight to Harvard, while two or three others attended parts of both functions. Nevertheless, for the first time in its twenty-year history, a significant number of new GOP members passed up Cambridge completely. The snub did not go unnoticed.

Democratic Party minders sent to keep an eye on proceedings admitted to being more than a little miffed at the Heritage Foundation and other conservative groups for going head to head with Harvard.

"Heritage is a fringe organization at best," said David Dreyer, the pony-tailed director of communications for Richard Gephardt, who was headed for a job in the White House. The opposition conference was part of a larger breakdown in civility between the two parties, and the GOP was responsible, Dreyer said. The more he talked about it, the madder he got.

"The Republicans want to tear down the institution of Congress, to make war against the Democrats," he fumed. "Their theory is if you go to an orientation organized by the party that runs Congress, you're coopted. If you don't, you're rebelling. That sounds just like the people who dominated the Left in the 1960s."

In the spirit of that bygone era, a group of protesters was marching around outside the window, chanting "Save American Jobs," a reference to the North American Free Trade Agreement and flight of American industry to Mexico and other points south. Campus security people looked very concerned. Harvard was apparently pro-NAFTA. Walkie-talkies hummed with instructions about how to contain the few dozen scraggly leftists—or were they rightists?—trudging in circles through the snow.

That's what college used to be like, but Harvard officials weren't selling nostalgia. They were selling *Harvard*, its research facilities, its bow-tied professors, its data-gathering skills in every conceivable field of human knowledge. When these congressmen and congresswomen become heads of committees with the power to fund special projects of national importance, the hope is they will remember this week of cram courses, and send a few multimillion-dollar grants to Harvard. Taking the money out of politics may reduce the influence of the lobbies, but it won't touch the connection between Cambridge and Congress.

During the 102nd Congress, Harvard, incidentally, ranked second among all universities in the number of free trips to campus it provided for members. Yale came in first; Stanford was third.

Republicans on hand said they found their experience not only educational but emotionally rewarding, particularly an evening of informal speeches during which each participant was encouraged to open up Oprah Winfrey–style about the plans and dreams, hopes and schemes that made them get into politics.

Rick Lazio, a New York Republican, brought tears to the eyes of listeners as he spoke about his late father's influence on his life. Ohio Democrat Ted Strickland was especially moved.

Even if Lazio was a Republican, he confided to a reporter, "I feel I understand him. We may disagree, but I could never hate him now, because I know what's in his heart."

Despite policy differences and partisan squabbles, the soul-baring at Harvard also served an institutional purpose, one that would eventually help all of these raw beginners become true Capitol Hill colleagues. It's okay to be political opponents. It's okay to go to the mat now and then for a special cause. In the end, what matters is the ability to compromise, to work together and to help each other stay in office.

Change is good, as long as it doesn't get out of hand, undermine relationships, or, worst of all, turn Congress over to *other* newcomers. Not even the most ardent freshman reformer wanted to see that happen.

If the trend established over the last ten years continues, 9.3 percent of the freshmen running for reelection in 1994 will lose. How vulnerable individual members are will depend on a variety of factors, not the least of which will be a perception by voters that many of those who once campaigned against

Congress have been terminally "congressionalized."

The freshmen had come a long way since that cold morning on the steps of the Capitol when many of them thought they were there to change the system. Three weeks later, they *were* the system. In the next election, the hard part for most of these 110 newly activated team players wouldn't be running against Washington. It would be running against Washington with *them* in it.

CHAPTER SIX

CAESAR'S PALACE
ON THE POTOMAC

Rev. Richard Halverson, D.D., ministers to the most expensive congregation in America. Halverson is the U.S. Senate chaplain, and it's his job to open each session with a brief message intended to pardon the act of lawmaking before it begins. On most occasions his little sermonettes are so tactfully out of touch with the real business of his flock that only the truly daffy even pretend to be listening. But as a new campaign season was about to begin, a time when incumbents were expected to get slaughtered at the polls like fatted calves, the situation called for spiritual intervention. And the good reverend, as always, knew exactly what to say.

"Sovereign Lord of history and the nations," he said, closing his eyes for dramatic effect, "we pray for the senators running for reelection. . . . Give wisdom to those who direct their campaigns. Give the senators special persuasion in speech . . . and provide wherever needed adequate campaign funds. We pray in His name through whom Thou dost promise to supply all our needs according to Your riches in glory. Amen."

Heads bowed and hands folded, Halverson's listeners not only enjoy hearing such prayers but fully expect they'll be answered.

By 1992, the average member of Congress had to raise $17,000 every week he was in office just to pay his or her election bills.

Praying may help. Each year special interest groups, including religious organizations, give lawmakers millions of dollars in campaign contributions, but even that amount barely begins to meet the ever-increasing need for more cash.

In terms of sheer man hours, filling up congressional coffers is probably the hardest work on the Hill. Former Colorado Sen. Tim Wirth said one reason he retired from Congress was a travel calendar that often kept him on the road fund-raising for four weeks every month, a tough life when you consider the Senate itself only meets in full session for *three* weeks a month.

Getting elected to Congress is the end of one campaign and the beginning of another. During his time in Washington, Wirth, one of the last original JFK look-alikes to leave office, raised over $8.5 million to win a total of seven congressional elections. Yet if he thinks six years is too long for a U.S. senator to be out begging for financial support, consider the poor U.S. representative. He only has *two*.

House members may have less time to get ready, but every lawmaker faces the same grueling schedule. Campaigns start the first day in office and they don't stop until the other guy concedes defeat, at which point the whole process begins all over again.

In the old days, senators and representatives could come to Washington and not worry about campaigning until two or three months before voters went to the polls. Anyone who did that today would be laughed out of town.

After only six months in office, the thirty-one senators elected in 1992 had already spent over $4 million on their next campaigns, still over five years away but very much on the minds of every one of them. The lawmaker who doesn't begin to finance his next election as soon as possible after his last one could lose valuable momentum that ultimately costs him his job.

While it's technically illegal for any member of Congress to use money provided for office expenses on campaign spending, the practical overlap makes it impossible to tell where one cost ends and the other takes over. But there's no law preventing politicians from paying their own campaign expenses, and most like to get off to an early start.

Expense reports for Campaign '98 filed with the Federal Election Commission during 1993 show that:

- Sen. Dale Bumpers, an Arkansas Democrat, spent over $2,700 from his campaign fund to rent an apartment in Little Rock that serves as Bumpers's primary Arkansas residence.
- Sen. Frank Murkowski, a Republican from Alaska, was reimbursed by his campaign fund for more than $15,000 in unspecified plane fare and other travel expenses, including $305 for an overnight stay in Tokyo.
- Sen. John Breaux, a Louisiana Democrat, who had $1.5 million left in his campaign treasury after his 1992 election, paid himself $106,925 for travel, restaurant, and entertainment expenses, all related to his reelection bid in 1998. Breaux also reimbursed himself $1,500 that he paid to attend Mardi Gras events and $1,050 for tickets to New Orleans Saints games.

Many lawmakers disguise the early launch of fund-raising efforts as "thank-you laps" around their districts or states, a chance to tell voters how grateful they are for their support and to remind them that the price of value-added representation is constant giving.

Less than ten months after winning a close election in 1992, Pennsylvania Republican Sen. Arlen Specter was back in the money hunt. Specter, who spent more than $9 million to retain his seat in the Senate, invited a few dozen high-end contributors to a Washington issues briefing with a lineup of guest speakers that included Bill Clinton's permanent campaign manager, James Carville. "Although the last election is not far behind us," Specter wrote in a letter to his supporters, "it is important to begin organizing now."

Specter was hardly the first politician out of the gate. House Majority Leader Richard Gephardt was also an early starter. The Missouri Democrat raised and spent slightly over $3 million to win his 1992 race, compared to his opponent's paltry

$375,000. However, Gephardt, whose legendary dullness gained national recognition on *Saturday Night Live* during the 1988 presidential primaries, was taking nothing for granted. At a time when incumbency offers no guarantee of job security, Gephardt began frontloading his 1994 House campaign with a big-buck reception only three and a half months into his new term.

The public thinks lobbyists are the ones chasing politicians, trying to stuff money into their pockets and fly them kicking and screaming to speaking engagements in Hawaii. In reality, it's the other way around. Lobbyists are the ones being chased. And while most don't play that hard to get, many resent being constantly typecast as the villains.

"Every time you turn around, some senator or congressman is after you to contribute to his campaign fund," said one lobby veteran. "The minute after you talk to one of them, there's a staffer on the phone, telling you to throw his boss a fund-raiser. If they're the victims, they get pretty good compensation for all their pain and suffering."

Some lobbyists on Gephardt's 163-person "steering committee" were reportedly asked to fork over $2,500 each, a cover charge that represented a potential payday for the honoree of more than $400,000.

What made the Gephardt affair so interesting wasn't the take but the timing, only weeks before the Clinton administration was due to announce a comprehensive campaign reform bill aimed at limiting the money spent at events just like the one held for Gephardt. The lawmaker picked by the White House to guide this important piece of good-government legislation through Congress? The Honorable Richard A. Gephardt.

Not so lucky with the timing of his fund-raiser two months later was Sen. Daniel Moynihan, chairman of the powerful Senate Finance Committee. Moynihan, up for reelection in 1994, invited supporters to pay $5,000 apiece to attend a VIP reception at the Rainbow Room in Manhattan's Rockefeller Center. In effect, lobbyists were being asked to give the maximum amount allowed by law. To show they'd be getting their money's worth, Moynihan dropped his befuddled-professor routine and sent out invitations that came right to the point.

"Most importantly," read the announcement, "Senator Moynihan is now chairman of the Finance Committee where he will oversee 55 percent of all federal spending and 98 percent of all revenue raising, as well as health-care reform and trade."

The fact that the fund-raiser was scheduled to take place a week before Moynihan's committee would start work on the 1994 budget was an added reason to give.

Hill veterans hadn't seen anything like it since 1988, when Moynihan's predecessor as head of the Finance Committee, Treasury Secretary Lloyd Bentsen, put the squeeze on lobbyists to pay $10,000 each to eat breakfast with him. Moynihan was selling himself as the man to see for everything from tax breaks to tariff concessions. What he hadn't counted on was a press leak, and the day after his reception made the news, Moynihan called it off without comment.

Congressional incumbents have never had to work that hard to collect money. Since their inception in the early 1980s, political action committees—those ingenious conveyors of cash created by big business, big labor, and big government to preserve and protect their bigness—have made it comparatively easy for law-makers, especially top party leaders and important committee chairmen, to accumulate all the resources they need to ward off bothersome challengers.

There are 4,000 PACs registered in Washington, and of the $678 million raised by House and Senate candidates for the 1992 elections cycle, more than 25 percent, or $180 million, came via PAC contributions. There are corporate PACs, trade union PACs, and sexual preference PACs. The liquor lobby has a PAC, so do beet farmers, animal rights groups, and day care providers. Every industry, religion, and recreation in America has a PAC to go with it. An outgrowth of the post-Watergate reforms, PACs were originally an attempt to clean up politics. Needless to say, it failed.

The latest effort to reform campaign finance by imposing limits on the intake of PAC money has only intensified the activity of lobbyists, who continue to have the same motivational influence on the legislative process as ukulele music has on hula girls. The economics is simple: Congress makes laws, and interested donors, through the use of applied capital, make sure that politicians in charge keep the special needs of their friends in mind.

Money in Washington is a by-product of relationships. The longer someone serves in Congress and the more relationships he establishes, the more money he's likely to accumulate to help him stay put. Capitol Hill has worked that way for years. But in 1992 something happened. The American voting public, the same coast-to-coast population that hundreds of millions of dollars are spent on every election, declared enough was enough. If the best government is a government that governs least, what a sizable portion of the U.S. electorate said was that no member of Congress should be allowed to govern at all once he's spent his allotted time at the capital till.

Given a chance to make their feelings known, 20 million voters in fourteen states cast ballots in favor of term limitations. That's more votes than H. Ross Perot got nationwide. As a result, 175 members of the House and Senate were put on notice that, barring court intervention, the countdown to mandatory retirement began the minute they were sworn in. Thus was created America's first class of time-released legislators.

Some backers of imposed term limits, like ex-Rep. James Coyne from Pennsylvania, think that restricting the number of terms any one person can spend in office will eventually produce the kind of Congress the Founding Fathers had in mind when they invented it, a legislature made up of amateurs predisposed by their lack of professional experience in Washington to do a good job, or at least not to be around long enough to develop into indictable offenders.

"Being in Congress should be like serving on a jury," reasoned Coyne. "Ordinary Americans are trusted to make complicated decisions in court all the time. We don't have career jurors. So why should we need career politicians? When I was in Congress I would hear people actually lamenting that they wished they had voted for this bill or that bill. But they didn't have the nerve because if they did, the National Rifle Association or some other special-interest group would cut them off. Here were individuals who knew what they were doing was wrong, but they needed the money to get reelected. . . ."

What newcomers to Washington soon discover isn't a government crippled by gridlock and red tape the way people outside the Beltway imagine, but a tax-supported Caesar's Palace on the Potomac where high rollers are indistinguishable from public servants, and anyone who bets on the House—or the Senate— almost always comes up a winner.

Congress is in the business of doling out tax dollars. Finding enough to give away never seems to be the problem. It's the distribution process that gets complicated. Money, however, creates the equivalent of a legislative express line, especially for people smart enough to put down a hefty deposit with their favorite elected officials.

Take the case of New York Yankee owner George Steinbrenner. Twice exiled from baseball, the first time for illegal campaign contributions to Richard Nixon, the second for making payoffs to a gambler as part of an extortion plot, Steinbrenner is a man whom public opinion might put in a league below politicians. Fortunately for him, personal charm has nothing to do with getting lawmakers to work in your favor once you happen to be on the preferred list of frequent contributors.

In 1987, Steinbrenner's Tampa shipbuilding business signed a contract to refurbish four Navy vessels for a total cost of $92 million. If the plan was to "low ball" the competition, it worked. In order to win government jobs, contractors often make purposely low bids, then when the bill exceeds the agreed-upon price, they file an appeal for reimbursement with the Pentagon to make up the difference. Steinbrenner filed such a claim after repairs to the four ships ended up costing him $37 million more than the contract called for. The Navy refused to pay, and he took them to court.

But Steinbrenner knew there was a better way to get financial relief than suing the government. So in 1992, he dispatched lobbyists on a visit to Rep. John Murtha of Pennsylvania and Sen. Daniel Inouye from Hawaii, respective Democratic chairmen of the House and Senate defense appropriations subcommittees. The Yankee owner's generosity over the years guaranteed his emissaries a warm welcome. Steinbrenner personally had given Inouye $4,000 for his losing bid to become Senate majority leader in 1992, and he sent the legal limit of $1,000 each to the two chairmen when they were last up for reelection. Steinbrenner's company PAC also had made contributions to both men.

After hearing their friend's tale of woe, his pals in Congress obligingly attached an extra $58 million appropriation to the Defense Department's 1993 budget. The amount covered the cost overrun on the ship contract and even gave Steinbrenner a bonus of $20 million more than he asked for in court.

Murtha called the settlement "an equitable solution" to the financial problems all shipyards are facing these days. To everyone in Washington it bore an all too familiar resemblance to business as usual.

"There is a 'For Sale' sign hanging on the United States Capitol," Tim Wirth said in a television interview shortly before retiring from the Senate. Freed from having to run for reelection, Wirth is also more or less free to tell the truth.

What's amazing is how relatively little it costs to buy into the kind of legislative assistance Congress puts on the market every day. A few thousand dollars here, a few thousand more there, and before too long it's possible to have your own congressional caucus on retainer.

The intermediary through whom this money moves is the lobbyist. As the name implies, lobbyists are the lounge lizards of Washington. While technically barred from pushing their clients' causes by direct contact with members on the House or Senate floor (unless they happen to be ex-lawmakers themselves), everywhere else politicians gather, from posh health spas to expensive golf courses, lobbyists are probably somewhere close by—and as long as it's legal—paying the tab.

In 1991, former House Ways and Means Committee Chairman Dan Rostenkowski combined work and fun at no less than nine pro-am golf tournaments around the country, many of them sponsored by companies with a direct interest in legislation before his committee. During one two-month period Rostenkowski found time to play in six different events, including the AT&T Open at Pebble Beach, the Kemper Pro-Am in Hawaii, and the Doral Ryder in Miami. No wonder *Golf Digest* magazine named the Illinois Democrat one of the sport's ten "most powerful people."

Clearly, it's an honor he well deserves. In addition to his grueling schedule of play, Rostenkowski has been instrumental in protecting the tax-exempt status of pro-am tournaments from the enemies of golf in Congress. When Rosty was hit with a multi-count indictment for kickbacks, PGA Tour Golf Course Properties donated $2,500 to his legal defense funds.

"We don't think there's anything wrong with getting them outside Washington to talk to real people," said one famous CEO of elected officials and out-of-town junkets.

But the "real people" lawmakers sometimes meet on such trips can get them in serious trouble. A few years ago, it was learned that lobbyists had entertained members of Congress and their staffs at woodland retreats in eastern Maryland, complete with booze, sex, and improper influence.

Another real-people excursion to Barbados by members of Rostenkowski's Ways and Means Committee in 1990 turned into a frequent-flyer fiasco of politically ruinous proportions. It all began when committee members, their spouses, selected aides, and military escorts deplaned for five days and four nights at a luxurious beachfront hotel. There, the committee entourage, traveling at taxpayer expense, rendezvoused with insurance lobbyists for tennis matches, scuba diving, and a total of seven hours' worth of briefings. Acting on an anonymous tip, a crew from ABC's *Primetime* was also there, with camera positions set up in five different hotel rooms for maximum coverage of offshore activity, much of it paid for by insurance company representatives.

"I think we showed people exactly how cozy and close knit

the relationship between lobbyists and congressmen really is," said Sheila Hershow, a *Primetime* producer, who posed as a tourist to get the story and several good close-ups, one showing an insurance lobbyist paying for congressmen to rent jet skis. The segment must have given *Primetime* co-host Sam Donaldson an idea. Four years later, Donaldson, according to the *American Journalism Review,* accepted $30,000 to give a speech at an insurance industry convention in New York.

"The idea that the press thinks these trips are junkets is absolutely ridiculous," protested former Democratic Rep. Marty Russo, whose 1992 opponent in the Illinois primary had campaign brochures printed with color shots of the Barbados trip. Russo lost. But he wasn't the only casualty. Congressmen Thomas Downey, another Democrat, and Republicans Ray McGrath and Guy Vander Jagt can also thank their exposure on ABC for ending their congressional careers.

And what lesson did they learn from the experience? Russo and Downey became lobbyists, McGrath, the president of a beer trade association, and Vander Jagt, a government affairs specialist with a big Washington law firm.

"When I lost, I was very depressed," said Vander Jagt. "I thought I would be devastated. With no politics, I thought it would be the end of the world."

In a way it was, but another one soon began. The fourteen-term Michigan conservative accepted a job offer from the legal firm of Baker & Hostetler, where his assignment is bringing in clients with legislative problems.

"We have beautiful offices," Vander Jagt declared. "The firm is very prestigious. . . . You really do retain lots of the perks and privileges. People still call me 'Congressman Vander Jagt,' and whenever I go to the Hill, the cops stop traffic."

The money, he said, isn't bad either. "I like to point out that the fellow who beat me tripled both of our salaries."

Cash contributions aren't the only way lobbyists try to woo votes in Congress. Being a professional in the trade means being a congressional friend, a consultant, and, with increasing frequency, a future coworker. The most successful lobbyists offer members a full range of services. They're lecture agents, investment advisers, and career counselors. Often senators and representatives have a closer relationship with lobbyists than they do with their colleagues and staffs, even their own families. And for good reason. It's lobbyists who keep them in business.

Take away the funds provided by PACs, lobby firms, and favor-seeking donors, and it would be impossible for members of Congress to pay their campaign bills—or their legal bills. Ray McGrath, Marty Russo, and Tom Downey, now lobbyists, all gave $5,000 to help their old boss, Dan Rostenkowski, pay his lawyers. But there's another attraction. Many lobbyists used to be elected officials, and many elected officials when they leave office will be lobbyists.

WHERE ARE THEY NOW?
Departed Members of the 102nd Congress
Working in the Washington Private Sector

HOUSE
Bill Alexander (D-Ark), counsel, McAuliffe, Kelly & Rafaelli, law firm
Beryl Anthony (D-Ark), partner, Winston & Strawn, law firm
Terry Bruce (D-Ill), vice-president for federal relations, Ameritech
Lawrence Coughlin (R-Pa), counsel, Eckert, Seamans, Cherin & Mellott, law firm
Robert Davis (R-Mich), consultant, Bob Davis & Associates
William Dickinson (D-Ala), consultant, William Dickinson & Associates
Thomas Downey (D-NY), consultant, Thomas J. Downey & Associates
Melvyn Dymally (D-Calif), consultant, Dymally International
Dennis Eckart (D-Ohio), partner, Arter & Hadden, law firm
Willis Gradison (R-Ohio), president, Health Insurance Association of America

Dennis Hertel (D-Mich), attorney, Hertel & Associates

Craig James (R-Fla), partner, James, Zimmerman & Paul, law firm

Ed Jenkins (D-Ga), consultant, Winburn & Jenkins

Jim Jontz (D-Ind), director, Citizens' Trade Campaign

Peter Kostmeyer (D-Pa), environmental consultant

Norman Lent (R-NY), partner, Lent & Scrivner, law firm

Mel Levine (D-Calif), partner, Gibson, Dunn & Crutcher, law firm

Bill Lowery (R-Calif), partner Copeland, Hatfield & Lowery, law firm

Raymond McGrath (R-NY), president, The Beer Institute

Matthew McHugh (D-NY) counselor to the president of the World Bank

Ron Marlenee (R-Mont), president, Capitol Consulting Corporation

Mary Rose Okar (D-Ohio), president, Okar & Associates

Richard Ray (D-Ga), independent defense and agribusiness consultant

Marty Russo (D-Ill), director federal relations, Cassidy & Associates

Richard Schulze (R-Pa), consultant, Valis Associates

Jerry Sikorski (D-Minn) public affairs director, Opperman, Heins & Paquin, law firm

Stephen Solarz (R-NY), adviser, Center for Strategic Studies

Robin Tallon (D-SC), government relations consultant, The Tobacco Institute

Guy Vander Jagt (R-Mich), attorney, Baker & Hostetler

Vin Weber (R-Minn), consultant, The Weber Group

SENATE

Allan Cranston (D-Calif), board of directors, American Committee on Russian Relations

Robert Kasten (R-Wis), consultant, Kasten & Co.

Warren Rudman (R-NH), partner, Paul, Weiss & Rifkind, law firm

Steve Symms (R-Idaho), consultant, Symms, Lehn & Associates

One of the things lobbyists have always done is raise campaign money, and all by itself that's made them people worth seeing on a regular basis. But even after they've collected enough reelection capital, congressional incumbents need to *win*, a goal achieved more and more often by buying into a program of wholesale sleaze. Some hire the services of slick campaign mudslingers to do the job; others take advantage of free dirt, also known as "opposition research," paid for by so-called "soft money" donations limited by law to political "education" projects.

Each party headquarters in Washington aids its candidates by supplying the local and national media with whatever information it can to expose an opponents' lesser-known weak points. There's an old saying that a politician should never be caught in bed with a live man or a dead woman. Today, just about any indiscretion, no matter how seemingly minor, could be the thing that tilts an election.

For former New Hampshire GOP Rep. Chuck Douglas, high on the Democrats' hate list in 1990, the lethal ingredient came in the form of a leaked item noting that Douglas's congressional parking space was occupied by a shiny new car with New Hampshire dealer's tags. No apparent transgression to the untrained observer, perhaps. But papers in his home state picked up on the story, and when the car turned out to be on "loan" from a Mercedes dealership, Douglas was caught red-handed with a prohibited favor. He later lost his parking space and his seat.

Party operatives, financed by campaign contributions mostly from large companies and associations, regularly comb through court records looking for anything they can use against the other side. In the late 1980s, after Democratic researchers learned that a certain Republican congressman was being sued by his male lover for giving him anal warts, they knew they had a potentially explosive issue on their hands. The problem was how to inject it in the campaign without having it backfire. Both political parties try to bury each other in bad publicity, but neither one wants to be seen as the source. After much deliberation over what to do with their big scoop, the Democrats decided the story was too risky to use and let it drop.

Access to lawmakers is directly proportional to the campaign contributions that lobbyists have traditionally used as a calling card. However, former crop-insurance lobbyist Paula Parkinson, accused of trading in a different currency, set off a sex-for-votes investigation in the early 1980s. Parkinson, who admitted bedding seven members of Congress, six of them Republicans, left Capitol Hill for Dallas to pursue a career in decorative plumbing fixtures, but not before blasting the political hypocrisy she blamed for driving her out of town. In a particularly memorable outburst, she accused an unnamed GOP lawmaker famous for his pro-life stance of once giving her $500 to have an abortion.

"My morals might be low," she told an interviewer, "but at least I have principles."

Voters cast their ballots for the finished product, not the work in progress lobbyists see every day. No one knows politicians like a lobbyist does, since no one else encounters them so often in their purest form, trading office visits for loot. Changes in the lobby laws may affect the basic closeness of that relationship. But in the time-honored tradition of Capitol Hill politics, not by much.

Hurrying to approve measures it knew would be changed by the House or else overturned in court, the Senate in 1993 passed a series of revisions in campaign spending rules that sound tough but in all likelihood will never take effect.

The Senate's new restrictions banned all PAC contributions and barred lobbyists from contacting lawmakers for a full year after giving them money. But that could be unconstitutional. The same goes for a proposed tax on candidates who refuse to comply with spending limits, and another section of the reform package that prohibits organizations from "bundling," that is, dispensing money donated by a group of contributors.

One phrase inserted into the bill shows how the whole thing was rigged to self-destruct on its first legal test. Striking down any part of the act, the wording goes, will cause the rest to "be treated as invalid" too.

Even accountability types, like Fred Wertheimer of the public interest lobby Common Cause, were predicting the Senate PAC ban would never stand up in court. Given the escape clause it contains, that would mean everything else in the law goes with it.

This is reform?

"Whenever the issue is money and campaign politics, there's always some doubt about what's really going on," said Ellen Miller, executive director of the Center for Responsive Politics in Washington.

Any law Congress writes for itself is bound to be full of loopholes, like the Senate's proposed one-year ban on contact between lobbyists and the lawmakers to whom they've given money.

"On the surface that sounds pretty strict," Miller said. "But any lobbyist can easily get around it by having a friend deliver the money. No law is broken and everybody's taken care of."

Another avoidance technique is delayed gratification. Senators serve six-year terms. They could meet with lobbyists, pick up a contribution, not see them for a year in accordance with the new law, and repeat the process all over again five more times before their next election.

Nebbishy Sen. Paul Wellstone, a Democrat from Minnesota, introduced an amendment to double the no-contact period to two years, which would still give lobbyists three opportunities to make their payoffs and lawmakers the same number of chances to take the maximum legal amount.

The House version of a campaign reform bill did even less to curb abuses, which wasn't surprising. If members of Congress were to ban PACs, bar contact with lobbyists, and cut campaign donations to a scaled down pittance, it wouldn't be long before they were out of work. That's because any campaign reform that hurts incumbents will have an equal and opposite effect on challengers.

"This is what makes campaign reform so difficult," said Miller. To really reform the system, the people who are in it would have to commit political suicide, and not even a crusader like Wellstone is going to advocate legislation that might get him voted out of office and sent back to teaching political science in the frozen North.

All of this concern over money means nothing, of course, to the growing number of millionaire House and Senate members. A total of twenty-eight Senators and fifty Representatives have a net worth of seven figures or more, and most are generous contributors to their own campaigns. In the House, where the two-year election cycle puts an extra premium on fast cash, the trend is particularly noticeable. Candidates for House seats in 1992 gave themselves over $54 million, almost twice as much as they did two years earlier.

The biggest spender was California GOP Rep. Michael Huffington, who laid out $4 million in personal funds. But that was just the beginning. Huffington soon announced plans to spend $15 million in the '94 Senate race against incumbent Democrat Dianne Feinstein, another Hill millionaire and equally disposed to spend whatever it takes to win.

Until they're forcibly evicted, the best places to find lobbyists are Capitol Hill lobbies. The most popular gathering spot is the vestibule outside of the House Ways and Means Committee. Known as "Gucci Gulch," this is the crossroads of the government's collected and spent wealth. If Congress wants to exact new taxes, rearrange its budget priorities, or do anything else it wants to do with America's income, the bucks start here.

Lobbyists and lawmakers usually work together behind the scenes. Some lobbyists have even been known to write entire bills for members, who introduce them without changing a word. It's rare when anyone in the profession gets to put on a performance in front of the full Ways and Means, and when one does, it's always a special occasion.

Hillary Rodham Clinton, though, was more than a lobbyist. The administration's health-care reform package was the single most ambitious and costly domestic spending plan since the Social Security system was adopted sixty years ago, and HRC was its chief architect and principal explainer.

Immediately after his speech to Congress on reforming the health-care system, Bill Clinton's one-of-everything cabinet fanned out across the country to promote the program to their various constituencies. In choosing his department secretaries, Clinton, like Noah filling his Ark before the flood, chose a representative from every ethnic, racial, and gender group in the nation; still, no one on his multicultural pep squad faced a tougher assignment than his wife.

As the acknowledged brains behind the president and the administration's designated driver, Mrs. Clinton took to the work like a suburban Super-Mom organizing a car pool. Health care was part of a larger mission, a larger involvement in the welfare of the nation, that she cited in her self-defining "politics of meaning" speech given in Texas a few months before.

Americans, she told her audience, were afflicted by "sleeping sickness of the soul. . . . We lack, at some core level, meaning in our individual lives and meaning collectively, the sense that our lives are part of some greater effort, that we are connected to one another, that community means that we have a place where we belong no matter who we are."

Not since Jimmy Carter's TV talk on malaise had anyone in public life offered such a grim diagnosis of the country's spiritual condition. "What do all our institutions mean?" Mrs. Clinton asked. "What does it mean to be educated? . . . What does it mean in today's world to pursue not only vocations, to be part of institutions, but to be human?"

So many questions. So many problems to solve.

"We are breaking new ground," she said, holding out hope that a remedy will be found. But "it's not going to be easy to define who we are as human beings in this post-modern world."

And it wasn't going to be cheap, either.

Yet what better place to begin the quest for meaning and the money to pay for it than the Ways and *Means* Committee?

Mrs. Clinton's job was to sell committee members and the rest of Congress on creating the biggest, most expensive feel-good bureaucracy in American history. Committee members were unfailingly polite, praising the First Lady for being "informed," "hard-working," and "delightful."

"I think in the very near future the president will be known as your husband. People will say, 'Who's that fella?'" gushed Chairman Dan Rostenkowski, evidencing exceptionally high spirits for someone facing indictment on charges of ripping off the House Post Office.

Even Republicans had nice things to say. "You're making a winning statement showing up here by yourself," said GOP Rep. Cliff Stearns from Florida.

Before long, with both Clintons entangled in Whitewater, appearing before Congress was the last thing on the First Lady's agenda. A scandal that included alleged money skimming, possible conflict of interest, and a dead lawyer—all somehow connected to the Oval Office—had GOP members panting to investigate, and Democrats doing everything they could to keep Clinton, Clinton & Co. as far from the Hill as they could. But now it was showtime.

Mrs. Clinton was only the third president's wife to testify before Congress (Eleanor Roosevelt and Rosalynn Carter were the first two), and she arrived armed with enough data to keep committee staffers busy adding and subtracting for months. Most interested in what she had to say were tobacco industry lobbyists, since the administration would be asking Congress to consider legislation that would triple the tax on cigarettes, from twenty-five cents to seventy-five cents a pack.

Because of Mrs. Clinton's tight schedule, each member's interrogation time was limited to two minutes. Questions by and large were of the slow-pitch variety that lawmakers normally reserve for their biggest corporate clients.

Rostenkowski's second in command, Florida Democratic Rep. Sam Gibbons, had been licking his chops for years, craving a shot at Rosty's chairmanship. Seizing the chance to sound like the leader he would be the minute the feds charged the big man, Gibbons wanted to know the unknowable. "How," he asked, "do we expect to achieve national savings with this program?"

Surrounded by a roomful of White House health care experts, most of whom didn't seem old enough to be plagued by anything worse than a bad-hair day, Mrs. Clinton answered that "additional revenue" would come from employers and from employees not currently contributing to any health plan. That seemed fair enough to Gibbons, who smiled gently down on Mrs. Clinton.

Rep. Fortney "Pete" Stark, a California Democrat and one of the wealthiest members of the House, was concerned about his mother. Would her Medicaid payments be cut? Would the Clinton health care plan protect his poor old mom?

"I have a mother, too, Mr. Stark," Mrs. Clinton replied, sounding a note of mild reproof. "And if we can't pass the mother test, we're not going to be able to succeed, are we?"

Mrs. Clinton was noticeably stricter with Republicans, many of whom had gone on the record criticizing administration reforms for being too costly and too bureaucratic. When Rep. Rick Santorum from Pennsylvania asked if the program might be implemented one phase at a time to test how well each part worked rather than adopting the entire plan at once, Mrs. Clinton's answer was a curt and absolute "No."

This was a lobbying campaign with a specific timetable. The administration wanted the package passed—as is—before the 1994 elections. Health care reform was set up to be the weapon Democrats needed to keep intact their congressional majority, significant parts of which were deemed open to Republican takeover in the wake of recurring White House ineptitude.

But first, Mrs. Clinton would have to defuse special interest opposition, much of it coming from lobbyists for the medical professions, as well as lobbyists for the tobacco industry, which was targeted for new taxes aimed at defraying a large part of the health plan's projected trillion-dollar price tag.

The tax "raises a fundamental question of fairness by singling out one product to bear the burden," said Rep. Lewis F. Payne, a Democrat from Virginia, where tobacco is a major cash crop. (Coming in second, according to some agricultural analysts, is marijuana.) Why not tax gun dealers or liquor distributors? Would the administration be open to discussing the impact of the higher tax on tobacco state economies? Payne asked.

"The president will keep an open door," Mrs. Clinton said. "But there *will* be a tobacco tax as part of this legislation."

Tobacco, she added, is the only product that "when used as directed, can have such dangerous consequences."

Mrs. Clinton said she would even like to see the tax discourage people from smoking.

The First Lady had pushed all the right buttons. She visited hospitals in one member's district, talked to cancer patients in another member's. She quoted emergency room data, amassed long-term care statistics, and when she was through, Rostenkowski planted a Chicago-style Polish-ward-boss kiss on her cheek.

"Hillary Clinton was the model of modesty, civility, family-minded understanding and concern," wrote columnist Meg Greenfield of *Newsweek* in a typical post-performance review. She had completely "disarmed" her interrogators, Greenfield noted. "The only thing many of them could think to do was burble on about how much they admired the work she had done. . . ."

In a Congress where cost projections have no relationship to actual spending, Mrs. Clinton's dazzling command of numbers and percentages left most lawmakers positively gaga, the kind of reaction only the best lobbyists get right before they score a bundle. Which is just what Mrs. Clinton was asking for. Health-care reform put one-third of the U.S. economy up for grabs. So it's understandable that her explanation of the "sin tax" funding structure left one nagging question that none of the lawmakers had thought to ask:

If the tax on cigarettes actually succeeded in getting Americans to stop smoking, as Mrs. Clinton had fervently hoped, where would the government find enough money to pay everyone's medical bills?

CHAPTER SEVEN

THAT'S INFOTAINMENT

"I don't even recognize Capitol Hill anymore," said Sid Yudain, nursing a drink at the bar and reminiscing about his old friend, former House Speaker Jim Wright. Yudain, who founded *Roll Call* newspaper in 1955, motivated largely by the assumption that life on the Hill was fun, now thinks good times in Congress are a thing of the past.

Just ask Jim Wright. Forced to resign from politics after charges that he used his position for personal gain, Wright was back in town to peddle his political memoirs, and that meant meeting the press for the first time since his hasty departure in 1989. One theme of the ex-Speaker's latest literary production is that he was driven from office by the media. Of course, being cited for sixty-nine violations by the House Ethics Committee—and getting caught trading copies of his previous book for illegal campaign contributions—had something to do with it too.

Congressional celebrities on hand for Wright's party were eager to second his innocent-victim shtick. "Yes, sir," said one angry lawmaker, he was "knocked around . . . harder than others have been."

The knockers in question were the thousands of television, radio, and newspaper reporters who patrol the Hill, waiting for lawmakers like Wright to step out of line. But the press corps has a conveniently short memory, and on this particular evening everyone seemed willing to forgive and forget—everyone, that is, except Yudain, who doesn't like what's happened to Washington journalism.

The old *Roll Call* did things newspapers today would never try. "We didn't have investigative reporting," Yudain said proudly. What the paper had were profiles of congressional cut-ups, jokes written by the later-to-be-famous Washington comedian Mark Russell (whom Yudain discovered working in a downtown strip joint), and weekly photos of pretty secretaries dressed in one-piece bathing suits.

Needless to say, those days are over. Reporters and members of Congress no longer play by the same friendly rules, and one big reason they don't is money.

In 1986, Yudain retired and sold *Roll Call* for $500,000 to Arthur Levitt, former chairman of the American Stock Exchange. Seven years later, when Bill Clinton nominated Levitt to be head of the Securities and Exchange Commission, the paper was put up for sale, and the London *Economist* bought it for an estimated $15 million.

Bigger investments in delivering the news mean a more cost-conscious approach to gathering it. As a result, the *Roll Call* of the 1990s is a far cry from the gag sheet Yudain once published. Gone are the cheesecake pictures and nightclub reviews, replaced by full-page corporate ads and special features on trade, transportation, and taxes. The twice-weekly tabloid has become as serious as it once was wacky.

Roll Call reporters start tracking upcoming congressional races more than a year before voters go to the polls. There are issue briefings, ratings of top staffers, and every time Yudain picks up a copy, which isn't often, it makes him long for the way things used to be.

Despite its reputation as Capitol Hill's hometown newspaper, *Roll Call* is no longer the pro-Congress pushover it used to be. While editors shy away from being the first to nail House and Senate wrongdoers, whenever damaging information is made public, they hardly ever hesitate to print it. After one *Roll Call* reporter came across information in a General Accounting Office study that indicated possible check-cashing irregularities at the House Bank, the paper began an investigation that eventually led to the closing of the bank and the resignation or defeat of dozens of members.

Yet ever mindful of the paper's readership as the scandal unfolded, *Roll Call*'s former editor James Glassman frequently appeared on television talk shows to defend the integrity of the House from Congress bashers. In Washington, the media giveth and the media taketh away.

If the legislative process is crisis driven, so is congressional news coverage, which tends to veer wildly from feeding frenzy to feeding frenzy with little time left in between for digestion. Nevertheless, there is a kind of Darwinian order to the process that every news organization in town instinctively obeys. The nation's capital is a vast information jungle where no single media outlet, regardless of how big and powerful it is, could ever hope to hunt down and consume everything on the menu. As in nature, rather than feeding off the same selections, competing news gatherers feed off one another. In such a way, territory is subdivided and stories are redistributed as they move from user to user up the news chain.

The Senate Press Gallery is a place where all species of media creatures come together, and on November 1, 1993, they turned out en masse for what promised to be one of those rare feasts with something for everybody. This was the day the Senate had set aside to take up the question of Sen. Robert Packwood's diaries, 8,200 single-spaced pages full of the author's most intimate thoughts on a wide variety of interesting subjects. By all indications, the session would *not* be just another day on the Hill.

Unwilling to surrender his writings, Packwood, then under investigation by the Senate Ethics Committee for sexual harassment, interrupted discussion of an unemployment benefits package a week before to let fellow lawmakers and the media know exactly what kind of material he'd been compiling for the last quarter century.

"My lawyer put out a statement indicating some of the things that were in the diary, including an extended affair that one senator had with a member of his staff and an affair that a staffer had with a member of the current congressional Democratic leadership. . . . I want to emphasize . . . I have no intention of using this for blackmail, gray mail or anything else. But I want the Senate to clearly understand what it is the Ethics Committee has demanded. . . ."

It was Packwood's preview of coming attractions, and exactly the sort of hype to guarantee saturation coverage. Two hours before the full Senate would meet to hear arguments for and against giving the Ethics Committee authority to pursue the matter in court, the press gallery was abuzz with anticipation. Earlier in the day, the *Portland Oregonian* had revealed that the ethics panel was looking into possible criminal conduct by the senator. The alleged infraction involved arranging a job interview for his ex-wife with Mitsubishi, the Japanese electronics company. This was just the kind of morsel that starts reporters' nostrils flaring, and data from the *Oregonian* article was stored in laptops as filler for the next day's editions of papers in Washington, New York, and Los Angeles. Like dominant species anywhere, news leaders on the congressional beat always eat their fill. But what they eat is often snatched from more active competitors just below them on the chow line.

The press gallery in the U.S. Senate consists of a four-tiered observation deck, and behind it an office area, with attached lounge, where journalists congregate to trade tips, take naps, and file their stories. With nothing to write about yet, shop talk turned to Packwood's romantic track record. Serious journalists, who pretend not to be interested in such things, had clearly done their homework. Using Ted Kennedy's statistics for comparison purposes, one newshound said he'd heard from a reliable source that Packwood had been stepping out on the Mrs. for the past twenty years.

"So what," said another. "At least he brought his dates home alive."

As senators slowly made their way into the chamber to decide what to do about Packwood's steamy jottings, reporters filled the gallery benches. Many appeared to take a vengeful enjoyment in just being there. Lawmakers, who never miss a chance to blame the media for their problems, now had to deal with an exposé written by one of their own. One journalist described the irony as "delicious."

The senators—all but a half dozen eventually showed up—were clearly uncomfortable with the task at hand. But if they let Packwood off the hook, as many no doubt wished they could, what would voters think?

The Oregon Republican had already been typecast in the media as a serial sex fiend. Female Democratic senators had played a large part, fanning anti-Packwood fires for months to raise campaign funds. Sen. Barbara Boxer, a Democrat from California, appointed to preside over a portion of the diary debates, was one of Packwood's most persistent critics, comparing him to Supreme Court Justice Clarence Thomas, the talk-dirty-to-me conservative whose long-term attempts to date law professor Anita Hill first put sexual harassment on the political map.

"Hill's spirit, if not her presence, was alive on the Senate floor," Boxer declared at a Washington fund-raiser. Among those who have benefited most from that spirit, Boxer wasn't about to let it evaporate.

"The end of the cold war," according to the *New York Times*, "has shifted the focus of political debate away from 'male' issues like national security and toward domestic problems, including those that women are presumed to know more about: health care, education and welfare reform." High on that list is also sexual harassment, a leading cause of cash donations to concerned candidates in both parties.

Demonstrating an almost otherworldly weirdness as the crisis dragged on, Packwood took the floor in his own defense, telling senators the story of how one of his female accusers had recently come to his office to apologize. She "put her arms around me, gave me a big kiss and said, 'You're wonderful.'"

It was a creepy yet touching moment. But at this point, to concede Packwood was anything but a complete pervert—and an obstructionist pervert at that—wouldn't do anyone any good. Women had been chased, maybe intimidated, and someone would have to pay, even if it took a trip to the Supreme Court before all the available evidence was in.

"We're not the Senate Committee on voyeurism," hollered the munchkinlike Barbara Mikulski, a Maryland Democrat and the only female member of the ethics panel. "We are not reporters from some scandal sheet. We are the U.S. Senate Committee on Ethics."

Thus assured, senators by a 94-to-6 vote agreed to let the committee take Packwood to court and turn his kissing spree into a full-scale federal case.

The Washington media thrives on such melodrama, and the Packwood case fit the requirements perfectly. In terms of actual coverage, politics isn't about personalities. It's about the themes associated with personalities, and the editors and pundits who set the agenda do so by deciding which themes play and which political careers play along with them. Agency reports, think tank studies, opinion polls, every fact and figure that falls under the general heading of news get filtered through the same review process.

"There's an unspoken conspiracy in this town that says the public can't be trusted with too many details," said pollster Alan F. Kay, who added that most political polls are designed not to determine what people really think but to confirm what poll takers would like them to think.

"The problem with polls is that they're easy to rig," said Kay, the MIT-trained founder of a nonpartisan survey organization called Americans Talk Issues. "The answers you get depend on the way you word questions. Include enough information and give people a wide range of choices, and you can get an incredible amount of wisdom."

When polls, such as those Kay conducts, reveal too much wisdom, the media and public policy establishment are quick to dismiss the results.

In March 1993, Kay's group released findings from a survey indicating that:

- 80 percent of those questioned favored cuts in salary and benefits for members of Congress.
- 77 percent favored limiting the amount of money candidates could spend on campaigns.
- 72 percent favored a balanced budget amendment.
- 70 percent favored the registration of lobbyists.
- 68 percent favored a one-quarter cut in the size of congressional staffs.
- 65 percent favored requiring broadcasters to provide free air time for the public discussion of issues.
- 59 percent favored the elimination of PACs.
- 58 percent favored allowing citizens to send mail to their congressional members free of charge.

Kay, who has conducted twenty separate surveys since 1987, concluded from this one that voters feel alienated from government and the political process. The *Washington Post* had a different reaction. It labeled the findings "unusual," quoting congressional scholar Thomas E. Mann of the Brookings Institution to back up its judgment.

"This is one of those cases where public opinion polling does more harm than good," Mann said. The principal fault of the survey, as he saw it, is that "it attaches a certainty to the ephemeral and unthinking reactions to change the system."

Inside the Beltway, outside thinking is always suspect, most of all when it contradicts experts in the field.

Once someone gets elected to Congress, his primary concern is finding ways to stay there. The same is true of journalists who cover congressional politics. In the wanna-be psychology of the profession, Washington reporters have a tendency to see their fame tied to that of the people they write about. The more important the political figures they cover, the more important the reporters who cover them. This is why the most negotiable currency on Capitol Hill, in the White House, or in any of Washington's news-producing centers is access. Reporters who can't get access to top politicians and behind-the-scenes advisers not only don't get the news, they don't get invited to talk about it on television.

Journalists want to be on the tube as much as politicians do, though not many will openly admit it. Part of the attraction has to do with a natural craving for stardom (heightened by the off-stage role reporters normally play), and part with the fact that TV has taken over the audience that once belonged exclusively to newspapers. After resisting the TV trend for years, the *New York Times* has retained a PR firm to get its top reporters on the air. Even America's paper of record realized it could use the exposure.

Appearances on programs like *This Week with David Brinkley*, *Meet the Press*, or *The MacNeil/Lehrer Newshour* can boost a print journalist's career in many lucrative ways, which accounts for the fierce competition among aspiring panelists and regulars. On *The McLaughlin Group*, a pioneer in the field of "yeller" journalism, the jockeying for position is notoriously intense. Host John McLaughlin, an ex-Jesuit priest, likes to be the center of attention, and when a word count of program transcripts once revealed that regular guest Robert Novak was talking too much, the syndicated columnist was soon gone. Novak later resurfaced as panelist on CNN's *Capital Gang*, hosted by Al Hunt of the *Wall Street Journal*.

The shows pay guests little or nothing, but being seen on them often leads directly to the corporate lecture circuit, network consulting and, for a lucky few, Hollywood.

Nina Totenberg (National Public Radio and *Inside Washington*) played herself in the movie *Dave*, and Michael Kinsley (the *New Republic* and CNN's *Crossfire*) portrayed a nerdy TV talk-show host in *Rising Sun*. Just as movie stars regularly come to Washington to give their views to the press and testify before Congress, top media celebrities have started playing fictionalized versions of themselves in films. Op-ed columnist Ben Stein, son of Nixon administration economic adviser Herbert Stein, followed his star all the way to La-La Land and a whole new career. Stein, who identifies himself at the end of his columns as "a writer and actor in Los Angeles," now lands parts in hit films like *Honeymoon in Vegas*.

Without access none of this would be possible. So when access is taken away, as it was after Bill Clinton decided early in his administration he didn't need news conferences to talk directly to the American people—after all, look how well he did in the campaign on MTV—everyone suffered. Most of all Clinton, whose popularity took a nosedive.

There are two ways to attract good press in Washington: Give reporters special treatment and give them dinner. On the advice of newly arrived presidential assistant David Gergen, Clinton did both, and it paid off.

For the top-of-the-line opinion makers, there were special invitations to private Executive Mansion feedings. On *The McLaughlin Group* in the midst of Clinton's make-nice offensive, panelists Fred B arnes of the *New Republic*, Eleanor Clift of *Newsweek*, Clarence Page of the *Chicago Tribune*, and Morton Kondracke of *Roll Call* discussed the guest list, sounding like kids comparing presents the day after Christmas. Although host McLaughlin, once a Nixon speechwriter, hadn't been selected, Barnes, who had, was positively giddy in the afterglow.

McLaughlin: "Issue One. Back on track. . . . Has Clinton turned the corner? I ask you, Freddy Barnes."

Barnes: ". . . He's finally learned to use the assets of the presidency. . . ."

McLaughlin: "Congratulations on getting in to see him. You finally got your line into the White House. . . . Thanks to David Gergen."

Barnes: "I'll take it any way I can get it. How many times have you been in to see Clinton?"

Clift: "John hasn't been in to see Clinton, but he's been in the White House. . . . The adage about Bill Clinton is true. His enemies get more out of him than his friends, and it's proven on this set."

Kondracke: "Eleanor wants an invitation to the White House."

Page: ". . . Hey, I'd like an invitation to the White House."

Kondracke: "I was invited to the same session as Fred and I

missed it. . . . I'm glad I did. Look what happened to you, Fred. You've lost all your sense of objectivity."

MCLAUGHLIN: "Ah, the power of the stroke, Freddy."

For the lumpen presidential press corps, meaning the 1,000 or so reporters holding White House media passes, there was a South Lawn barbecue, complete with a semi–self-deprecating stage appearance by Mark Gearan and the Clinton communications staff (à la Nancy Reagan's bag-lady rendition of "Secondhand Rose") that turned their reputation as a bunch of arrogant yuppies into a song-and-dance number set to the tune of "Margaritaville."

> Nibblin' on sound bites,
> Watchin' the press fight
> All of those pencils chasin' a leak
> Schmoozin' reporters
> From our large quarters
> Come through the hallway, you'll find what you seek.

In the old days, most politicians and members of the press had a relationship that didn't need any mediating PR campaigns. Elected officials took reporters into their confidence. In return, reporters kept certain information out of the papers and off the air.

Journalists still protect favored politicians when potential bad news strikes.

"Bimbo eruptions" had been a regular occurrence for Bill Clinton since the campaign, but most newspapers and network news organizations weren't nearly so eager to pursue stories about Clinton's low-rent womanizing as they were when the womanizer was, say, Sen. Robert Packwood, and the women were college-educated professionals. After the conservative *American Spectator* magazine published a lengthy article in January 1994, detailing Clinton's marital infidelities while governor of Arkansas, the *Washington Post* initially buried the story in its national news section, and the *New York Times* ignored it entirely. Two days later, both papers ran Mrs. Clinton's defense of her husband's behavior on the front page.

Following the media's backdown from the Gennifer Flowers story after the Clintons' 1992 appearance on *60 Minutes*, there was a virtual embargo on reporting about Clinton and sex. It was still in effect two years later when a former Arkansas state employee, Paula Jones, accused Clinton of sexually harassing her while he was governor. Even though she had more witnesses to back up her charges than Anita Hill had when she started the uproar against Clarence Thomas, Jones's allegations, first made at a Washington conservative gathering, were dismissed by many news outlets. It was only after Jones filed suit against Clinton in May 1994, claiming he had asked her to perform oral sex—Clinton "lowered his trousers and underwear exposing his erect penis and asked Jones to 'kiss it'"—that the mainstream media began running the story.

For twelve years, the largely liberal Washington press corps had been covering a conservative White House. Now that there was a Democrat in the Oval Office, it was hard not to be protective.

"Truth is, the press is willing to cut Clinton slack," said Eleanor Clift, "because they like him and what he has to say."

By the time Paula Jones took legal action, once-friendly reporters had switched to attack mode. Clinton, not Packwood, was Washington's most oversexed politician. NBC News could claim first place in the bad-taste race by featuring *Tonight Show* host Jay Leno on *Meet the Press*. With columnist David Broder and moderator Tim Russert tittering in the background, Leno told not one, but *two* penis jokes.

All of a sudden, the president was officially vulnerable.

When revelations about Whitewater forced the *Washington Post* and other news organizations that had backed Clinton to step up their coverage of his Arkansas finances, some blamed their original lack of investigative zeal on ethical restraint. After being routinely scooped by the Moonie-owned *Washington Times*, the *Post* ran an editorial-page column explaining how meticulous fact-checking, not political bias, made it appear the competition was getting ahead.

"We had the fundamental facts in the paper way ahead of anyone else," reporter Howard Schneider said in defense of the *Post*'s tendency to bring up the rear on Whitewater. "We thought there was no need to regurgitate what we already reported," he added. "We were 'behind' by virtue of being ahead."

There was a time when every reporter on Capitol Hill worked exactly the same way. Covering Congress was like covering the hometown ball club. What happened in the game was news. What happened off the field wasn't. The sportswriters and the players were on the same team. They drank and caroused together, and in an era before anyone worried about conflict of interest, neither side ever imagined it was the public's right to know.

Then, in the 1970s, a new breed of journalists came on the scene. Fueled by missionary zeal rather than Jack Daniel's, they didn't socialize with the people they wrote about, and therefore held them to a different standard of accountability than their predecessors had. Old-timers saw reporting as a higher form of taking dictation. For newcomers it was roughly the same thing as looking for clues at the scene of a crime, and any politician was a potential suspect.

It didn't take long for members of Congress and members of the Fourth Estate to become enemies. As the gulf between the two widened, the press developed a certain sense of ethical and intellectual superiority. After Abscam, Koreagate, and dozens of other similar indiscretions, the real Washington adversaries weren't Republicans and Democrats, but politicians and journalists. At the higher levels of both professions, they may attend the same exclusive parties and live in the same upscale parts of town, but that doesn't mean they can ever be friends.

Still, there are exceptions. When former Ways and Means Chairman Dan Rostenkowski was hit with a seventeen-count indictment for misuse of government funds, media pundits hurried to his defense. Conservative Robert Novak said on CNN that even if Rostenkowski was guilty as charged, giving him a prison sentence would be "a distortion of reality." Rosty, who chose to fight the charges against him rather than cop a plea,

was, in the words of David Broder, "a warrior" with "a passion
. . . to govern." A *Chicago Tribune* columnist called Rostenkowski "a giant" under attack "by pygmies."

But in politics, it's the giants that always make the best targets.

"You can't trust reporters," said the press secretary for a Senate Democrat, summing up the general feeling on the Hill
toward the media. "No matter how friendly you are, if they ever
get a chance to fuck you, they do it."

As a public service prank, *Roll Call* once published the mug
shots of a dozen congressional correspondents under the headline "Know Your Enemy." The underlying message was not lost
on lawmakers, their managers and staffs.

GOP campaign strategist Ed Rollins learned his lesson after
the 1993 New Jersey gubernatorial election. Following a dramatic win by Republican Christine Whitman over incumbent
Democrat Jim Florio, Rollins couldn't help gloating. And why
not? In managing Whitman to victory, he had beaten the
Democrats' reigning campaign genius James Carville. But in a
traditional post-election meeting with reporters in Washington,
Rollins told the press more than he should have. Putting a new
twist on the old practice of buying votes, he bragged that he had
used campaign funds to keep voters away from the polls.

"We went into black churches and basically said to ministers
. . . 'We see you have already endorsed Florio. That's fine. But
don't get up in the Sunday pulpit and . . . say it's your moral
obligation to vote on Tuesday, to vote for Jim Florio.'" In
return, Rollins told reporters, payments totaling $500,000 were
made to the ministers' favorite charities.

Rollins also said money was given to Democratic organizers,
many of whom had been paid to get out the vote by the Florio
campaign. "How much have they paid you to do your normal
duty?" Rollins said he asked them. "We'll match it. Go home, sit
and watch television. . . . I think to a certain extent we sup-
pressed their vote."

Paying people to vote wasn't news. That happens all the
time. Paying them *not* to vote—that *was* news. Rollins, who
managed Ronald Reagan's 1984 presidential campaign and

briefly headed Ross Perot's bid for the presidency in 1992, instantly became the most underhanded political consultant in the business. But to everyone who knows how the game is played, his mistake wasn't buying off ministers, it was telling a roomful of reporters about it.

Consultants and journalists are used to serving each other's special needs. Both see themselves as smarter than politicians, and since they're the only ones "who know what's going on," they play by their own set of rules. Consultants dish their favorite reporters exclusive campaign insights and reporters make their favorite consultants look like geniuses. If Rollins had told his walking-around-money story to one or two chosen writers over drinks, chances are it would have never made news.

That's what he did at a Washington dinner party when he laid the scoop on veteran columnist Roland Evans and Margaret Warner of *The MacNeil/Lehrer Newhour*. He also mentioned his New Jersey exploits to Mary Matalin, a cable TV talk-show hostess and Carville's then-fiancée, now wife. Neither of the recipients reported what they'd heard. It was only when Rollins repeated himself in the more competitive environment of a media breakfast speech that his revelation became a scandal.

Within days, however, he was telling a different tale. In a sworn deposition, the veteran political operative said he had made everything up, driven to deceit by a campaign of "psychological warfare" against his arch-rival Carville.

Playing his own version of good cop/bad cop, Rollins both accused and excused himself of wrongdoing. His boast about payoffs, he explained to attorneys, was (a) "the most irresponsible act that I've done in thirty-two years of political government service," and (b) part of "an inside the Beltway bullshit game that I've become a victim of."

And what made that "bullshit game" so much fun in the first place?

"In the world of political consultants," Rollins said, "I had star quality. . . . I had people interested in meeting me as much as meeting [the people he worked for]. And I did the same thing my old boss used to do. I'd shake hands, smile, act like I was your lifelong friend, and move on."

Then he opened his big mouth.

But "there was a subset game going on," Rollins added. It was a case of "one-upmanship" between "super consultants [that] backfired. . . . The ultimate revenge was that Carville got to me."

Well, not quite.

Reporters got the ultimate revenge. If lying to voters is standard practice in campaigns, lying to the press is a sin punishable by the worst sentence any Washington insider can imagine—being permanently Nixonified in every media mention, up to and including an obituary—all for what Rollins described as "two minutes of words that I wish, and will wish for the rest of my life, I could take back."

If star athletes don't like reporters, they don't talk to them. In Washington, that's a luxury few politicians can afford. They need reporters to promote them and quote them. Without news coverage, they might as well not exist. But given the inherent dangers in the process, elected officials are always looking for risk-free ways to get their message across.

Presidents have tried it with fireside chats and Saturday morning radio addresses. Those, however, are one-way formats that don't allow for all-important audience feedback, a crucial component in any political sales pitch.

Enter Larry King.

King began his CNN show, *Larry King Live*, in 1985, with the idea that he would function not as an interrogator but as a facilitator, helping his guests talk to cable viewers all over the world. This celebrity-friendly environment was the ideal setting for politicians, particularly in 1992, when the program became a virtual video press release. Presidential contenders appeared and reappeared free of charge to make announcements and state their positions, as King, dressed in his trademark rolled-up shirtsleeves and suspenders, supervised the call-in questions. Here, right in the middle of Washington, was an alternative to the traditional news grilling most candidates dread. The high-visibility showcase was the newsmaker's counterpart of the Home Shopping Network; instead of diamond rings and tennis bracelets, it offered viewers presidential hopefuls and other assorted vote seekers.

"This is the meeting place, this is where they come," King told fellow talk-show host Charlie Rose.

When Vice-President Al Gore challenged Ross Perot to debate on the eve of the North American Free Trade Agreement, the one venue they could both agree on was *Larry King Live*.

"A vice-president can debate a citizen on national TV. Wow! What's next?" wondered King, who was originally asked by David Gergen to emcee a debate between Perot and Lee Iaccoca, a meeting of the minds that never came off.

Perot had used King's show as a personal soapbox many times over the past year. But the problem with the program's do-it-yourself framework is that guests who weren't careful could end up doing it *to* themselves. Which is exactly what happened to Perot, whose petulant Pappy Yoakum performance helped the White House push the NAFTA bill through Congress.

King lets his guests be guests. He also lets them sell whatever products they've brought with them. So when Jim Wright came to town, King's show was one of his first stops.

KING: "You knew this book would be controversial."
WRIGHT: "I expect it will. . . . But the purpose . . . Larry, is not to shed heat; it's to shed light. I'm not out with a vendetta against anybody. I've just got a story to tell."

And if the story needed an extra promo, King was happy to accommodate.

KING: "There's a big book party here tomorrow, and two former Speakers are going to be there. . . . Mr. O'Neill and the current Speaker Mr. Foley. And I'm going to be there, too. Thank you very much, Jim."
WRIGHT: "Thank you, Larry."

Now that's complete coverage.

CHAPTER EIGHT

HOME ALONE

Most of the women who worked for former Democratic Rep. Jim Bates from California agreed with their boss's position on the issues. It was his position on *them* they couldn't stand.

Other congressmen have been just as annoying as Bates in their pursuit of female staffers, but few have been as persistent. During his eight years in office, Bates thrived on a regular routine of grabbing attractive secretaries and hugging them, as he put it, to give himself "more energy." He asked them to sleep with him, commented on their breast size and rear ends. But Bates didn't stop with hugs and lewd remarks. One woman revealed how he liked to attach himself to her leg, which he would straddle as they discussed legislative business. And that wasn't the only way the congressman wanted to get physical. Another female staffer told a reporter that Bates informed her he often thought about hitting an office assistant "until blood trickled from her mouth."

Bates harassed his male aides too, throwing temper tantrums almost on a daily basis. For years, no one complained, fearing if they did their careers on the Hill would be ruined. Then in 1987, two women, who couldn't take it anymore, filed charges against Bates with the House Ethics Committee. The outcome surprised no one. After hearing the case, the congressional panel sent Bates a letter asking him to apologize to the women and learn how to behave himself.

"I think I made a mistake," admitted Bates, who lost his 1990 bid for a fifth term. "I didn't really know what sexual harassment was."

That's understandable. Senators and representatives live in a world immune from such concerns, and the longer they live in it the more immune they become.

"Congress is like a big fraternity house," said a female Senate staffer. Make that Animal House. *Roll Call* newspaper reported in 1988 that 90 percent of Congress that year was made up of former fraternity brothers. Which made sense to syndicated advice columnist Ann Landers, who observed: "Most men who seek political office are extroverts. They're joiners by nature. They recognize the value of fraternities, where they can develop their people skills . . . and fraternities go after such men."

Male bonding, talking dirty, and chasing women—activities long associated with what goes on in college fraternities—have always been favorite pastimes in Congress, and, despite the ever-present risk of scandal, most members still behave as if they're big men on campus. When he was asked why he hired so many ex-beauty queens to work in his congressional office, Rep. Charles Wilson, an eleven-term Democrat from Texas and once engaged to Miss World, replied: "You can always teach 'em to type. But you can't teach 'em to grow tits."

The congressional attitude toward sexual harassment may be changing, but it's not changing fast enough to suit many female employees. From tales about lawmakers begging their secretaries to sleep with them for the good of the nation to stories of drunken attacks, it's clear that Capitol Hill is not just a place where laws are made.

Here's an account of a night on the town with the Senate's premiere playboys, Chris Dodd from Connecticut and his buddy Ted Kennedy, before they went on semi-inactive status. Dodd and Kennedy were notorious party animals—once Kennedy attended his office Christmas bash in drag, pretending to be Iran-contra pinup Fawn Hall. But one night in 1985 the two Democrats sank to an all-time low. The incident occurred in La

Brasserie, a Washington restaurant, and was later retold by *New York Times* reporter Michael Kelly in *GQ* magazine:

"It is after midnight and Kennedy and Dodd are just finishing up a long dinner in a private room on the first floor of the restaurant's annex. They are drunk. Their dates, two very young blondes, leave the table to go to the bathroom. The dates are drunk too. . . . Betty Loh, who served the foursome, also leaves the room. Raymond Campet, the co-owner of La Brasserie, tells [another waitress Carla] Gaviglio the senators want to see her. As Gaviglio enters the room, the six-foot-two 225-plus-pound Kennedy grabs the five-foot-three, 103-pound waitress and throws her on the table. She lands on her back, scattering crystal, plates, cutlery and lit candles. Several glasses and a crystal candlestick are broken. Kennedy then picks her up from the table and throws her on Dodd, who is sprawled in a chair. With Gaviglio on Dodd's lap. Kennedy jumps on top and begins rubbing his genital area against hers, supporting his weight on the arms of the chair. As he is doing this, Loh enters the room. She and Gaviglio both scream, drawing one of two dishwashers. Startled, Kennedy leaps up. He laughs. Bruised and angry over what she considered a sexual assault, Gaviglio runs from the room. Kennedy, Dodd and their dates leave shortly thereafter, following a friendly argument between the two senators over the check."

Not all women, it should be noted, find amorous attention from lawmakers to be this unpleasant, though few have gone to the lengths of a staffer named Dorothy, who tape-recorded Michigan Democratic Sen. Don Riegle's remarkable ability to mix business and pleasure during their many office make-out sessions.

RIEGLE: "I love you."
DOROTHY: "Don, I love you and I'll always love—"
RIEGLE: "And I'll always love you. . . . I . . . I . . . God feel such super love for you. By the way, the newsletter should start arriving."

Shortly after this recording was made, Riegle, who had a wife and three children at the time, dumped Dorothy, got a divorce and married another woman who worked in his office.

There are more than 19,500 congressional staffers, and while the vast majority have never had to pry a congressman off their legs or take dictation from a nude senator, they all know what it feels like to be overworked, underpaid, and exploited.

Staff members answer constituent mail, write speeches, and research important issues. They also act as chauffeurs, party hostesses, and pet walkers to the many dogs and cats of Congress. An intern working for former Democratic Rep. Jerry Sikorski from Minnesota wasn't only required to take her boss's dog for walks, she once was ordered to take it to the vet's to be artificially inseminated.

Hill types by and large don't seem to mind such duty. Preconditioned by high ideals and a belief in self-sacrifice, the more ambitious among them thrive on it. To serve the boss is every congressional staffer's main function, and it's rare in this age of chronic complaining to find many unwilling to throw themselves body and soul—well, at least soul—into the task.

Only Hollywood movie studios require a comparable degree of groveling. That's because Hollywood and Washington are one-industry company towns where advancement through the ranks is a by-product of sucking up. Granted, talent counts for something, but the most useful skill is knowing how, where, and when to kiss ass. On Capitol Hill the challenge can be immense. Since anyone could someday reign supreme, kissing *all* ass is the operative rule of thumb.

Staffers are trained to show reverence and respect to their bosses, who are always described to constituents and other visitors by their title. *"The senator is busy." "The congressman will see you now."*

They may have been lawyers, college professors, or car dealers in their previous lives, but once they arrive in Congress, all elected officials are elevated to the status of instant VIPs. Their mere presence is an event. Their very words make history. And among their assistants and aides they can do no wrong, even if they happen to be caught red-handed in the most embarrassing scandals imaginable.

Loyalty is big on the Hill, and whenever a member of Congress gets in trouble, staffers are expected to close ranks and rally to his or her side. At the height of his trials and tribulations over claims that he had sexually harassed, then intimidated some two dozen former female staffers, Sen. Robert Packwood's staunchest defenders were female members of his *present* staff.

In a 1990 memo to Democratic Sen. Chuck Robb of Virginia, his then-press secretary tried to warn his boss that stories circulating about Robb's behavior "raised questions" about his judgment and credibility. The memo, entitled "Womanizing," went on to point out that despite Robb's denials it was well known that he had engaged in "oral sex . . . with at least a half-dozen women."

A few years earlier, Robb himself deftly addressed the oral-sex question in a carefully crafted memo of his own: "I'd have to acknowledge that I have a weakness for the fairer sex," he wrote, "and I hope I never lose it. . . . But I have always drawn the line on certain conduct [despite being around] some very alluring company. . . . I haven't done anything that I regard as unfaithful to my wife, . . . the only woman [I have] had coital sex with in the 20 years we've been married."

Once, Robb admitted receiving a nude massage from an ex-beauty queen, but steadfastly maintained that the rubdown was purely therapeutic. "First Clinton didn't inhale," went one joke, "then Robb didn't insert."

After the memos fell into the hands of reporters, Robb was forced to respond, which he did in a letter to Virginia Democrats just prior to announcing his 1994 reelection bid against Iran-contra defendant Oliver North, another ex-Marine.

"I am clearly vulnerable on the question of socializing under circumstances not appropriate for a married man," he declared, and then suggested that if his wife, Lynda Bird Johnson Robb, had forgiven him, so should voters, assuming not too many of them linked "socializing" to oral sex, a crime punishable inder Virginia's sodomy laws by twenty years in prison.

Like certain primitive tribes that worship the procreative powers of their leaders, some congressional staffs celebrate their boss's sexual prowess. Republican Sen. Strom Thurmond from South Carolina, now in his nineties, has fathered so many children he's picked up the nickname "Sperm" Thurmond. A well-known but perhaps exaggerated story is that his staff once gave him a baseball bat as a birthday gift. As one reporter explained, the joke was that after he dies, the undertaker will need it "to kill his dick." A fitness nut, Thurmond is fond of his studly reputation.

No senators or representatives could make it through the day without the constant care and guidance staffers provide. In the schedule-intensive environment of Capitol Hill, it's the member's staff that's responsible for getting him where he's supposed to be, when he's supposed to be there. Yet sometimes it's a case of the blind leading the blind. A former Pennsylvania congressman was once scheduled to give a speech in a hotel, and instead of going through the front door, aides led him through the service entrance. After following staffers around in the dark for a while, the lawmaker mistook a lighted swimming pool for the dance floor and fell in.

Many believe that if term limits are imposed on Congress, staffers will be the only ones left who know how a bill becomes law. The picture of aides someday running the House and Senate is legitimate cause for concern. But anyone who thinks that's the wave of the future hasn't been to the Hill lately. Staffs *already* run things, often directly, guiding their bosses around like nitwits, and sometimes indirectly through such double-edged management tools as the leak.

The Hill operates like a police state, with everyone busy reporting on everyone else. Take away the resulting leaks, and you take away a vital source of news and misinformation. Leaks are strategically planned to make members look good or look bad, depending on the leaker's motives. In the right hands, leaks can also be lethal interoffice instruments of revenge, the only way for browbeaten staffers to get even with their cruel and callous superiors. In a city where knowledge is power, a well-placed item leaked to the media at just the right moment can do an amazing amount of damage.

It was a leak that ruined the brief career of former Rep. Ernie Konnyu from California. Elected in 1986, Konnyu was done in by staff informers a short time later. According to a leak, the conservative Republican was attending a political event in his district when he told a female staffer to remove a campaign button from her sweater since it was calling undue attention to her small breasts. The story started a cottage industry of similar Konnyuisms, nearly all of them leaked by staffers who doomed their boss to defeat after one term.

Leaks to reporters about Anita Hill's closed-door testimony to the Senate Judiciary Committee forced her to go public with charges that Supreme Court nominee Clarence Thomas had harassed her while she worked on his staff at the Equal Employment Opportunity Commission. During hearings that followed, constant leaks helped to provide a solid weekend of televised dirt and gossip. Republican Sen. Alan Simpson from Wyoming, one of Hill's most persistent critics, claimed that he was getting leaked information about her "over the transom."

Leaks also played a significant role in the Packwood case. When it was learned that the veteran Republican was about to resign in the midst of an Ethics Committee investigation, committee staffers leaked word of his plans to the Justice Department. Government lawyers promptly issued a subpoena for Packwood's famous diaries, thus cutting off any legal escape route he might have and forcing him to stay in the Senate and face his accusers.

"We need to buoy him up and sustain him and press him to our bosom," Sen. Simpson said of Packwood, adding that the

Ethics Committee should find and punish the staffer responsible for the leaks.

There is a natural tendency in congressional politics to love the leak, when it serves a desired political purpose, and hate the leaker, when he doesn't. That explains the reception given to Clinton nominee Morton Halperin by some members of the Senate Armed Services Committee. Halperin, a former protégé of Henry Kissinger, was named to the new job of assistant secretary of defense for democracy and peacekeeping, part of America's post-Cold War nice-guy role in world affairs. But Halperin's background raised doubts about his ability to contain leaks.

When he was a National Security Council staffer in the Nixon administration, his phone was tapped by the FBI, which suspected him as the source of leaks about secret bombing raids in Cambodia. Later, he supported Daniel Ellsberg, famed leaker of the Pentagon Papers, and Philip Agee, whose book on the CIA leaked the names of agents overseas, one of whom was subsequently murdered. In the 1970s, Halperin also defended *The Progressive* magazine when the liberal journal published detailed instructions on how to make a hydrogen bomb.

Although the FBI never proved that Halperin had leaked classified material, to those opposed to his nomination the man was a human sieve. The *American Spectator* called the former boy wonder a "traitor to his nation," and Senate conservatives managed to muster enough support after two days of hearings to send the appointment back to the White House, which later withdrew the nomination.

If the capital of the mightiest nation on earth were suddenly taken over by an army of twenty-year-olds, it wouldn't look much different than Capitol Hill does right now.

Stroll down the corridors of power, and the first thing you notice is the incredible number of young people. In the 1960s, the first commandment of the student rebellion was "Don't trust anyone over thirty." In Congress, the rule these days seems to be "Don't *hire* anyone over thirty." Everywhere, youthful workers, well groomed, attractive, and politically plugged in, are busy carrying messages or retrieving information. There's a great temptation to call them glorified errand boys and girls, but to do so is to miss an important point: In politics, that's what everyone is.

Hill help is along for the ride. Which is why so many cling to their jobs for dear life. A staffer's destiny is directly linked to that of his or her employer. As long as the boss is on top, they're on top. When the boss takes a tumble, so do they.

The case of former House Sergeant-at-arms Jack Russ reversed the process. After a series of patronage appointments Russ became supervisor of the now-closed House bank. When a check-bouncing scam ended his career in 1992, dozens of the bank's best congressional customers took a political fall with him. Russ, who turned up mysteriously shot in the cheek after the scandal broke, got two years in prison for writing more than $75,000 in bad checks.

Working for someone whose only concern is his political popularity "can really do a number on your head," said a former House administrative assistant who has moved on to a key subcommittee. With the arrival of the permanent campaign, congressional politics is so consuming and the personalities it produces so demanding that a normal life ceases. That's especially true for the most faithful staffers who are on call round the clock.

Members of Congress, like all politicians, need constant reassurance, and the people they most often turn to for stroking are their office staffs. The bond that results can be intensely personal, so personal at times it's romantic.

But in politics there's a thin line between love and hate. Many staffers would do anything for their senators or representatives, up to and including marrying them, while others, fed up by their boss's chronic desire for pampering, wouldn't give them a pot to pee in, literally.

Republican Sen. Arlen Specter from Pennsylvania, whose unpredictable outbursts make him one of the worst people to work for on Capitol Hill, once told his staff he needed a place to stay while his house was being painted. Under some circumstances it might be considered an honor to have a U.S. senator camp out at your place for a few days. But apparently not when the senator is Specter, who informed staffers that anyone wishing to put him up would have to provide a private bathroom. There were no takers.

Congressional power is a seductive force, even for those trained to resist its magnetism. A female journalist from Europe, who found herself drawn uncontrollably to Democratic Sen. John Kerry, couldn't believe the humiliations she endured over the course of their brief affair. Dates planned around Kerry's tight schedule began at midnight, following important political functions where the bachelor from Massachusetts couldn't be seen in the company of a 25-year-old reporter. With workday meetings out of the question and Kerry often away on weekends, most of their little time together was spent in bed, where she was invariably pressed into service soothing his ego.

The woman soon tired of the arrangement and dropped Kerry for a member of Pink Floyd.

The gamble staffers make is that their bosses will be reelected, climb the seniority ladder and take them along too. Unfortunately, that dream often gets thwarted by defeat at the polls or else hard-to-please staff directors and jealous congressional wives, a growing number of whom now work in their husbands' offices as unpaid volunteers and close advisers on personnel matters. One way for House and Senate wives to make sure their spouses keep their libidos in check is through vigilant on-site monitoring.

In this respect, some wives work harder than many of the lawmakers they're married to. Heather Foley, wife of House Speaker Tom Foley, is famous for controlling access to her husband. Annette Lantos and her husband, Democratic Rep. Tom Lantos, may be the closest thing on the Hill to co-legislators. Working on a voluntary basis, Mrs. Lantos, a cousin of Hollywood beauty specimen Zsa Zsa Gabor, occupies a corner in her husband's

House office from which she oversees scheduling, tends to her own favorite issues, like animal rights, and generally keeps a close eye on all comings and goings with her toy French poodle Gigi.

There are members of Congress who need watching, and there are others who need finding. As a special service to his party, former House Speaker Jim Wright used to assign trusted staffers to pick up and deliver certain heavy-drinking Democrats with the tendency to get loaded just before big votes. Republican staffers performed the same duty on an as-needed basis. House Minority Leader Bob Michel liked to hang out at his favorite Capitol Hill bar to tipple and sing until closing. One evening he reportedly had such a good time that aides were summoned to take him home. The next day the Iran-contra scandal broke, and it was mid-afternoon before assistants had Michel in any shape to meet reporters.

Ex-Republican Sen. Gordon Humphrey of New Hampshire presented his staff with problems of a different kind. Humphrey was notorious for his regular disappearing act. All senior senators have "hideaway" offices, secret suites in the bowels of the Capitol where they can retreat whenever they want to be alone. Lyndon Johnson turned his into a private saloon. Others have used their hideaways to conduct clandestine discussions with lobbyists and get-togethers with their girlfriends. Humphrey, something of a recluse by nature, made his a hideout, keeping his whereabouts a mystery to all but a few trusted staff members and communicating with his main Senate office by personal computer.

For an institution devoted to bringing the order of law to bear on the nation as a whole, Congress itself appears to be in a perpetual state of disarray. Although senators command more work space than representatives, all Hill offices, where the real business of governing goes on, are about as organized as the average attic. Desks are crammed into corners, phones set up on boxes, and closets used as everything from mailrooms to resource centers.

Staffers say the payoff for spending ten to twelve low-wage hours a day wedged into such surroundings is the chance to rub shoulders with greatness, perhaps if they're lucky to be great themselves, like the dozens of staffers who *have* gone on to long and rewarding careers in politics. Bill Clinton started his climb to the top as a Senate messenger.

Hopes like that can seem depressingly slim when measured against the daily drudgery of life as a Capitol Hill lackey. Still, it's easy to see why the cream of America's civic-minded youth is drawn there. The wide hallways of six House and Senate office buildings are lined with flags and filled with fast-moving foot traffic. There's a sense that important decisions are being made behind every closed door. But since most members will go to any lengths to avoid having to decide anything, what's more likely to be going on is a lot of yelling and screaming.

In exchange for their dedication, hard work, and optimism, staffers are usually treated like servants. One congressman makes his staff peel his oranges; others use theirs to pick up dry cleaning. When Newt Gingrich's morning coffee doesn't contain sugar and cream to his exact specifications, he reportedly goes into fits of rage. If he doesn't get his way, Democratic Rep. Toby Roth from Wisconsin throws telephones.

Female members can be just as bad. After meeting an Australian feminist at a conference in Europe several years ago, Maryland Democratic Sen. Barbara Mikulski was so taken with the woman that she invited her to move to America and run her congressional office, where the newly radicalized Mikulski and her friend proceeded to make life so miserable for staffers most of them quit.

Not many, however, can top the congresswoman who once asked her entire staff to submit letters of resignation. She assured worried workers that the letters were strictly symbolic, her way of signifying a fresh start to voters back in her district. But when all the mail was in, she changed her mind and got rid of everyone.

Who would put up with such mistreatment?

Anybody who thinks working in Congress is a noble calling and "doesn't mind being shit on for a good cause," said a former House staffer who switched from politics to journalism, but still fears the wrath of his ex-employer.

All political work is essentially temporary—and permanently threatening. To a degree that would probably surprise most average voters, the good life in the nation's capital isn't all it's cracked up to be. People who live according to election results have a concept of job security that makes migrant work look like a tenured position. Every dip in the public opinion polls is good reason to panic. Nowhere else in the U.S. labor market do people spend more time polishing their resumés than they do in Washington.

Everybody in government thinks he or she is on the verge of defeat, deactivation, or dismissal, including federal bureaucrats who can only be terminated if they show up for work naked demanding the violent overthrow of democracy, and even then it would take so long to process the necessary paperwork, they'd probably be on the job till they reached retirement age. That's because federal employees are protected by civil service rules and regulations adopted more than a century ago designed to shield them from the harsh realities of politics. Workers on Capitol Hill should be so lucky. No such rules have ever applied to them.

Created in 1883, two years after a disgruntled office seeker assassinated President James Garfield, the Civil Service Commission was intended to depoliticize the federal workforce and act as a watchdog over the "merit system," assuring that government jobs went to the best qualified applicants instead of the best connected.

The only merit system that counts on the Hill is politics. Over the years, members of the House and Senate have systematically exempted themselves from nearly every labor law on the books, including the National Labor Relations Act of 1935, the Fair Labor Standards Act of 1938, the Equal Pay Act of 1963, the Civil Rights Act of 1964, the Age Discrimination Act of 1967, the Occupational Safety and Health Act of 1970, the Americans with Disabilities Act of 1990, and the Family and Medical Leave Act of 1993.

The congressional philosophy of employment is not much different from that in the fast-food industry, where low wages and an endless supply of teenage job applicants make wholesale abuse the order of the day. Given what they do for a living and what their bosses do *to* them, Hill staffers may constitute the most elite exploited workforce in America. Certainly they are among the most frightened.

In a 1993 survey taken by the Joint Committee on the Organization of Congress, 44 percent of House staffers and 40 percent of those in the Senate said they would be reluctant to complain about working conditions, believing that any official investigation wouldn't be worth their "time and energy." Almost half of all those responding cited the damage going public might do to their careers. They also said they didn't think they would be given an honest hearing by the congressional Office of Fair Employment Practices, which handles complaints from Hill staffers. From 1988 to 1993, the OFEP received 1,200 inquiries from Hill workers, but only sixteen formal complaints. Of those, four cases made it all the way through the review process, with only one being decided in the employee's favor.

A study of congressional compliance with labor laws by the independent Employment Policy Foundation found coverage "sporadic and woefully inadequate." As a place to work, most experts conclude, Congress is essentially unchanged from what it was a hundred years ago, only now there are more places to eat.

But even restaurant employees complain of on-the-job abuse. Recently, several female food-service workers in the Senate dining room won an out-of-court settlement in a case against their supervisors, who for years called the women "sluts," "bitches," and "whores," tore off their dresses, and stuffed the women head-first into trash cans.

Two congressmen, Christopher Shays, a Connecticut Republican, and Dick Swett, a Democrat from New Hampshire, have introduced legislation that would apply all civil rights and fair labor laws to the legislative branch. That means that the House and Senate would finally have to obey laws they expect the rest of the nation's employers to live by. But with the congressional record on self-reform less than impressive and members unlikely to surrender enforcement of any new protections to outsiders, Congress seems likely to remain a nice place to visit but a horrible place to work.

CHAPTER NINE

THERE GOES
THE NEIGHBORHOOD

It was a typical Saturday night on Capitol Hill—dangerous without being life threatening, anyway not yet. As usual, criminal activity was at a temporary standstill. Except for a few scattered stickups, most practitioners of serious violence were on their seven o'clock dinner break.

Weekends in Washington's worst neighborhoods, places with genteel-sounding names like Mayfair Mansions and Kenilworth Gardens, tend to follow the same pattern. Even the murder capital of the United States has occasional intervals of down time. Nevertheless, the statistics showed that one segment of the criminal element was hard at work: Eleven days into 1992, and there were already fourteen homicides. At this rate, the city was on a pace to break its own annual record by Labor Day.

Crime isn't running rampant in Washington. Few things operate on a more dependable schedule. In some sections of town you can set your watch by the comings and goings of local troublemakers. This is one place where the crackheads, carjackers, and kill freaks all keep regular hours, and anyone with the slightest instinct for self-preservation knows when it's time to duck for cover.

The District police were expecting another busy night. Which is one reason many of them call weekend duty "prime time." Not only was Washington's murder rate of 80.6 homicides per

100,000 residents—the highest in the country—attracting coverage from the big network news shows, it also meant extra hours on the job—and that meant extra money.

Law enforcement professionals may hate crime, but in Washington it's hard to find any who don't like overtime. On an average weekend the sheer volume of wrongdoing makes generous allotments of OT a major part of every cop's regular take-home pay. An arrest means paperwork, and that, plus subsequent court appearances, is where the real money is. Booking an unruly wino can take four or five hours. Processing somebody picked up for a little freelance street surgery often takes a whole shift and then some.

For a city with so much crime—5 percent of the population is under some form of court-ordered supervision—it might seem reasonable to think police would have the in-house phase of the business down to a science. Think again. One problem is a lag in technology. The D.C. Police Department doesn't have computers. It *had* computers, but gave up the experiment when most of them were stolen. As a result, records are kept the old-fashioned way—with ballpoint pens and carbon paper. "You can tell which guys are making the arrests," explained an officer whose penmanship has drawn consistent praise. "Their hands are always blue."

A more serious cause for concern is the misapplication of manpower. Half of the city's 4,200-person police force isn't even out chasing criminals. They're administrators, who have to work late themselves just to keep track of everyone's overtime. It's a big job. In one year, 1990, the city paid out a total of $22 million in federally subsidized police overtime wages. A dozen detectives alone accounted for more than a million dollars. Throwing money after mayhem is an old Washington tradition, and while the bonus work hours have not had any noticeable effect on curtailing the city's continuing murder spree, they have definitely increased the monetary benefits that come with cleaning up afterward.

Yet "cleaning up" may not accurately describe what takes place in the aftermath of most Washington crime. The city currently sports a 25 percent arrest rate in first-degree murder cases. That represents a drop from 97 percent in 1948 and 80 percent as recently as 1986. The rapid increase in the number of homicides has meant less time for investigation and fewer convictions in court. From 1986 to 1990, District police sent 938 murder cases to the U.S. attorney's office for prosecution. A total of one-third were dismissed. That's roughly twice as many as in other cities.

Tucker Carlson of the Heritage Foundation has studied the problem and traces it back to the police department's recruitment process, a haphazard series of preferences and exemptions that have helped to produce a virtual open-admissions policy. In 1988, the city's police academy eliminated final exams after 40 percent of the new trainees flunked. At the time, community leaders protested the tests were racially biased against blacks, who now make up more than three-quarters of the force.

Following three, sometimes four, sometimes five months of instruction in basic law enforcement, D.C. police recruits can graduate—and nearly 100 percent do—with no questions asked.

"Never mind memorizing the words in the Miranda warning," said Carlson. "For all anyone knows, these people don't understand the difference between right and wrong."

The fact that Carlson works for Capitol Hill's biggest right-wing think tank almost guaranteed that his findings would be ignored by the city government. Local officials had the same reaction in 1990, when a special commission headed by economist Alice Rivlin, now Bill Clinton's budget director, concluded that Washington's police department was a classic study in wasted money and sloppy procedures.

The city accepts new recruits with juvenile arrest records. Former police instructors say that illiterates and people diagnosed as "borderline retarded" have graduated from the police academy. The consequences aren't hard to miss. The most frequently cited reason for Washington's low murder conviction rate is botched or otherwise insufficient police work. Some cases never even make it to court because prosecutors can't read the arrest reports.

Maybe the best indication of the department's declining performance came in 1992 when thirty-six police officers were indicted on charges ranging from homicide to kidnapping. In one case, an on-duty street patrolman, found guilty of forcing a woman to perform oral sex on him, had this to say during his interrogation:

QUESTION: Did you at any time inform [the woman] that if she didn't give you a blow job . . . you would lock her up?

ANSWER: You have to see my girlfriend and you can answer that. . . . Why would I want a smelly bitch giving me a blow job when I got a beautiful girlfriend?

A year later, an FBI sting operation netted a dozen D.C. cops charged with accepting $80,000 in payoffs for protecting fake shipments of cocaine. Several of the arrested officers were captured on videotape boasting they had sold drugs prior to joining the force. Two of the men even bragged they had once worked as contract killers.

This is the protective environment in which Washingtonians live. The nation's capital is a classic example not just of a breakdown in law and order but of its systematic disappearance. The problem is particularly acute on Capitol Hill where all the supposed causes of crime—poverty, drugs, and a ready supply of easy victims—come together in an area approximately half the size of Central Park.

Congress has its own 1,100-person police force to guard government buildings and direct traffic. But the Capitol police, despite being armed to the teeth with the latest in anti-terrorist weaponry, have neither the training nor the manpower to venture into areas outside their limited official jurisdiction. So members of Congress, like everyone else in Washington, have to rely for their safety on D.C.'s finest.

In the squad room, out back by the gas pump and wherever

else officers at the First District Substation gather to unwind, most of them seem to know more about each other's paychecks than they do about what's going on in the streets. In that respect it's not much different from other Washington police precincts. Sill, the One-D-One, as it's called, is a round-the-clock pressure cooker. Covering Capitol Hill from the Southeast Freeway to H Street and from Union Station to the Eastern Market, One-D-One is probably the most politicized free-fire zone in America.

Home to elected officials from around the country as well as a new breed of cold killer from the tenth grade, Capitol Hill has become the kind of place where even a simple walk to the bus stop has terminal implications.

"I used to be a cop," said Colorado Sen. Ben Nighthorse Campbell, a Cheyenne Indian and a former Olympic gold medalist in judo. That wasn't much help, however, when someone stuck a pistol in Campbell's face outside a Capitol Hill grocery store and ran away with his wallet. Campbell figured he got off easy. It could have been worse.

The wife of North Dakota Sen. Kent Conrad was attacked by a man with a gun after parking her car in front of her Capitol Hill town house. When she refused to hand over her keys, the gunman, angered by her failure to cooperate, pushed her into the street where she was almost hit by a truck.

Hundreds of others weren't so lucky. There was the lawyer who was killed while driving near the Capitol when his car was sprayed with gunfire from a playground. There was the congressional aide who was shot through the heart during an attempted robbery outside his apartment. And then there was Tom Barnes, a 25-year-old Senate staffer whose murder in January 1992 touched off renewed hostilities between Congress and the District of Columbia over crime and self-determination.

Barnes, like many who work on Capitol Hill, was eager to do something important. In 1991, he got a job as a intern in the office of Sen. Richard Shelby. The Alabama Democrat, a friend of the Barnes family in Tuscaloosa, had known Tom since the day he was born. Within a year after joining Shelby's staff,

Barnes was promoted to legislative assistant and seemed to have a promising career ahead of him. But that was before he decided to move to Acker Street, on the Hill.

Urban renewal had come slowly to Acker Street, and the results only emphasized Capitol Hill's split personality. The dozen or so Acker Street houses that have been rehabilitated are all lived in by whites and look like cellblocks with designer steel doors and bars on the windows. The houses where blacks live have far less curb appeal. But despite their different living conditions, everyone who ventures outside, regardless of race, is equally exposed to street crime.

Barnes and Toof Brown, his roommate and fellow-worker in Shelby's office, didn't think of themselves as inner-city pioneers. They were just glad to find an affordable place to live. And like many first-time residents on Capitol Hill, they were only vaguely aware of the dangers awaiting them in their new neighborhood.

Washington is shaped like an upright diamond with the lower left-hand portion missing. Rock Creek Park, a lush woods that runs in a straight line from the Potomac River to the northernmost boundary with Maryland, cuts the city in half. Most of Washington's wealthy white population lives west of the park, where the homes are expensive, incomes substantial, and neighborhoods relatively crime free. The area east of the park, where the population is predominately black, is just the opposite. Communities are run down, unemployment is high, and crime, especially violent crime, is epidemic.

In 1993, there were two murders in the largely white region west of Rock Creek Park. East of the park, there were 454.

Capitol Hill appears at first to be an exception to the rule. Compared to the surrounding neighborhoods, the Hill looks like an island of civility. But the elegant old row houses and serene tree-lined streets that give the area its turn-of-century charm also hide the many threats that go with living there, threats that new arrivals sometimes overlook.

That was the case when Tom Barnes decided to walk to a convenience store to buy a cup of coffee. At the corner of Acker and

Seventh Streets, a half-block from his house, Barnes was fatally shot in the head.

Police initially thought he was the victim of a hit-and-run driver, a natural assumption since he was found lying right in the middle of the intersection. But when they put him in the ambulance, medics noticed that the lower back portion of his skull had been blown away. At the Washington Hospital Center, a life-support system kept Barnes alive for four days.

With no suspects arrested in the case, calls were made for increased police protection for residents of the Hill. If someone on his way to buy coffee could become a murder victim, anyone could.

Newspapers in Barnes's home state blamed his death on Washington lawlessness. "Murder has all but grown commonplace in the shadows of monuments to liberty and justice," editorialized the Foley, Alabama, *Onlooker*. "Legislative help is needed to prevent the shameful bloodshed on the streets of the nation's capitol from spilling over to the backroads of Baldwin County."

Even the Washington media, which report crime statistics as if they were sports scores, found something particularly chilling about Barnes's murder. That it had occurred so close to Congress raised inevitable questions about what lawmakers were doing to stop violence on the city's streets and in their own backyard. And those questions in turn prompted lawmakers to ask District officials what they were doing about it.

The District of Columbia's lone congressional delegate, Democrat Eleanor Holmes Norton, undertook immediate damage-control measures. "I make it my business to call every member [who has problems in the city], since I'm the one who lives here and represents here," she said. Norton had called Barnes's mother in the hospital and later reported that "she sounded very upbeat . . . She didn't blame the people of the District . . . There was no self-pity, no lashing out at the city."

But if Barnes's mother didn't lash out over her son's death and the slow police work that followed, others did.

"Like much of the violence that plagues this city, there is no motive, no suspect, no answer," said Shelby. "Indiscriminate senseless violence can strike anyone, anytime. The horror is that we are powerless to protect our friends and families against individuals who have no respect for life."

Another Acker Street resident, former Rep. Claudine Schneider, called the shooting an "isolated incident." Then added, "I don't think there is any safe place in D.C."

To live in Washington means living with danger, and not just the predictable kind that occurs in bad neighborhoods. In the District, because good and bad neighborhoods can often be separated by a single street, any place is dangerous. People have been shot cutting their grass by drive-by strangers. Shoppers have had to dodge bullets outside of fancy stores. And in one grim incident a few years ago that surpassed even Washington's standards for random violence, a gunman with an automatic rifle opened fire on a swimming pool full of little kids, wounding six of them.

Start a discussion about crime in Washington and before long it leads into another subject that inflames passions on all sides of the issue—race. And when city officials and members of Congress get involved, the back-and-forth charges of racism and incompetence are all that you hear.

District politicians do not like Congress. When they run for office, they campaign against the "overseers" on Capitol Hill, and when they get elected and start having problems, the House and Senate are always to blame. Washington officials pretend they manage their own affairs. But it's Congress, which bankrolls the city with close to $650 million in annual appropriations (one-fourth of its local yearly budget), that still has final approval over every local law.

One oversight committee and two subcommittees do the work, and it's rare to find a lawmaker who wants to serve on any of them. An exception is Norton, whose principal function is making speeches in favor of D.C. statehood, an issue that could only make sense in a city of government workers.

Logic says that Washington, D.C., given its meager tax base, could never be self-supporting as a state. Certainly, Norton won't be much help. It was revealed during her first campaign for the congressional delegate's job in 1990 that she and her then-husband owed the city more than $80,000 in unpaid back taxes. But District voters are a forgiving group. They elected Norton anyway.

Statehood also happens to be one of Rev. Jesse Jackson's favorite issues, although any cause that gets him on television will do. In one demonstration, Jackson, Norton, and assorted local officials blocked traffic on Capitol Hill, demanding that a reluctant Congress make Washington the fifty-first state. Jackson, who calls D.C. statehood the most important civil rights issue in America, said it was time for supporters "to put our bodies on the line." As a small, mostly black, crowd cheered, Jackson then helped to tip over what looked like the world's largest urine sample. It turned out to be a barrel full of iced tea from the House cafeteria, a symbolic reminder of the Boston Tea Party, yet for Jackson the statehood fight is hardly a give-me-liberty-or-give-me-death kind of issue.

If Washington becomes a state—the name already selected, from a list that included "Douglass" and "Utopia," is "New Columbia"—Jackson will surely be elected governor, or more likely one of its two senators. He already goes by the title of "shadow senator" for the District, and has used the unpaid position—Jackson's actual source of income is one of the true mysteries of Washington politics—to push his way into Congress in a manner few, if any, duly elected officials appreciate. Jackson has made speeches on the Capitol steps, and has tried to persuade the Senate to give him floor privileges and office space, say Hill insiders. He even refuses to walk through metal detectors in the Capitol building, something required of everyone but senators and representatives.

When Jackson pleads for D.C. statehood, what he's really

pleading for isn't independence, it's a job, not only for himself but for the thousands of other future employees needed to run the new state. Since there are no present plans to drop the city government if statehood is granted, what would prevent Washington from having two separate governing units? Or even more? As a state, D.C. (which already employs one out of every nineteen Washingtonians) would have to have counties, and each one of those would need its own bureaucracy. Government is Washington's only natural resource, and once statehood was granted, every able-bodied adult living in the city could be eligible for a government job.

Norton herself has provided a hint of what all this self-determination might cost. According to the National Taxpayers Union, the spending implications of legislation she sponsored halfway through the 103rd Congress (much of it aimed at benefiting the District) came to $563.2 billion. That's $63.2 billion more than the Clinton administration proposed collecting over a five-year period to help reduce the deficit.

The District's fiscal problems are directly related to its crime problems. As the city loses population and businesses to the safer Maryland and Virginia suburbs, its tax base also goes down. In the face of constant revenue shortfalls, District officials have had to resort to more and more desperate money-making schemes. They have tried and failed to enact a commuter tax, a special tax on lawyers, and a surtax on doctors' fees. One plan, an effort to introduce casino gambling, failed when it got no support in Congress. Another called on the State Department to pressure the government of South Korea to pay reparations to the District. The reasoning had a familiar ring, given Washington's long history of living off federal entitlements. The city was owed the money, some council members declared, because Korean immigrants were buying up neighborhood grocery stores and depriving other minority residents of economic opportunities.

Several years later, when those same Korean merchants were being robbed and killed in disproportionate numbers during a crime wave that made national news, the city council opposed a plan to call in the National Guard, claiming it would be bad for Washington's image and hurt its campaign for statehood.

Tom Barnes's murder was not helping matters either. The shooting had galvanized anti-statehood sentiment all over the Hill. Not since former Washington Mayor Marion Barry was caught snorting cocaine in an FBI sting had members of Congress been so outspoken in their criticism of city government leaders, who retaliated as usual with charges of racism.

Washington's electric chair had been unplugged for nearly forty years, but seven months after Barnes's death, Shelby proposed legislation that would give local juries on homicide cases the option of sending convicted murderers to jail for life or handing them a death sentence.

Led by Shelby, a group of Republican senators, including the tough-on-crime trio of Strom Thurmond from South Carolina, Jesse Helms from North Carolina, and Orrin Hatch from Utah, had tried to impose a death penalty law without giving District residents any say in the matter. That was the way Congress used to do things. But in a deal worked out with former Sen. Brock Adams, then chairman of the District of Columbia Appropriations Committee, a possible losing floor fight was avoided by agreeing to put the measure on the November 1992 ballot.

A husky Southern lawyer with a fastidious comb-over haircut, Shelby introduced the bill with an emotional speech on the Senate floor.

"When I received the call that Tom Barnes had been shot, it changed my life," he said. "And it changed my attitude about the violence in the District of Columbia forever. . . . I regret that it took a tragic event to open my eyes. . . . Tom's murder has encouraged me to do what I can to reduce the city's crime rate. However, Tom is not the only one for whom I'm doing this. Too often, when we address the issue of capital punishment we tend to think more about the rights of the criminals and we forget about the victims. Therefore, I would like to take a few minutes to read the names of every murder victim in the District of Columbia in 1992. . . . As I read this . . . keep in mind that all these murders have occurred . . . in less than seven months . . . within a few blocks of where we are at the moment."

The list contained 248 names—among them Victim No. 38, Maggie Comfort, a one-year-old child, Victim No. 223, Willie Berry, 73-year-old grandfather—and by the time Shelby had finished reading them all, the city's body count no longer sounded like simple mathematics.

"While the death penalty alone may not stop all the violence in the District of Columbia, I believe it makes a forceful statement," he said. "It says we have had enough. . . ."

Shelby, a former four-term congressmen, is a staunch conservative, a fact that has alienated him from many Democratic causes. Actually, on most issues that separate Democrats and Republicans, Shelby might as well be in the GOP. He's pro-business, anti-entitlement, and once voted against making Martin Luther King's birthday a national holiday.

But his Republican predecessor, Jeremiah Denton, a cranky Vietnam POW, made Shelby look like Mr. Sensitive. Once during a Senate hearing on wife rape, Denton grabbed a microphone and blurted out: "Damn it, when you get married, you kind of expect you're going to get a little sex." *Congressional Quarterly*'s 1988 election tout sheet said Denton had failed "to keep in touch" with his Alabama constituency.

So far, keeping in touch with the folks back home hasn't been a problem for Shelby, who rises to the defense of the South on a regular basis. On one occasion, he opposed an extension of the Voting Rights Act, claiming it unfairly penalized Alabama and other Southern states. But nothing he'd done in the past even came close to having the kind of instant impact his death penalty referendum had.

When Shelby introduced the bill, there was an immediate outcry from city officials that Congress, in particular a member of Congress from the South, was meddling in local affairs. Speaking to an audience of downtown ministers, Washington Mayor

Kelly denounced the death penalty bill and the conspiracy of "congressional dictators" behind it in language that had her listeners clapping and shouting "Amen."

"Just as Moses told the Pharaohs: 'Let my people go,'" she said, "we must say to Congress: 'Let our *city* go!'" Kelly is an ardent proponent of statehood for the District, and likes to dress up the issue in biblical parables. In this case, the technique worked perfectly.

Black churches play a major role in Washington politics. Church congregations vote, and politicians court them constantly. Ministers are Washington's ward bosses, and the bigger their churches, the more votes they control.

"We have a crisis on our hands," Rev. Reginald Green told his congregation at the Walker Memorial Church in one of the city's worst crime areas. "A Congress that is only concerned with themselves is trying to impose their will on the District of Columbia."

Some ministers, Green among them, pointed out to their parishioners that Jesus Christ himself had been a victim of capital punishment.

Polls showed voters to be evenly divided on the question. But with no one actively campaigning *for* the death penalty bill, the airwaves and town meetings belonged to the statehood forces, who were vehemently opposed to the measure. "Thou Shalt Not Kill" posters began to appear on phone poles. But the mobilization had little to do with morality. If the referendum passed, local politicians would be the big losers. A "Yes" vote for capital punishment would validate criticism by anti-statehood conservatives in Congress that the city couldn't run its own business, although if the most important business of any city is protecting its citizens, clearly it couldn't.

Washington's murder rate may have been leading the nation, but according to police statistics, somebody walking down the street in the District was thirteen times more likely to be robbed than killed. Rape and assault were also popular pastimes. There were many ways the city's criminal class could make life uncomfortable, and very little law-abiding citizens could do about it. Which, some frustrated District residents admitted, was reason enough to cast their votes for the death penalty.

As election day drew closer, Shelby became the target of everyone from outraged talk-show callers to ex-Mayor Marion Barry, freed from prison after his drug conviction and campaigning for a city council seat with a colorful African wardrobe and new name, "Anwar Amal." A white senator from Alabama leading a pro-capital punishment drive in a city that's 70 percent black was a situation tailor-made for a last-minute racial offensive. Eleanor Holmes Norton led the final charge, comparing Congress to a lynch mob and Shelby to something like the Grand Wizard of the Ku Klux Klan.

"Senator Shelby took no interest in the District's homicide problem until someone close to him got killed," Norton sputtered in one radio interview. "People need to know that he comes from one of the worst states for executing black people."

A provision never mentioned by opponents to Shelby's bill would give the mayor of Washington the power to commute any death sentence to life imprisonment, which, considering the liberal nature of District politics, almost guaranteed that no offender would ever face execution. But a concession to the Senate on any point might be seen as an admission that people in power weren't doing their jobs.

It's not often that anyone convicted of murder in a Washington court ever serves a full sentence. And since the death penalty or life in prison without parole would obviously impose a much harsher punishment, local politicians found themselves in the somewhat awkward position of having to defend their hometown murderers.

If the congressional bill became law, said Norton, the city, which no longer had the necessary equipment to perform executions, might have to contract with states like Alabama, Mississippi, and Georgia to carry out sentences—and, she added, "execute mostly black people."

Norton was pushing all the buttons. The death penalty was no longer a religious issue, or even a racial issue. It was a matter of civic pride. The law Washingtonians were being asked to approve, a law being forced on them by some senator from the same state as George Wallace, would not only inflict cruel and unusual punishment, it would send the business out of town.

Washington murder statistics were bad enough, but the complaint among many in Congress was that local leaders and the District's police department had become immune to violence and the toll it was taking on the community.

"I'm not sure," Shelby said, "that people around here appreciate what it is to murder someone anymore."

Shelby, whose anti-crime campaigns had carried predominantly black districts in his home state, was having serious trouble getting out the message that the death penalty was designed to serve the public good in the District. A big part of the reason was the *Washington Post*, so sensitive to charges of racial bias that it often doesn't even identify prison escapees by color. "Death Penalty Fueled by Fear," read a typical *Post* headline. *Post* op-ed pieces accused Shelby of resorting to racially oriented scare tactics to lure voters. But what could be scarier than the three or four murder stories the paper ran every day, often buried as two-paragraph "filler" items under the foreign weather report in its Metro section?

With Barnes's killer still on the loose, capital punishment was getting more publicity than Marion Barry's political comeback. But then, Barry was a shoo-in. The vote on the death penalty was too close to call. If the bill passed, Shelby and others said, it would be more than a vote for law and order. It would be a vote of no confidence in local leaders and the District government and maybe, Shelby hoped, the beginning of the end for the D.C. statehood issue.

Shelby and several others cosponsoring the referendum were advocates of "retrocession," that is, giving all the land now known as Washington—save a small enclave for museums and federal government buildings—back to the state of Maryland, which originally contributed half the territory to create the District of Columbia. The other half came from Virginia, which took back its portion in a dispute over slavery in 1846.

Returning the District to Maryland is not a popular political option on either side of the border, particularly in Washington, where the government job loss would be significant. District politicians, like politicians everywhere, don't want less government. They want more. And letting anti-statehood forces dictate terms on life-and-death issues like capital punishment was no way to get it.

The turnout on Election Day '92 was larger than expected. A random tour of polling places seemed to indicate that the death penalty question apparently had gotten out the vote. At one school in a black precinct, the line of people waiting to cast their ballots stretched around the block. But crowds were also heavy in white areas. Outside a church in Georgetown people milled around talking about capital punishment. No one admitted voting for it, but most agreed something had to be done to stop the murders. The city, said an elderly man in a tweed jacket with elbow patches, was getting so dangerous he was afraid to walk his dog. "We have to send a message," he added, but he didn't say to whom.

When the votes were counted, the capital punishment question passed in only 11 of the city's 140 voting polling precincts. That all 11 precincts happened to be located in white neighborhoods was seen as a sign that the city's racial divisions were deeper and darker than most people thought. In Anacostia, a predominantly black section of town, where forty-six murders had been recorded in the four previous years, almost 80 percent of the voters opposed the death penalty. In Shaw and Cardozo, equally dangerous neighborhoods, 75 percent rejected it.

All told, 67 percent of the District's voters—most of them from the areas hardest hit by crime and violence—said "No" to capital punishment, and "Yes," apparently, to turning the other cheek.

The outcome, Norton declared, was a victory for home rule. But everybody knew it was also a victory against Congress, one of the few fights with Capitol Hill the city has ever won.

"Shelby did us a favor," D.C. City Council member John Ray told reporters. "I think the vote would have been a lot closer, or might have even gone the other way, if citizens had put it on the ballot."

Shelby did not take the loss in stride, and weeks afterward was still mad.

"The defeat sent the wrong message," he said, sitting behind his desk, folding and unfolding his big hands as though he might wring someone's neck. "It says criminal justice is not important to us. That's exactly what some of these politicians are saying. They don't want Congress to interfere. . . . Well, Congress will interfere. . . . This is the nation's capital, and what's going on is a cryin' shame."

Almost one year after Tom Barnes's death, a special FBI task force on unsolved crimes made an arrest in the case, proving, some said, a theory that cops and prosecuting attorneys have about murder. It's not strangers who kill people, it's friends, family members, and next-door neighbors. This time the evidence pointed to a man who lived across the street from Barnes. The motive, as in much of D.C.'s random violence, was unclear.

Several months after Barnes was killed, Acker Street residents were shocked to find that someone had dumped a bucket of blood-red paint on the spot in the intersection where Barnes's body was found. The police said later it was probably kids.

"The level of tension in the neighborhood following Tom's death was pretty high," said Toof Brown, Barnes's roommate, who moved to another part of town. Capitol Hill, Brown said, was a nice place to work, but he didn't want to live there anymore.

In its own response to rising crime rates, the Senate in late 1993 passed, among other get-tough measures, legislation requiring a mandatory life sentence for anyone convicted in federal court of three violent felonies. It also refused to ban capital punishment sentences imposed by federal courts for crimes committed by defendants under the age of eighteen.

Almost 50 percent of Washington is made up of government property where such laws would apply, but the city's most lethal neighborhoods, including most of Capitol Hill, are outside federal jurisdiction. And as if to emphasize that point, during the week the Senate debated its anti-crime package, the District averaged one murder per day.

"It's a mistake to think we're talking about a normal city," Shelby said. "This is the nation's capital, and people come here thinking they'll be safe. . . . There should be signs on the roads leading into town to let them know how dangerous it is."

CHAPTER TEN

IT'S NOT <u>WHAT</u> YOU KNOW

If a ritzy black-tie dinner held at the Library of Congress a few years ago had been a book, the cataloguing department would have shelved it under:

Capitol Hill . . .

Politics . . .

Nocturnal.

The occasion was a tribute to the late Averell Harriman, American ambassador to Moscow, and the timing, a few months after the coup attempt that ended the Soviet Union, was just as impeccable as the late honoree's diplomatic portfolio. So many of Harriman's colleagues from the crusade against communism turned out, it could have been a victory party. George Kennan, the father of the containment theory, was there. So were former Defense Secretary Robert McNamara and retired CIA director Richard Helms.

Unfortunately, the passing years had not been kind to these geezers-*terrible*, some of whom were having trouble just moving from the open bar to the hot hors d'oeuvre table.

"Oh, my," said Harriman's ageless widow Pamela, now American ambassador to France, as she wistfully surveyed the room. "I *do* wish Averell were here."

In a way he was. The noted envoy had been dead for five years. Yet with his letters, memos, and other writings recently opened for scholarly inspection several floors below in the library's manuscript room, you could say that Harriman, an adviser to a half dozen presidents, wasn't just in the building, he was still being consulted.

Overseeing this get-together of past and present Washington insiders was Librarian of Congress James H. Billington, one of the city's most purposeful partygivers.

In the nation's capital, the theory goes, it's impossible to have too many friends or attend too many parties. The skill comes in picking the right ones, and that's where Billington, who excels in applied cocktail circuitry, puts his real talent to work.

Washington parties aren't meant for fun, but for doing business, an opportunity for the powerful to access each other outside the confines of the office, and for the less powerful to attach themselves to higher-ups who can help to advance their careers.

The business of Washington isn't business as such. It's self-promotion. "What could be better professionally than to be on a first-name basis with a cabinet member?" asked *Washingtonian* magazine gossip columnist Chuck Conconi. For serious Capitol Hill climbers, it's getting that same cabinet member to take an interest in their careers and introduce them to *other* important officials, until they eventually know everyone in town they need to know.

The rapid turnover and natural attrition common in politics make Washington's social scene a daily showcase of ambition, and with one of the city's most impressive party venues at his disposal, Billington could put his administrative aspirations on display in ways others only dreamed of.

His main goal, announced shortly after he took office in 1988, was to increase the library's outflow of information by installing a complex computer delivery system that would make everything in the vast collection available to users across the country. The plan had the endorsement of many in government. "I see a time when a child can come home from school and instead of playing video games, he can plug in to the Library of Congress," said Vice-President Al Gore, long a staunch supporter of high-tech communications.

Libraries are supposed to dispense knowledge, and the Library of Congress has always been a leading innovator in the field. But Billington had another more controversial objective, one that put him on a direct collision course with his chief economic benefactor and most important customer.

He wanted to do business.

To earn money for the financially hard-pressed library, Billington wanted to start _selling_ data to commercial users—book publishers, on-line services, and cable TV networks—the same data most of them were accustomed to getting for free, then selling themselves. It was a bold idea aimed at making the library less dependent on congressional funding. But at the same time it was bound to anger the multibillion-dollar information industry, whose lobby has considerable pull with Capitol Hill lawmakers.

There was ample precedent for what Billington wanted to do. NASA markets some of its services to private buyers, so do other federal agencies. The Library of Congress, however, doesn't happen to be a federal agency. It's a wholly owned subsidiary of Congress, and as such a jealously guarded piece of political property.

To be successful, Billington would not only have to line up hard-to-find backers in the House and Senate, he would have to push a 5,000-person library workforce in ways bureaucrats don't normally like to be pushed.

This particular idea had one other drawback—namely, its author, who appeared to have forgotten an important distinction between him and his congressional bosses. They were elected. He was appointed. Members of Congress trade favors for votes. Billington had nothing to trade but fancy finger food and high-end chit-chat, a handicap that would put his plan, no matter how many millions of dollars in taxpayer savings it generated, on shaky ground.

"We are trying to accomplish in our time what Thomas Jefferson wanted to do when this place was founded," said Billington, blissfully undaunted by the ordeal ahead. "Jefferson believed that in order for an open society to operate as it should, you have to have an ever-increasing knowledge base. To make knowledge available, we have to keep modernizing our institutions. It's easy for libraries to fall behind and drift into a genial decline. I, for one, don't subscribe to the notion that it will happen to this one."

The Librarian of Congress is supposed to be above politics. Yet in order to turn the institution into the kind of retail outlet he wanted, Billington would need to mount a concerted political offensive, the first phase of which began with invitations to potential allies to stop by for drinks and dinner.

The night of the Harriman party, Billington was working the crowd with his usual charm, only this time there was an added incentive to be friendly. The room was literally crawling with research material. Sporting a rumpled tuxedo and an acquisitive smile, Billington was out to add whatever he could to a collection that included the original draft of the Declaration of Independence, a handwritten copy of the Gettysburg Address, and the personal papers of twenty-three presidents and 1,000 members of Congress. Should any of his VIP guests want to leave something to posterity, he would be more than happy to take delivery.

This was a normal outing for Billington, who always seems to be tracking down something. That was the case when he was attending an international library conference in Moscow in August 1991, just in time to catch the coup that eventually toppled the communists.

While others ducked for cover, Billington, a Russian expert of international renown, was busy organizing a leaflet collection project. The literature being churned out by hardliners and reformers alike created a street-sweeping opportunity of historic proportions, and Billington sent staffers out to bring back every flyer, bulletin, and manifesto they could find. The result was a printed record of three days that changed the world and another prize addition to the library's holdings.

Unlike most Washington offices that pour out endless reams of printed matter, the Library of Congress sucks it in like a giant vacuum cleaner. With its stacks open to any item deemed useful in "advancing . . . the cultural life of America," the library's current dilemma is an inevitable by-product of its overall purpose.

To keep up with the growth of knowledge, it must keep growing. And to do that means having more room and more money, two things it's been running out of since the first day it opened almost 200 years ago, with $5,000 in federal funds earmarked "for the purchase of such books as may be necessary for the use of Congress and for putting up a suitable apartment for containing them."

The Library of Congress was the first government think tank. Today, with an annual budget of $400 million and an inventory of 100 million items on 532 miles of shelves, it's more like a mental mega-mall stocked with enough information to keep inquiring minds occupied well into the next millennia.

Books, even such priceless specimens as a Gutenberg Bible, are hardly its only resource. There are 180,000 movies, dating back to the earliest known motion picture, *Fred Ott's Sneeze,* directed by Thomas Edison in 1893. Among its more than 14 million prints and photographs is the famous 1903 shot of the Wright brothers' first airplane flight. There are 39 million manuscripts, 12 million newspapers and technical reports, 10 million records in computer databases, 8 million microforms, and 4 million maps, charts, and atlases. In addition, the library houses the Congressional Research Service, a private fact-finding center for members of the House and Senate, and the U.S. Copyright Office, which each year registers (for a modest fee) more than a half-million written works.

As soon as they're made public, however, all these numbers are out of date. The library's mammoth collection increases by one item every five seconds, or about 6,000 pieces of information every day. Most of it ends up somewhere inside three buildings on Capitol Hill; the rest is sent either to a facility in Maryland or a storage site built into the side of a Pennsylvania mountain.

Washington is a city of paper trails, and one of the longest ends at the Library of Congress. Figuring out where it goes after that is Billington's biggest challenge. Figuring out where to begin is his second biggest. As much as one-third of all library material—nobody seems to know the exact amount—is uncatalogued, meaning it hasn't been given a number and shelved, and therefore is of no practical use to anyone. With so much inventory arriving and the current staff able to process only a small fraction of it, the problem is obvious. The flow of information is out of control.

"That's not true," said a library spokesman. "We have it under control. We just don't know where to put it."

Officially referred to as "arrearage," the uncatalogued mass has taken on a life of its own, and, like all things in Washington, has grown in size according to available funds. So it's only natural that Billington should want more.

Every federal bureaucracy needs a mission, ideally one that expands in scope each year to justify increased levels of congressional support. Taming arrearage was Billington's. He had promised Congress that he would have the mess straightened out by the end of the century. Trying to manage vast amounts of essentially unmanageable paper products is standard Washington work, and no one questioned Billington's commitment to the task, only his chances for success. Considering the sheer volume of incoming items, the backlog might never be eliminated. Unless, of course, the library could start selling data and use the earnings to attack arrearage full force.

Pacing around his penthouse office, which overlooks the U.S. Capitol building across the street, Billington had a lot besides books on his mind. The tall and tweedy ex-Princeton professor, given to turning conversations into lectures, faced a wide variety of daily challenges, among them thieves who walk off with a fortune in literary treasures. The most notorious, Robert Merrill Mount, a self-described "Victorian gentleman," now serving time in prison, made a brief career out of stealing rare signed manuscripts and selling them to autograph dealers.

Another nuisance is homeless visitors who sleep in hallways and wash themselves in library rest rooms. The street people, who compete for space with legitimate users, are called "special patrons," and Billington has authorized a whole set of guidelines for handling them. Infractions that merit getting kicked out of the building include: "offensive personal hygiene," "defecating and urinating in public," and "bathing in fountains." Libraries are no longer the exclusive domain of people who keep their clothes on in public.

"I came here as a lifelong library user," said Billington. "I soon discovered that the management needs of this institution and the intellectual resources of the people in it were disconnected. One of the things I want to do is get the champagne out of the bottle, and by champagne I don't mean just the merely 100 million items in the collection. I mean what's in the heads of the people who work here. That entails having a more efficient organizational structure, and maybe even bringing forward a more corporate attitude."

It's that attitude that led to Billington's plan to begin commercial user fees, and opponents faced with paying the bills were not pleased.

"The Library of Congress is a tax-supported institution," said Carol Henderson, deputy director of the Washington office of the American Library Association. "We don't want it to act like a business."

But that's what Billington wanted it to become. As a first step, he instituted a massive reorganization of the staff, a move assuring that thousands of irate library workers would do everything they could to stop him. The Library of Congress is a typical Washington bureaucracy, which means procedure matters more than results, and when a procedure, any procedure, is threatened, retaliation can be swift.

There are two kinds of government bureaucrats: the politically appointed kind, whose tenures are limited in duration, and the career kind, whose civil service jobs can be theirs for life.

It was the second variety that posed the greatest threat to Billington's success. Long-term bureaucrats, who live in constant fear of having their positions transferred, downgraded, or, in their worst possible nightmare, abolished, don't like things to change.

Following his arrival, Billington declared that the Library of Congress was in urgent need of restructuring and hired the Arthur Young consulting firm to recommend what steps should be taken. That would have been the normal thing to do in any private-sector company. In Washington, where businesslike efficiency is frowned on, it's a prescription for a rank-and-file uprising.

"Mingling management issues with budget questions increases . . . suspicion," warned a Brookings Institution study on federal productivity. Many government employees, the report went on, see performance reforms as "witch hunts to cut their salaries and criticize their work." Library of Congress workers reacted to Billington's proposals as if he were coming after them with bloodhounds.

Historian Daniel Boorstin, who called Billington "the perfect man" to succeed him as librarian, practiced a standard Washington management style of combining lofty aims and benign neglect. Boorstin wrote books and let the library run itself. Billington took a different approach. He subdivided and rearranged old divisional hierarchies, making library personnel answerable to nine different service units, each one of which reported to a management team that in turn reported directly to him.

The library's new organization chart looked like an aerial view of a craps table, with bars, circles, and arrows defining the different service areas and the relationship of each one to Billington. No librarian in the history of the institution had ever done anything this corporate.

Like Bill Clinton, Billington was a Rhodes scholar, a great many of whom seem to gravitate to careers in Washington. Which should come as no real surprise. Rhodes scholars are good at playing politics. That's how most of them got to be Rhodes scholars to begin with.

"Jim and I went over on the boat together in 1950 and have been friends ever since," said former Rep. John Brademas, president emeritus of New York University, who met Billington while the two studied at Oxford. "We were a couple of eager and optimistic young Americans at a time when that's what Americans were. . . . I don't think there was ever a doubt in anyone's mind that Jim had the candle power to do big things."

Billington came to Washington to head the Wilson Institute, a center of Sovietology during the Cold War. It was his anti-Marxist leanings that endeared him to the conservative political establishment in the early 1980s, even while his obsessive interest in Russia made many wonder what made him tick.

As U.S.-Soviet relations improved, Billington's service was much in demand at the Reagan White House. His knowledge of Russian jokes helped to liven up Ronald Reagan's summit conference exchanges with Soviet President Mikhail Gorbachev, and Billington got along so well with Nancy Reagan that she recruited him as a personal adviser in her dealings with Mrs. G. The points Billington scored with the Reagans played a big part in getting him named to his present job.

Alas, the same schmoozing skills that worked at White House receptions did not translate well to his job on Capitol Hill, where Billington came off as a stuffed-shirt dictator. His hopes to revolutionize the way the library did business sounded a snooze alarm in every department. Many employees who had been peacefully gathering dust for years came back to life. Some wrote letters to members of Congress. Others called reporters. Everywhere staffers gathered, they grumbled with resentment and plotted guerrilla campaigns against their boss.

Complaints to Congress met with a particularly warm reception. Lawmakers love tales of mismanagement in government agencies. It gives them a chance to investigate and, if they're lucky, torture some hapless official in public. The Library of Congress, long a source of conflict between the academic snobs in upper management and the workers under them, offered the ideal target for a close-to-home inquisition.

Seizing on claims that Billington's promotion policy violated equal opportunity guidelines, one subcommittee gave a library employee a temporary job until it could look into her charges. Few members needed any extra incentive to go after Billington. Politicians dislike intellectuals for the simple and well-founded suspicion that intellectuals feel the same way about them. Congress is a place for schemers, not thinkers, and when the two mix it up, the schemers usually win.

"Billington is a visionary," noted one library staffer who went to court to have his old job restored. "But he can't translate his visions into any coherent policy, and he hasn't surrounded himself with people who can."

What he surrounded himself with instead was show business. Billington started a media campaign designed to convey the idea that the Library of Congress was a fun place. The centerpiece of his effort was a slick television special. In one segment, magicians Penn & Teller took the audience on an amusing romp through Harry Houdini's personal papers. In another, Julia Child tested dishes from the library's rare recipe collection. Ted Koppel from *Nightline* played a part. Billington used glitz as a campaign tool the same way members of Congress do.

He also launched a fund-raising drive to help pay for the library's many programs and exhibits, all threatened by congressional cutbacks. The primary vehicle for bringing in donations was the James Madison National Council, an association of moneyed backers who, for a minimum of $10,000 a year, get to attend library meetings and, of course, parties. At the upper end of the scale, a $100,000 contribution buys a three-year membership. For $1 million, a donor is recognized as a "Jeffersonian" and made a lifetime member of the library's select inner circle of prime benefactors.

The Madison Council was Billington's brainchild, and he persuaded dozens of wealthy Americans to join, people like communications mogul John Kluge, the richest man in the United

States, *Washington Post* publisher Katharine Graham, and financier Laurance Rockefeller, whose last name literally means money in the bank.

Unaffected by campaign spending limitations and other nagging restrictions on how much capital he could raise, Billington was doing something no member of Congress could ever get away with, signing up rich donors without any interference from the Federal Election Commission. If a senator or representative went after fat cats the way Billington did, he'd have his ass in a sling. Which meant jealous lawmakers were all ears when library workers started turning up with their gripes.

"Sure they were jealous," said one Hill insider. "Why shouldn't they be? They don't care about making the library pay for itself. . . . They see all this money being handed out and they automatically start wondering why they're not getting any."

Billington looked like a man making a bundle by letting rich supporters sip wine and pretend to be smart. And now he wanted Congress to let him sell information, too! Even members who admired Billington's brains thought that was pushing it too far, especially for a guy who never had to beg for change at election time.

Meanwhile, back at the library a vicious war of slurs was coming to a head. After Billington hosted a group of celebrity drop-ins, a mock advice column in the library employees' newsletter made it clear that problems between administration and the staff had turned openly hostile.

"My boss has to 'entertain' prominent people who are interested in the library. Sometimes this simply consists of 'show and tell' . . . sometimes it involves more elaborate touring of the buildings, wining and dining, etc. . . . My problem is that on more than one occasion I have seen my superior display an incredibly short fuse. He blows up when the slightest thing does not go his way. . . . I'm afraid this might give a very bad impression to the very people he is trying to impress."

The rude reply: "Let's hope the library's not trying to rival the National Zoo for live-action drama."

"This is a government agency," Billington said of the in-house unrest. "Change is a long slow process. It doesn't happen overnight."

Every year, federal administrators appear before Congress to have their budgets reviewed. For most, it's a simple in-and-out process, a few questions, a pat on the back, and the traditional check-signing ceremony. Billington's visit was shaping up to be an indoor barbecue.

For months, lobbyists had been bombarding lawmakers with complaints, all of which could be boiled down to a single item of bad news: Let the Library of Congress be run like a business, and not only would the entire communications industry be adversely affected, it would be like handing over a multimillion-dollar high-tech enterprise to someone who makes Daniel Patrick Moynihan, the Senate's most insufferable know-it-all, look like one of the boys.

Billington, who underestimated the forces massing against him, immersed himself in concept polishing.

"We're an enormous throw-away society," he mused. "My task lies in the area of preservation, to preserve memory but also to make memory relevant to a highly present-minded mentality in this town and in America in general. . . ."

By the time he was scheduled to appear before Congress to justify his user-fee request, Billington's interrogators had been thoroughly briefed by all parties opposed the venture.

"The crucial issue facing the Congress regarding its library," Billington informed the senators, "is whether to provide national electronic access or to relegate the institution to the status of a passive warehouse of materials accessible only to those who come to Washington. . . .We need a wider range of funding devices to meet the needs of the institution and the people we serve."

Services the library provided free of charge, Billington pointed out, are repackaged and sold by private companies. In effect, what he was looking for was congressional authority to take back profit from the lucrative market that library resources helped to create.

But since many of the companies in that market were affiliated with influential lobbies and PACs, elected officials weren't about to let Billington set up government-approved competition.

The problem was that the idea could save taxpayers money, and even if virtually no taxpayers were paying attention, Congress couldn't just say "No." For that, outside justification would be needed, and Billington provided that all by himself.

When he had trouble coming up with specific prices for services and other sales information, Sen. Conrad Burns, a Montana Republican, saw an opening. Billington, he said, wouldn't make a very good businessman.

"Stay a *librarian*," Burns advised.

As the name implies, the Library of Congress belongs to *Congress*. Lawmakers weren't going to let it dabble in private enterprise, no matter how much economic sense it made. If there was any selling to be done, members of Congress would take care of it, and they didn't need Billington's advice on salesmanship.

His business plan was through.

For someone not used to being put in his place it was a stunning defeat. Afterward, Billington was even hinting that he might retire. He didn't want to stay on as librarian until they hauled him out "in a drool bucket," he told a reporter.

Had this been some other city, Billington might be too embarrassed to show his face in public. But this is the nation's capital, a town of infinite comebacks. It didn't take him long to return to the party circuit where all was forgiven. Besides being a launchpad for lofty ambitions, the Washington social scene is also a permanent safety net for fallen egos. Someone may be shot down by Congress or bounced around in the press. As long as he minds his manners and still has an important job title when the dust settles, he can always hobnob with the establishment.

A few months after his Senate appearance, *Washingtonian* magazine named Billington to its "A-List" of the city's 100 "top hosts" and "best guests." Criteria for selection included proximity to power, media heaviness, and "intellectual glitter." The latter category was Billington's.

Department store heiress Betsy Bloomingdale, Nancy Reagan's best friend and a member of Billington's select Madison Council, confirmed his continuing social significance.

"He's such an exciting man," she said following a council soiree. "Whenever he talks about something, you're glued to every word. . . . He's so smart."

Even if he did think he could slip one past Congress.

CHAPTER ELEVEN

LIGHTS, CONDOMS, ACTION

The 1993 Gay, Lesbian, and Bisexual March on Washington had to be one of the most thoroughly organized demonstrations in the history of modern protest. From on-site crisis intervention to a Braille calendar of events, planners thought of everything. There was even a notice in the official program asking participants to refrain from wearing "scents, colognes and perfumes so that this special occasion may be accessible to people with chemical sensitivities and respiratory problems."

Obviously, somebody forgot to tell that to Dykes on Bikes. Heedless of the tough emissions standards, more than 100 of the female motorcyclists, their exhaust pipes throbbing, roared into town the night before the big march to lead a candlelight procession of lesbians from Dupont Circle to the Washington Monument.

The bikers gunned their engines, and 10,000 lesbians from all walks of life took to the streets. But the center of attention on the one-mile route wasn't the impressive chopper formation. It was "Super Pussy," as marchers called it, a huge homemade vagina carried aloft like something out of a pornographic Macy's parade.

"We made it ourselves," said one of the half dozen women holding up the gigantic sex organ.

Everywhere along the parade route, straights and gays alike watched with equal fascination as Super Pussy passed by.

"When people have to deal with a lot of grief, they develop a sense of humor as a coping mechanism," said a female psychotherapist from Boston, who added that "showing your hurt can have a therapeutic impact."

Impact, of course, is what demonstrations are all about, and the lesbians, many of whom went topless, were stopping traffic and onlookers at every intersection. Contingents from around the country carried signs and banners identifying their organizations. "Chicago Dykes Rule" read the message on a big, purple bedsheet. Some in the march shouted "Bull Dykes Unite . . . Fight, Fight, Fight." One beefy demonstrator, her bare breasts bouncing up and down defiantly, led a group from New York in a chant that got right to the point: "Don't Fuck Men. . . . Don't Fuck Men." Which made sense. After all, these *were* lesbians.

The rally had the kind of "take-back-the-night" motif common in recent protests against various forms of male sexual aggression. Yet many of the lesbians who filled Pennsylvania Avenue appeared just as anxious to pick up babes as any guy on the singles-bar circuit.

The lesbian parade, like the rest of the gay march, was more than a challenge to the political system. It also put the Washington media to the test. News coverage of the event estimated the number of participants and included the standard quotes from organizers, but not a single newspaper or television report mentioned the one thing that stood out most of all. Super Pussy.

The *Washington Post*'s media critic Howard Kurtz blamed this and other similar omissions in overall march reporting on a brand-new set of reverse taboos. "In an age of hypersensitivity," he wrote, "the operative motto seems to be 'When in doubt leave it out,' even if crucial information is consigned to the cutting-room floor." Kurtz wondered if the same reporters and editors would have been so restrained in what they showed and told if the gay rights march "had been an anti-abortion demonstration, with the most extreme protestors holding up pictures of fetuses." His conclusion: "Probably not."

One news outlet that covered events uncensored was C-Span, the Capitol Hill cable network whose philosophy, summed up by a company spokesperson, was "Show it all." To satisfy the needs of addicted viewers and to fill air time, C-Span regularly televises federal agency hearings, newspaper editorial conferences, and just about anything else remotely related to government. Once it broadcast a bus ride by new Republican members of Congress from Washington to a meeting in Annapolis. Yet not even C-Span's six hours of uninterrupted coverage could capture the full scope of a march that touched on so many aspects of sexual self-expression.

The problem wasn't unique to news gathering. If sex is the most *special* of all special interests, it's also the most complicated to address in terms of federal policy. Government is a public activity; sex is a private one. During the gay march, it was just the opposite. Sex was out in the open, and government, or at least government officials, all seemed to disappear.

"Where are our so-called leaders?" shouted one speaker at a gay wedding ceremony held in front of Internal Revenue headquarters. "We want some action. . . .Where are the people whose salaries we pay?"

As usual, most of them were away for the weekend.

Some destinations make such perfect sense that it's hard to imagine ending up anywhere else. If you want to see a show, you go to Las Vegas. If you want to get mad, you go to New York. And if you want to make a show out of getting mad, you go to Washington. From farmers and environmentalists to poor people and animal lovers, there isn't a group, movement, or coalition anywhere in the country that hasn't made the trip. But no mass demonstration had ever challenged the body politic the way the gay march did. Clearly, this was not your usual sign-carrying, slogan-screaming afternoon of unrest.

Washington has had so many protest marches that a convenient format has evolved. First, there are speeches on the monument grounds; then a parade past the White House, with indignant fist raising for network coverage; next comes a mass gathering at the Capitol, followed by more speeches and network overhead shots, before participants head off to lobby their senators and representatives.

Making an impression on elected officials is largely a matter of getting as many people as possible into TV camera range. Politics is always a numbers game, and politicians, who can count better than anybody, respond best to big crowds. The gay march attracted one of the biggest crowds on record—a half-million by some counts—that parts of it were hanging out of hotel windows. But size in this case was part of the trouble. All groups have demands, and the long list that gay organizers brought with them contained more than a few built-in political risks.

According to the official platform, marchers wanted:

- A cure for AIDS
- No mandatory HIV testing
- Legalization of same-sex marriages
- An end to censorship
- Repeal of the ban against gays in the military
- Unrestricted safe and affordable alternative insemination
- Passage and implementation of graduated age-of-consent laws
- An end to the exploitation of youth
- An end to sterilization abuse
- Development of a national needle-exchange program
- An end to institutional and internal racism
- An end to anti-Semitism
- An end to discrimination based on sexual orientation in all programs of the Boy Scouts of America
- Restoration of the self-determination of all indigenous peoples and their cultures
- An end to economic injustice in this country and around the world

Every demand—and there were dozens more—came with its own constituency, and during four days of events each constituency put on teach-ins and mini-demonstrations to showcase its particular cause.

There were Gay and Lesbian Pilots, Queer Scouts, Lesbian Physicians, Gay and Lesbian Judges, Gay Men of Color, Lesbian

Republicans, Older Lesbians for Change, Lesbian Latinas, Drag Queens United, Gay Libertarians, Lesbian, Gay and Bi-Sexual Urban Planners.

The Queer Earth Conclave met at the "P" Street Beach to form something called an "Eldritch Circle," described in the program as a "ritual to reflect the diversity of gay spirituality, to honor our gay ancestors and to empower the participants to work for change."

Presbyterians for Lesbian and Gay Concerns conducted a seminar in a local church to "examine passages from the Bible commonly used against homosexuality and to explore interpretations of scripture that support the gay lifestyle." Appropriately, the Commerce Department auditorium was the site of a sadomasochism conference and marketplace sponsored by a group calling itself the Leather Fetish Contingent.

"Business is great," said one exhibitor of bondage and domination apparel whose own outfit appeared to be held together entirely by zippers.

All were in town to let the government know, as members of Queer Nation kept shouting, "We're queer and we're here," a variation of the same declaration every special interest makes to Congress. That's what lobbying is. One group comes to Washington and tries to get the government to treat it better than other groups. This time, though, the aim was to get the government to treat gays, lesbians, and bisexuals the *same* as other groups.

But that effort was complicated by political considerations that seemed simple compared to the identity crises some protesters brought with them. Several people gathering for a premarch drag show on the Mall called themselves "transgender lesbians," men who had been surgically altered and now want to be with women. If that was the idea, why did they have their male parts removed?

"I didn't want be with *those* kinds of women," said one of the former men.

Since the Clinton White House and gay rights activists were in general agreement on many key questions, march organizers turned their attention to Capitol Hill, where support for gay issues was less enthusiastic. In 1989, federal funding for a traveling exhibit of erotic photographs by Robert Mapplethorp sparked a series of heated confrontations between liberals and conservatives. Republican Sen. Jesse Helms became the archenemy of culture by threatening to cut off government support for the arts because of the Mapplethorp show.

On the House side, ex-Rep. William Dannemeyer from California said he wasn't only worried about "pornographic" art exhibits but about what he saw as the moral implications behind them. During an angry exchange on the floor over a proposal to put restrictions on government grants, Dannemeyer compared America to Germany prior to World War II.

"The movie *Cabaret*, which depicts the Weimar Republic during the 1920s, tells the whole story of what's going on," he said. "That movie showed the growth of toleration for homosexuality in Germany. . . . Let's not kid ourselves. Pornography and homosexuality are not . . . the cause of decline. They are the symptoms of moral decay in a society that has lost its standards."

A relatively obscure member up to this point in his seven-term congressional career, Dannemeyer made a name for himself as unofficial spokesman for the anti-gay faction in the House, a role the conservative Republican used to denounce homosexuality at news conferences and in speeches. Once he even put a detailed explanation of gay love-making techniques in the *Congressional Record*, claiming it was the public's right to know what "homosexuals do."

The passages described orgies and "other activities peculiar to homosexuality . . . such as . . . inserting dildos, certain vegetables and light bulbs" into areas not usually mentioned in government publications.

Reaction among Dannemeyer's colleagues ran from shock to anger. One outraged colleague, Rep. Andrew Jacobs, an Indiana Democrat, asked the House Ethics Committee to investigate Dannemeyer and in the process clarify standards "for placing . . . unspeakable remarks in the *Record*."

Dannemeyer's chief opponents in the House were Democratic congressmen Barney Frank and Gerry Studds from Massachusetts, the only two openly gay members of Congress. Both Frank and Studds exited the closet in front-page sex scandals that could have ended their careers, but they survived and became leading spokesmen for gay rights.

In the 1970s, gay sexual encounters proved politically disastrous for two former Republican Congressmen, Bob Bauman from Maryland and Jon Hinson from Mississippi. Bauman was charged with soliciting sex from a 16-year-old boy. Hinson was picked up for fellating a Library of Congress messenger in a House men's room. Neither lawmaker was reelected.

Studds avoided a similar fate in 1983, when he was cited for having sex with a 17-year-old male page. Refusing to beg forgiveness, as Bauman and Hinson had, Studds, a popular figure in his liberal district, took the direct approach, challenging the definition of sexual wrongdoing. "I do not believe that a relationship which was mutual and voluntary; without coercion [and] without any preferential treatment expressed or . . . implied constitutes improper sexual misconduct," he told his colleagues.

The tactic succeeded, and following a House censure, Studds resumed his duties. At the same time, another lawmaker, conservative ex-GOP Rep. Dan Crane of Illinois, who had admitted having sex with a female page, got little support in his district and resigned in disgrace.

One practical result of the Studds-Crane scandal was a complete revamping of the rules under which the Hill's hundred or so teenage pages live, work, and most of all play. A strict nighttime curfew was put into effect, and to keep the youngsters safe from lecherous lawmakers, a new Congress-proof page dorm opened.

If Studds had embarrassed the Democrats, the Barney Frank affair gave them fits. After it was revealed that a male prostitute had been doing business out of Frank's Capitol Hill apartment, the usually abrasive Harvard-trained lawyer pleaded that he was the wronged party. Frank met hooker Steve Gobie through a personal ad the congressman had placed in a Washington gay newspaper in which he referred to himself as "Hot Bottom." But it was Gobie, Frank said, who seduced and betrayed *him*.

"I was a loser. I lost money and I was embarrassed," Frank confessed at a Boston press conference the day after the *Washington Times* broke the 1989 story of his two-year liaison with Gobie. "I thought I was Henry Higgins," Frank explained, comparing what he claimed were his efforts to reform Gobie, whose criminal record included felony convictions for selling cocaine and corrupting a minor, to those of the professor in *My Fair Lady* who transformed a young cockney girl into the toast of London society. Frank employed Gobie, whose only discernible talent was selling sex, as his "houseboy," chauffeur, and personal aide.

Liberal columnist Mark Shields advised Frank to quit. Norman Ornstein of the American Enterprise, perhaps the most quoted authority in Washington, said: "The more Frank is in the news, the more he hurts the Democratic Party because the American public already believes the Democrats are out of sync with the nation's values."

The *Boston Globe*, which had always endorsed him, called on Frank to resign from Congress "for his own good and the good of his constituents." But Frank refused to go.

Instead he sent a letter of apology to supporters in his home state, admitting "What I did was wrong [but] it did not affect my public decisions or any public business." Frank told *Newsweek* that it was easy for Gobie to "con" him because as a gay member of Congress he had been deprived of "any kind of healthy emotional life." In a tactic later used by Sen. Robert Packwood to ward off accusers, he also dropped a hint that Gobie's Capitol Hill prostitution service may have had members of Congress among its clientele.

"I don't know who he's going to say was in my kitchen," Frank said. "I'm vulnerable and other people are vulnerable."

While Frank psychoanalyzed his relationship with Gobie,

many Democrats supported him publicly, praising his hard work, dedication, and candor. Several liberal House members even defended him on the House floor, an obvious contrast to the cold shoulder GOP conservatives gave Ohio Republican Rep. Donald "Buzz" Lukens when he was arrested in Columbus for having sex with a female teenager.

The difference in treatment had less to do with degrees of moral turpitude than a sexual-political double standard. Lukens and other non-gay lawmakers caught in the act were seen as dirty old men, whereas Studds and Frank were seen as victims. The gay lobby, a growing source of Democratic campaign contributions, played a key role in helping members understand the distinction. In Congress every reputation has a price. And while Lukens's may not have been worth that much, Frank's certainly was.

Privately, dozens of Democratic lawmakers wished Frank would pack up and leave, but few were willing to jeopardize their financial relationship with gay supporters by going on the record. How much influence the gay lobby could exert was particularly noticeable in the Ethics Committee, whose task it was to determine whether the Massachusetts Democrat had broken House Rule XLIII, clause one, which states that members must conduct themselves "at all times in a manner which shall reflect creditably on the House of Representatives."

For eight months, the twelve-member panel was split along party lines over Frank's punishment. Should he be given a mild reprimand or a much harsher censure? No matter what was decided, Frank's chief nemesis, William Dannemeyer, was waiting in the wings, ready to ask the House to expel him.

Finally, the committee recommended a reprimand based on two transgressions, neither of which involved sex. Frank, they decided, had fixed parking tickets for Gobie, and had written letters on congressional stationery to Gobie's parole officer. Dannemeyer's subsequent attempt to remove him from Congress failed, and after the full House voted to accept the Ethics Committee's recommendations, Barney Frank, officially decloseted and politically immune to future scandals, was free to take up the cause of gay rights in Congress.

During the 1992 presidential campaign, Bill Clinton, who received millions of dollars from gay contributors, had promised that if elected he would open the armed services to homosexuals. Almost as soon as Clinton took office, he tried to make good on his pledge. In response, conservative groups and other concerned citizens began bombarding the House and Senate with phone calls opposing the plan. The scale of public protest surprised even those who helped organize it. At one point, 50,000 calls an hour—most of them against lifting the ban—jammed congressional switchboards. In a matter of a few days, something that had never been an issue in the campaign was Clinton's first major test of strength on Capitol Hill.

On one side of the debate were the president and the gay lobby. On the other, the Joint Chiefs of Staff and its veteran allies in Congress. It was the new administration vs. the political establishment, and no two individuals better epitomized the values at odds than the two Southerners in the center of the controversy.

For Bill Clinton, the Rhodes-scholar chief executive who had avoided the draft, opening the military to gays was a civil rights question. For Democratic Sen. Sam Nunn of Georgia, who lists his occupations as "farmer and lawyer" and chairs the Senate Armed Services Committee, it was a matter of imposing liberal social policies where they didn't belong.

As Nunn worked behind the scenes to defeat Clinton's plan, Clinton went public to build a consensus among traditional Democratic support groups. Before long, the terms of the argument shifted from abstract notions about justice, equality, and patriotism to concerns about gays and straights in the service using the same shower facilities.

Nunn had wanted the job of secretary of state, but flatly denied that being passed over in favor of Warren Christopher had anything to do with his opposition to Clinton's proposal.

Clinton, on the other hand, accustomed to getting his way as the governor of Arkansas, showed he wasn't afraid to take on opponents in Congress. When Sen. Richard Shelby, the conservative Alabama Democrat, ridiculed Clinton's stimulus package, the White House showed him who's boss by eliminating several dozen NASA jobs in his home state. The president was twice as mad at Nunn. But the powerful chairman had the Pentagon on his side.

After Nunn took committee members and network camera crews on a tour of naval sleeping quarters, Clinton changed his original open-admissions proposal to one that would allow gays to serve provided they didn't announce their gaiety on military property, or, as Barney Frank put it: "As long as they didn't yell Fire Island in a crowded latrine."

The news was delivered by Defense Secretary Les Aspin, a former congressman with an advanced degree from Oxford. Clinton needed somebody to take heat from the generals as well as the gays, and Aspin was the obvious candidate. A stoop-shouldered sad sack whose body seemed molded to fit behind a government desk, Aspin lasted a year on the job before he was given a medal and relieved of his duties.

Gays, needless to say, felt betrayed by the compromise. The don't-ask-don't-tell rule agreed to by the president and Congress actually put the administration on the opposing side in several court cases involving gay service personnel who broke the rule by "telling."

Clinton, some gay leaders said, had taken their money—an estimated $7 million in campaign contributions—and run. The final insult came when organizers of the Gay March on Washington invited the president to join their big parade and they were informed he'd be out of town.

The religious right has raised millions of dollars by marketing Felliniesque gay-parade videos, and several crews from churches around the country were in Washington to videotape the mother of all gay parades. However, compared to other gay marches this one, even with its contingents of leather people and drag queens, was notable for its middle-of-the-road mildness.

One aim of march organizers was to make a good political impression. With endorsements from the NAACP, Amnesty International, the American Civil Liberties Union, the Socialist Workers Party, and the National Organization for Women, here was protest in the great tradition, even if parts of the march looked more like a campy version of the Rose Bowl Parade. There were bands with cross-dresser drum majorettes, military units, even a celebrity in a convertible, actor Dick York, the out-of-the-closet co-star of the 1960s television sitcom *Bewitched*.

"It's a great to be gay," he called out to a crowd at Fifteenth and Pennsylvania Avenue, where a group of anti-gay protestors held up a banner that read: HAVE FUN IN HELL.

One of the few unexpected moments of street theater took place at 2 P.M., when hundreds of members of Queer Nation, an organization that seemed to be in a perpetual state of whistle-blowing hysteria, suddenly collapsed along the parade route in a dramatic AIDS die-in.

A march on Washington is purely for show, and the gay march was one of the biggest shows the city had ever seen. To carry any political weight, though, the demonstrators' demands had to be hand delivered to lawmakers and, considering what some of those demands were, that would require a carefully managed lobbying effort.

"We have to side step the special-rights language," said Marla Stevens, whose job it was to help prepare more than 3,000 first-time gay lobbyists to meet their senators and representatives. "That's what killed us in Colorado."

This time, said Stevens, the political drive, organized by the Human Rights Campaign Fund, the National Gay and Lesbian Task Force, and other groups, would be much less confrontational. And to keep misunderstandings to a minimum, she and her assistants passed out a list of do's and don'ts for those new to influence peddling.

- Present your views in a clear and concise manner
- Dress appropriately
- Be on time

"We have found that parents make enormously effective lobbyists," Stevens explained. "It's hard, even for people like Jesse Helms who opposes just about everything we stand for, to look a mother in the eye and say, 'I don't care about your son or daughter.'"

Helms wasn't among the seventy-one senators who eventually signed an agreement not to discriminate against gays in hiring, but Nunn was.

Stevens said she wasn't about to censor any of the lifestyles represented in the gay community; still she admitted, some do pose a slight problem as far as lobbying is concerned.

"We told everyone to wear standard attire. But when people come in leather or in drag, we try to mix them in with mainstream types. I don't really think it bothers too many politicians. Someone wore leather to the White House, and the president didn't care."

Stevens is a full-time lobbyist for gay issues and visits lawmakers in state capitals around the country. She's gotten to know why they call it lobbying.

"I've spent half my life in hallways. That's what it takes. Political change in this country is meant to be a slow and considered process. . . . I never feel like I'm wasting my time. . . . I think we're moving in a direction that's right for the country, and we're doing it the same way every other successful organization does, by getting out and meeting the people who make laws."

But not everyone in the movement believed in gradualism.

With the deadline approaching for the White House to submit its plan on ending discrimination against gays in the military, Queer Nation decided "it was time pull out all the stops." Begun by playwright Larry Kramer in the early 1980s, Queer Nation is the performance wing of the gay movement, and when it comes to psychodrama anything goes.

The first member of Congress to feel the effects would be retiring Democratic Sen. David Boren of Oklahoma, who was charged with opposing "issues as diverse as AIDS . . . and immigration." Boren, according to Queer Nation spokesman Michael Petrelis, was an "anti-gay closet case," an irresponsible claim he planned to reveal in the first-ever "outing" of a U.S. senator.

Speaking to a handful of reporters in a meeting room across the corridor from Boren's Senate office, Petrelis said that Queer Nation "unequivocally believes" that Boren is the unnamed politician attacked by Michelangelo Signorile in his book *Queer in America*. For proof, he brought along copies of a 1978 article in the *Tulsa World* in which an opponent accused Boren of being gay during a bitterly contested Senate race. Boren denied the accusations and won the election.

Petrelis said it was necessary to raise the charges again because "now is the time to play political hardball." Exit the *New York Times*.

As other reporters left the room, it was obvious Queer Nation's game plan had backfired. Fifteen-year-old newspaper clips don't make the best evidence to start a major sex scandal. But the episode did raise a larger tactical question: Is it wise politics to turn off the same elected officials whose votes you need to win?

"Lobbying is an art form," said Marla Stevens. "You have to figure out what messages politicians need to hear, then learn their decision-making styles."

And there's another valuable lobbying lesson she's picked up over the years.

"As much as possible," she said, "we try to keep sex out of it."

CHAPTER TWELVE

ALTERED STATES

In 1929, when Chief Justice William Howard Taft persuaded Congress to appropriate $10 million for the construction of a Supreme Court building, the portly former president, as usual, was thinking big. For over 100 years, the highest court in the land had been a tenant in the basement of the U.S. Capitol, and Taft was determined that the new headquarters should be no less awe inspiring than the Parthenon.

Cass Gilbert, the architect chosen for the job, had already designed three state capitols as well as the world's first skyscraper, the Woolworth Building in New York, so he understood Taft's lofty vision. People should look up to the law, Taft believed. When they saw the Supreme Court of the United States, they should be reminded of Greek gods, not ambulance chasers.

Time would tell.

After a brief stop at the metal detector, entering Gilbert's court today is like being admitted into a maximum-security church. There's one set of guards to open the doors, another to usher spectators to their seats, and another to make sure none of them says a word. In a building where the hallways still have hand-lettered "Silence" signs, only people on official business have the right to be heard.

The court is in session Monday through Wednesday from the first Monday in October until the end of June. When John Marshall presided as chief justice almost two centuries ago, oral arguments could drag on for days. Now each side gets thirty minutes, and when a tiny red light starts flashing in front of the attorney's table, lawyers have to stop talking and sit down. The justices are on a very tight schedule, so tight that once when a case ran a few minutes into the noon-to-one lunch hour, Chief Justice William Rehnquist issued a formal apology to his eight fellow jurists, promising it would never happen again.

A Supreme Court hearing bears no resemblance to an ordinary court trial, where attorneys call witnesses and ask questions while the judge sits and listens. Here it's the other way around. The justices ask all the questions, and when they think a legal precedent is being overlooked, slighted, or abused, they tend to ask a lot.

Some attorneys, all dressed up for the occasion in cutaway coats and striped pants, hardly get a word out before a justice leans forward in his luxury La-Z-Boy and starts giving him the third degree. As other justices join in, citing cases and quoting decisions, an argument that took years to prepare can be reduced in a matter of minutes to background noise.

At this level of law the important thing is not what's said, but what's written. In the lower courts, the outcome of a case depends on the jury verdict. There's a winner, a loser, and that's that. In the Supreme Court, who did what to whom is less significant than the legal issue involved.

Any case that gets this far, regardless of the actual facts, raises some basic question of right and wrong that the justices feel requires their weighty attention. In the 1970s, an important copyright decision grew out of the case of a circus performer who got shot from a cannon.

The Supreme Court is the last stop in the American legal system, and like last stops anywhere it tends to be a catchall for strange people with strange problems. A case brought by Rev. Jerry Falwell against Larry Flynt—the former accusing the latter of libel for publishing a satirical ad in *Hustler* magazine that claimed Falwell once had sex in an outhouse with his mother—

was accorded the same thoughtful consideration as any dispute involving state governments, great universities, and multibillion-dollar corporations.

Connected to the public by the Word of Law, Supreme Court justices are America's answer to the ancient prophets, but instead of foretelling the future, they shape it by opinions pondered over for months and delivered in the form of printed pamphlets. Few are ever widely read. Yet the fact that people actually obey them is one of the miracles of democracy.

The relationship between the Supreme Court and the other branches of government can be nasty and contentious. The concept of judicial review gives the court the ultimate authority to say "Yes" or "No" to every bill that Congress passes and the president signs into law. And in a town where the working principle is "Let's think about it," that's not only an awesome responsibility. That's entertainment.

It was a Supreme Court decision on "executive privilege" in 1974 that cleared the way for impeachment proceedings against Richard Nixon. The court has declared so many congressional acts to be unconstitutional that it sometimes seems the two bodies aren't even in the same country, let alone across-the-street neighbors.

The only time Supreme Court justices are even polite to members of Congress is when they appear before them to answer questions during their confirmation hearings. The justices like to pretend to be above the messy business of politics, but if they hadn't been smart politicians when slots opened up on the Big Bench, all of them would still be pounding their gavels in obscurity.

The justices may be creations of the political system, but they don't like to show it, which is why they can be particularly tough in matters dealing with other works of political creativity. And they got their chance in 1993 when a group of voters from North Carolina challenged the constitutionality of one of that state's newly redrawn congressional districts.

• • •

After every ten-year census, state legislatures around the country take up the task of redrawing the boundaries of their respective congressional districts. The aim is to make each one conform to changes in the population so that every district in the state is roughly equal in the number of voters it contains. This process is supposed to be free of partisan manipulation. In practice, that's not how it works.

Since the party controlling the state legislature also controls the shape of each district, politics is often the only consideration. And when the North Carolina legislature redrew the boundaries of the 12th Congressional District, there was more than the usual amount of political art work involved.

Congressional incumbents dread reapportionment even more than they dread the sudden appearance of a camera crew from *60 Minutes*. At least *60 Minutes* has an audience. If the boundaries of their districts are changed, they may not have *any*. Old districts might be redrawn to include new voters, or, what's even worse, combined with another incumbent's district, forcing two veterans to fight it out in a winner-take-all battle of musical chairs for a single seat.

The power to redesign a voting map is the power to make or break careers in Congress. For years party bosses exercised their authority over the process like controlling interest in a job-placement service. Most state legislatures were once run by machines that pounded congressional districts into any shape they wanted, the idea being to concentrate friendly voters in certain areas and spread around unfriendly ones in ways they could do the least harm.

The scheme worked especially well in the South, where it was augmented by poll taxes, reading tests, and other barriers used against black voters to dilute their political strength. At one time the North Carolina constitution allowed blacks to vote only if they could prove they were descended from Confederate Civil War soldiers. As a result, before 1992, despite representing 20 percent of the state's population, blacks never made up a majority in any of North Carolina's congressional districts.

The Voting Rights Act of 1965 changed that by requiring Southern states to create special congressional districts designed to increase the chances of minority candidates. When the courts first took up the "one man one vote" issue in the early 1960s, congressional districts in Louisiana, Tennessee, and several other states had been unchanged since the turn of the century. Civil rights leaders called the new plan a fair way to correct the flaws in the old system. But North Carolina's controversial 12th Congressional District, designed to comply with 1982 amendments to the Voting Rights Act, raised legal questions that an attempt to remedy one political injustice had only succeeded in causing another.

The number of seats in the House was fixed by law in 1912 at 435, in effect making the Congress a closed shop. Congressional seats are distributed among the states according to population, and since populations are always changing, so is apportionment. In 1900, representatives from Ohio, Michigan, Indiana, Illinois, Wisconsin, and Minnesota made up almost one-fourth of the House. But the Depression and World War II spurred a population shift to the South and West that gradually changed the political dominance of middle America.

In the 1920s, Sunbelt states from the Carolinas to California had a total of 90 seats in Congress. By the 1992 elections, that number had jumped to 166—more than one-third of the entire House—with the biggest chunk, 52 seats, going to California. But California's 12 percent share of the House still doesn't beat Virginia's all-time record of 19 seats in the 1790s, which represented 18 percent of the total.

In most Southern states, large minority populations were routinely divided among several districts. After reviewing a Mississippi case in 1969, the Supreme Court found that "subtle, as well as obvious" attempts to minimize the political influence of blacks had produced discriminatory district boundaries throughout the state.

Later in a similar case, the court ruled that in order to prove a congressional district was purposely designed to exclude black voters, there had to be evidence of intentional discrimination. The justices clarified the proof requirement in 1986, when they decided that North Carolina's failure to elect a single black representative to Congress in nearly 100 years was all the evidence needed to show that the makeup of the state's districts had violated the voting rights law.

In the wake of that ruling, Democratic and Republican legislatures, often with guidance from Washington, went to work to meet new standards for minority representation. Using videographic technology that allowed them to pinpoint party strengths and weakness, politicians redrew districts in ways that would have given old-time bosses a power rush.

Computer-age political science eliminated guesswork and afforded the ruling party in states under court order the means to put a lock on every minority district. Legislatures still isolated black voters, only this time it was to maximize their strength rather than minimize it. A total of sixteen Southern and border states have been required to submit revised district maps to the Justice Department for approval, but, as recent court challenges have shown, that hasn't always guaranteed compliance with the law.

Currently, there are fifty minority districts represented in Congress. One of them, Maryland's newly created 4th, which takes in parts of the Montgomery County and Prince George's County suburbs near Washington, met all the federal standards, even though the upper and lower portions of the district are joined by a suspiciously thin line of minority neighborhoods along the eastern edge of the District between the two counties.

The courts approved the configuration of the Maryland district because it satisfied the requirement of basic "compactness," a concept recognizing that while congressional districts may look like inkblots, they should look like reasonable inkblots.

But North Carolina's 12th District stretches the theory of compactness to its limits, and beyond. The district, which looks less like an inkblot and more like an extended drip, runs along a 170-mile route through ten counties in the central part of the state from Durham to Gastonia, taking sharp right and left turns at strategic points along the way to pick up dozens of black communities. At some locations, the district is no wider than the four lanes of Interstate 85—and at others, it's no wider than two lanes.

If the 12th District didn't exist, not even Rand-McNally could have invented it.

The state legislature's first remapping attempt in 1991 was rejected by the Justice Department because the plan contained only one minority district. The next effort, which contained *two*, was given the okay, even though the finished product raised a few eyebrows in Washington.

At first the courts seemed to overlook aesthetics when it came to the creation of districts whose sole purpose was to help minority candidates win elections. But as more districts took shape, taking on stranger and stranger shapes in the process, it was inevitable that some would have to return to the drawing board.

In congressional politics, geography is destiny. That was certainly true in 1992 when voters in North Carolina's two new minority districts elected Rep. Eva Clayton and Rep. Mel Watt, both Democrats and both black.

What is distinctive about the 12th District, represented by Watt, a Yale-educated lawyer, is that for all of the territory it covers, it only takes in carefully chosen sections of certain communities. "It depends on how you define community," Watt told *Congressional Quarterly*. "It makes a lot more sense to define congressional districts in terms of communities of interest than in geographic terms."

Even before the 12th District was established, critics were crying "reverse" gerrymandering. If it had been wrong to create white majority districts in order to dilute the voting power of blacks, it was equally wrong to create black majority districts that have the same effect on white voters.

So said five white North Carolinians who sued the state, challenging its redistricting plan on constitutional grounds. But their case raised another question. By packing a minority district with black voters, had the legislature discriminated against minorities elsewhere in the state by removing black votes from other districts?

Although the Supreme Court's spectator section is generally filled with tourists, few have any idea what's going on. A quick survey revealed that none of those lined up to watch the North Carolina case had ever seen a district voting map before, but when several people outside the courtroom were shown the one in dispute, all seemed to notice the problem immediately.

"This looks ridiculous," said a woman from Ohio, voicing an intuitive grasp of the issue the justices were being asked to resolve. A New Jersey man, visiting Washington with his family, thought the 12th District looked like "modern art," an insightful observation, since that's exactly what making special districts has become.

As the justices filed into their seats, their arrival was announced by a court guard, wearing a rent-a-cop blue blazer and gray slacks. "Oyez, oyez," he proclaimed, which is French for "Hear ye, hear ye," although one official in the court's press office confessed she had no idea what it meant. After a brief reminder of the time-limit rules, Rehnquist told Robinson Everett, the lawyer representing the group opposed to the current makeup of the 12th District, to begin his argument.

"As our complaint seeks to make clear," Everett said, "this case poses the basic issue of how far a legislature may go in seeking to guarantee the election to Congress of persons of a particular race. Perhaps the best evidence is here in the form of a map."

The *map*. In a case based largely on looks, the weird configuration, which, Everett suggested, had violated every principle of redistricting and reapportionment, was a strong piece of evidence.

"Tell me," said Justice John Paul Stevens, "exactly what principles does it violate?"

"Well," replied Everett in a mellow Southern accent. "It violates the principle of compactness. . . . I will also include contiguousness."

"Compactness" and "contiguousness," while they may not be as well known as other concepts in election law, could soon become just as important in deciding how Americans vote and who they vote for.

Stevens was visibly confused. Wasn't the 12th District of North Carolina contiguous?

"Well," said Everett, seeming to draw a connect-the-dots picture in the air, "it's contiguous in a very marginal sense of the word. If there's any significance to contiguous other than, say, a point—one point where there is an infinitesimal contact—*that* violates contiguousness. Certainly it violates compactness no matter what the test is."

As the attorney went on to describe in detail the cartographic strangeness, Justice David Souter interrupted, as he often does, and tried to frame the matter in a legal context.

"So your argument . . . really isn't it . . . doesn't it rest. . . . [ahem, ahem] . . . I take it that any of these principles have been mandated either by the authority of this court or by any other authority that we would recognize. . . . Then isn't your case really based on the violation by which this particular configuration supposedly was justified?"

"That's the key to it, Justice Souter," agreed Everett, one of the five original plaintiffs in the suit and happily sensing in Souter a potential ally.

But the justice was just warming up. "Aren't they assuming that all black people will vote for a black representative, and therefore are drawing a district with a certain number of blacks in it on the assumption that since they're black, they will vote for a black representative?"

Souter, whose head barely rose above the bench, then rocked forward dramatically in his chair.

"That's using race," he announced triumphantly, "not for

community, but for the stereotypical conclusion that if you're white you will vote for a white and if you're black, you'll vote for a black."

"Justice Souter," beamed Everett, "that's exactly right!"

This line of questioning activated Justice Antonin Scalia, the court's most outspoken open-mike conservative. The prohibition against attorneys telling jokes does not apply to justices, and Scalia takes full advantage of the opportunity whenever he can.

"What about drawing lines based on registered Republicans as opposed to registered Democrats?" he inquired. "Can you do that? . . . Does the Voting Rights Act apply to Republicans?"

"Not to my knowledge," answered Everett, sounding a little nervous.

Scalia enjoys making fun of congressional writing, which is often legally sloppy, and the Voting Rights Act was one of his favorite targets. In 1991, he argued that amendments to the act covered only the election of "representatives," as the language stated, and not of local judges, as commonly understood. If by "representatives," Congress was referring to all elected officials, he commented in a dissent, then the law would also apply to "fan-elected members of baseball All-Star teams."

"Does the Fourteenth Amendment apply to Republicans?" Scalia snapped at Everett.

"I didn't think so," answered the lawyer.

"You didn't *think* the Fourteenth Amendment applies to Republicans!" Scalia shot back. "You think it's *okay* . . . to discriminate against Republicans. . . . That's very interesting."

Everett looked relieved when the red light went on, indicating his time was up.

The justices seemed to have exhausted all their energy on the plaintiff's case, and when the government's side was presented by Justice Department attorney Edwin Kneedler, most just sat back and listened. Kneedler, who looked as though he'd been awake all night perfecting his delivery, was up to the occasion. He recited the history of the law, provided data on its applica-

tion, and defended the basic idea behind the 12th District, calling it a valid remedy to correct "a pernicious evil."

Sometimes, he concluded with reference to the map, "It has
been necessary to adopt broader measures to prevent . . . purposeful discrimination, and it is on that basis—"

Red light.

The Supreme Court is the pinnacle of the justice system, and
this was one of those cases that would require the kind of wisdom William Howard Taft had in mind when he had the place
built.

Three months later, the justices had made up their minds. By
a vote of 5 to 4, they agreed with the plaintiffs on two of their
basic assertions: that North Carolina's redistricting plan segregated voters according to race and that the map used to do so
looked "bizarre."

Justice Sandra Day O'Connor, in the majority opinion, wrote
that "racial gerrymandering, even for remedial purposes, may
balkanize us into competing . . . factions; it threatens to carry us
further from the goal of a political system in which race no
longer matters."

O'Connor went on to say, "We believe that reapportionment
is one area where appearances do matter. . . . A reapportionment plan that includes in one district individuals who belong to
the same race, but who are otherwise widely separated by geo-
graphical and political boundaries, and who may have little in
common with one another but the color of their skin, bears an
uncomfortable resemblance to political apartheid."

Voting with O'Connor in the majority were Chief Justice
Rehnquist and Justices Anthony Kennedy, Scalia, and Clarence
Thomas, the court's lone black member.

Like most Supreme Court decisions on controversial political
questions, this one drew a quick response from politicians, especially from members of Congress whose careers could be directly affected.

In a press release, Rep. Mel Watt, whose political future hung in the balance, said the ruling only created confusion.

"By focusing its attention on the way North Carolina's 12th District looks, the Supreme Court seems to have ignored . . . discriminatory intent," said Watt, who believed the "decision will have little . . . value in terms of establishing a precedent for other cases."

But that hardly calmed the anxiety in Democratic circles, or the glee among Republicans, who saw a chance to have other minority districts declared invalid—and maybe turned into GOP House seats as a result.

One of the most irate critics of the court's decision was law professor Lani Guinier, whose White House rejection for a job in the Clinton administration had made her a celebrity. In her controversial writings, Guinier seemed to suggest she would favor the court's decision. In one of her articles she stated that minority districts "may perpetuate inequities" by "isolating black constituencies" and thus limiting their ability to bargain for increased political power with other groups of voters.

What could make more sense? It's hard to imagine what Clinton, or for that matter Guinier's conservative opponents, found so alarmingly radical.

But this was not the same position she took after the North Carolina ruling. In a speech to the NAACP, Guinier said, "In the name of race neutrality they were able to establish a constitutional right to challenge the district, which had in fact been drawn to remedy 100 years of exclusive and white domination. . . . The district looks funny, and what does that mean? That the district looks black. When the focus is on appearance we do not win. . . . I was history because of my strange name, strange hair, and strange writing. . . . In other words, if you're black you don't fit in."

Guinier may have a point. In Congress, though, what counts more than racial equality is winning elections, and when the outcome can be virtually guaranteed going in, all the better. If judges become strict constructionists and start applying the "compactness" theory to new congressional districts, voters wouldn't be the losers, politicians would be.

The strange shape of so many minority districts says something about race relations in America. But not what most people may think. The reason it's hard to create such districts without resorting to Salvador Dali techniques is because racial integration in many parts of the country is making large concentrations of minority voters harder to find.

Politicians like to ghettoize the electorate into uniform blocs: urban blacks, suburban whites, and rural poor. It makes elections easier to manage, and thus easier for those already in office to stay there.

Automatic incumbency isn't a product of social diversity or mixed opinion. Which is why voting districts that look like the one in North Carolina have less to do with past racial injustice than with modern-day political ambition. It wasn't racism the loudest critics of the court's decision were worried about. It was reality.

CHAPTER THIRTEEN

LIFE AFTER CONGRESS

For several days after first arriving in New York City, former California congressman Tony Coelho actually found himself wondering where money comes from.

"It really had me confused," he said, looking out the window of his office at Wertheim Schroder & Co., an international investment firm he joined shortly after quitting Congress in 1989. "There were dozens of stores and restaurants on every block. How did they all stay in business?"

That's when the ex-head of the Democratic Congressional Campaign Committee—and once his party's most prolific fundraiser—realized that in New York all commerce is essentially vertical.

"The customers are up there," he said, smiling and pointing to the skyscrapers high above his mid-size executive suite. The experience taught Coelho a valuable lesson about life after Congress: Getting to the top in his second career would mean applying everything he'd learned about money to a whole new economic architecture.

There was a time when almost any former member of the House or Senate who wanted to could parlay his contacts into a comfortable job as a Washington expert. That's still true in some cases, especially for leadership types like Coelho who come with political connections most companies drool over. But for others, the future employment picture may be changing.

If the anti-incumbent turnover on Capitol Hill continues at its present pace—the last elections resulted in a 25 percent departure rate—more politicians than ever before will be reentering the work force. And with little to sell besides access, the competition could soon become fierce.

Coelho may be fortunate to have beaten the rush. But his easy transition from Washington to Wall Street had nothing to do with luck. For that, he credits his eleven years of hard work in the House where he raised more than $34 million in campaign donations and became what he calls a trained and tested "people person"; make that a people-with-money person.

"It all comes down to a matter of trust," he explained. "What counts is your ability to get people to believe in you, and if you do, they'll bring business your way." It was the same in Congress, with one big difference.

"In Washington, people trusted me and never had any idea what I did with their money. Here, they can keep track of it every day."

Within a year after joining Wertheim Schroder, Coelho produced over $160 million in new accounts, many from the same labor organizations and special-interest groups he collected donations from in politics. "I always have my tentacles out all over the place," he said, only now they're wrapped around $6.5 billion in assets. Big campaign contributors like the Sheet Metal Workers, the Electrical Workers, and the Ladies Garment Workers Union happily hand him funds to invest.

When Coelho gave up his House seat in the midst of a junk bond scandal, over eighty campanies wanted to hire him. He could have gone into television, consulting, or corporate communications. Just narrowing down the list of possibilities to three final choices took several months.

"I wanted to prove to myself that I possessed personal abilities that had nothing to do with politics," he said, looking back on his job hunt. But he noted with obvious pride that his most salable skills came straight out of Congress.

• • •

Capitol Hill, in fact, provides the best job-training program in government. But unlike Coelho, who only spends part of each week in Washington, many recent congressional alumni never left town. Not counting those retiring on generous inflation-proof pensions, of the 121 departing members in 1992, more than 40 percent followed the path of least resistance into "government relations," otherwise known as lobbying.

"There's an absolute flood of ex-members," said lobbyist Victor Schwartz, who views the phenomenon as an inevitable result of the current reform movement, which has created a buyer's market in used elected officials. "The ones that are thoughtful and knowledgeable hold their value. They're the diamonds. But there are an awful lot of bozos out there too."

Former politicos can be found in trade associations, consulting firms, and law offices. A few of the bigger names have opened companies of their own. Ex-Rep. Vin Weber from Minnesota became the Weber Group; ex-Rep. Thomas Downey from New York is Thomas Downey & Associates.

While awaiting sentencing on federal extortion and racketeering charges, former Massachusetts Rep. Nicholas Mavroules busied himself with some "limited strategic consulting" out of his home.

Not many professions are better than politics at preparing their dropouts and losers for potentially rewarding new careers doing basically the same thing they did in their old ones. In reality, all most of them need is a phone and they're schmoozing for dollars all over again.

The constantly revolving door between the legislative branch and the private sector always swings faster after elections, when lame-duck lawmakers get busy advertising themselves to potential employers.

Anti-lobbying legislation that took effect in 1993 prevents former members of Congress from engaging in business on the Hill for one year after leaving office. Nevertheless, in a line of work where reinventing yourself is an ongoing process, the wait amounts to a mere rest stop on the road to greater earning power.

With seven-figure salaries the prize, it doesn't take long for most to restart their engines. Here's a letter written by former Republican Rep. Chuck Douglas following his 1990 election loss and mailed to seventeen law firms in Washington and Boston.

Dear Managing Partner:

Having just been defeated in an upset race for re-election to Congress, I am now looking to renew my life in the law. As a member of Congress grandfathered under existing rules of ethics, I may begin any representational work without delay. . . .

From 1970 to 1974, I served as a lobbyist for private clients and the governor of New Hampshire. From 1985 to 1989, I represented the New Hampshire Mortgage Bankers Association and the New Hampshire Homebuilders Association in our legislature. . .

I enjoy the practice of law and wanted to contact you to open up this new and exciting possibility for both of us.

Sincerely,
Chuck Douglas

The "new and exciting" possibility referred to by Douglas is part of a political economy that makes lobbyists and other access agents among the best paid middlemen in the business. "We're the lubricant that makes the machinery run better," brags Victor Schwartz. "Government wouldn't work without us." Schwartz loves what he does. But crossover elected officials shy away from the lobbyist label.

"Lobby? That's certainly not what the position is all about," outgoing Democratic Rep. Glenn English of Oklahoma told the *Washington Post*. In late 1993, English announced he would be vacating the House seat he'd held for eighteen years to become president of the National Rural Electric Cooperative Association. As chairman of the House Agriculture subcommittee, he had close dealings with NRECA, an organization of telephone and electricity companies that spends about 10 percent of its $90 million annual budget on lobbying.

"I have devoted much of my service in Congress to improving rural opportunities and the quality of life," English said at a good-bye press conference. "[Joining] NRECA will afford me the chance to continue these efforts on a nationwide scale."

And quitting Congress in mid-term gave English the chance to leave politics without losing an election. That's a distinction that means a lot in a city that loves winners.

When he was in the House collecting and dispensing millions of dollars in political contributions, Tony Coelho's Capitol Hill office was known as "the confessional." It was, former colleagues recall, a place where they could go to get things off their chests.

As chairman of the DCCC, Coelho, who once studied for the priesthood, not only handed out money to House members but also listened to their sins. People came to see him with financial problems and family problems, in many cases telling him more about themselves and their troubles than they ever intended.

In the quid-pro-quo world of Washington, politicians who wouldn't trust one another with their car keys trusted Coelho with their deepest, darkest secrets. What he gave them in return, he said, wasn't penance but "compassion" and "inner peace," often accompanied by generous campaign donations from the party bank.

Political money, for Coelho, was never just cash. It was a sign of belief, a symbol of something far greater than access or clout. Whether it came from individual voters, big corporations, or other politicians, money was part of a bond that joined people to one another and to causes they believe in. The more money, the stronger the bond, and the stronger the bond the greater the likelihood it would never be broken. Which is why ex-senators and representatives often go to work for the same businesses they once protected and/or hit up for cash in Congress.

No plea for campaign contributions had ever been so elevated. Coelho had succeeded in putting the dirtiest business in politics on the same moral plane as giving money to the missions. The spin was so high-concept, it was almost spiritual.

The chief source of Coelho's power in Congress, aside from his close relationship with hundreds of members, was his ability to produce huge amounts of so-called "soft money," the polite term for corporate and private donations earmarked for party activities rather than candidate spending. The impolite term might be "payoffs," but Coelho never considered incoming cash a gratuity for services rendered.

In his six years heading the DCCC, Coelho raised soft money from labor unions, trade associations, and other special-interest groups. Pamela Harriman personally gave him thousands of dollars, including a $400,000 interest-free loan to pay for a state-of-the-art party communications center. Soft money built the Democrats' new headquarters in Washington; it paid for legal advice and network air time. Soft money didn't make the Democrats as rich as the Republicans, but it came close. And Coelho was the chief paymaster.

Coelho became one of the leaders in his party despite the fact that he had less seniority than half the House Democrats. "His relentless pursuit of influence [has left] a few of his potential rivals wondering what hit them," reported the 1988 edition of *Politics in America.*

There was no end to Coelho's schemes for collecting funds. One of his most lucrative was a come-on known as the Speaker's Club, which, for annual fees up to $15,000, gave lobbyists the opportunity to serve "as trusted and informal advisers to the Democratic Members of Congress."

Tony Coelho knew how Washington worked. A six-term congressman from Northern California farm country, he was a virtual soft-money machine, and, with his own personal PAC, the pastoral-sounding Valley Education Fund, a reliable dispenser of payments to needy candidates.

Then came the scandal.

In 1986, Coelho bought $100,000 worth of Drexel Burnham

Lambert junk bonds, the high-risk, high-yield investment vehicle popularized by Drexel's infamous financial planner Michael Milken. The deal was financed in part by Thomas Spiegel, a Beverly Hills savings-and-loan executive, and while Spiegel's $50,000 loan to Coelho was perfectly legal, it had the appearance of an attempt to buy political favors, which Coelho denied. The investment earned him $12,000 during the six months he owned it. It wasn't in the same category as Hillary Clinton's $100,000 windfall in cattle futures, but it still raised a lot of eyebrows.

When the junk-bond purchase first made headlines in May 1989, Coelho called it an accounting error. Later, after the true nature of the deal came to light, he abruptly announced he was giving up his congressional seat and ending his climb up the House leadership ladder. The move was hailed as a selfless gesture by nervous Democratic party officials, still reeling from revelations about Speaker Jim Wright, whose financial activities had also forced him to quit.

In a year when congressional misdeeds seemed to erupt every week, the two resignations just days apart sent shock waves through the Hill. This wasn't just a couple of unlucky members caught with their pants down. Coelho and Wright represented an entire decade's worth of wheeling and dealing by hundreds of lawmakers in both parties.

For Wright, who went back to Fort Worth to speak, consult, and build an exact replica of his House Speaker's office, most of the harm his case could do was already done. His fruitless pleading before the Ethics Committee was said to have left the hearing room carpet covered in knee prints. "Let me give you back this job you gave me, as a propitiation for all this season of bad will," he said in a bitter farewell speech to the full House. "Let that be total payment."

But Coelho, whose rapid departure helped him circumvent a full-blown ethics probe, was credited with saving the institution and his party considerable embarrassment. "Some people say I used it as an excuse to get out, and it might have been," Coelho conceded, reflecting on a decision that relieved anxious friends and foes alike. "I knew I couldn't stay."

After leaving his job, Coelho blamed the media for fanning the ethics controversy, pointing out that Congress was cleaner than ever. "When I came here twenty-five years ago the cash flowed freely," he told the *Los Angeles Times*. "If you wanted certain things done, you handled it with cash." Politicians "didn't have to disclose anything, and they got away with everything."

Many who had watched Coelho work said he would do well in the world of private, as opposed to public, finance. And he has. After four years at Wertheim Schroder, he's president and CEO of the company's multibillion-dollar investment services, where his job is providing the same kind of personal attention to people's money needs as he did in Congress—only on a much larger scale.

Wertheim Schroder counts some of the country's richest corporations among its clients. It takes $1 million just to sit down and talk business.

"People have to feel confidence in what you're offering, whether you're managing funds or taking care of them with legislation," said Coelho. Remove the element of trust, and you have nothing to sell. The problem is that trustworthiness is one of those qualities that takes years to establish.

"The thing that intrigues me . . . is how important relationships are. . . . You have strong relationships that convert into business, and you maintain them because it's good business. That's politics. That's the investment world."

In his office at Wertheim Schroder's Manhattan headquarters, Coelho keeps two books on prominent display: a Bible and a collection of meditations entitled *A Truthtelling Manual and the Art of Worldly Wisdom*, written by a seventeenth-century Spanish Jesuit. The latter volume was a present from hotel heir Baron Hilton, who shares an interest in the religious order Coelho once wanted to join.

"That book got me through my crisis," said Coelho as he flipped through the pages. After a brief search, he found the passage he was looking for.

"'Never cry about your woes,'" he read. "'To make lamentation only discredits you.'"

The author, Baltasar Gracian, the sort of Machiavellian monk the Jesuits were famous for producing, warns against whining about insults and bad press. "A man of sense," he wrote, "will never publish abroad, either the slights or the wrongs he has suffered, but only the honor in which he is held, for it will serve better to constrain his friends and restrain his enemies."

The junk-bond scandal may have left his altar-boy image tarnished, but Coelho survived the ordeal—thanks largely to the impeccable timing of his exit—and even used it, he claimed, to strengthen himself for the rigors of his career change, which actually weren't all that rigorous, to hear the behind-the-scenes activity that paved the way.

Wertheim Schroder managing director Alan J. Blinken was in Mexico City when he heard the news of Coelho's resignation from Congress. "I knew we had to have him," said Blinken, who phoned Wertheim Schroder president Steven Kotler, who immediately got in touch with Coelho.

The phone call, one of dozens Coelho received that day, made an impression. Blinken had been a fund-raiser for Vice-President Al Gore's 1988 presidential campaign and admired Coelho for his politics and financial savvy, especially, said Blinken, for the way he saw "money as a way to do good." Coelho's congressional ethics problems in Washington did not concern him.

That's now the same reaction of many who know Coelho, even Republicans, who were the main victims of his soft-money offensives. Rep. Newt Gingrich, who once said Coelho had "raised extortion to an art form," these days considers him a valuable source of tips. Coelho said he also had gotten to know and like the late Richard Nixon, another politician whose ethics were called into question.

"It began before I left office," he recounted, acknowledging that the relationship might have seemed strange to some people. "We didn't see eye to eye philosophically, but there are lots of things we talked about." One of them was money.

But the friendship may have gone deeper than that.

"Tony is our Dick Nixon," said one prominent lobbyist. "They're both from California. They were both driven from politics. And both probably felt no one ever truly understood them. I think Nixon saw a lot of himself in Tony and vice versa."

After Washington, life has a way of smoothing out the political differences between Democrats and Republicans. As the need to be reelected is replaced by the need to get rich, old adversaries not only find themselves seeking each other's advice but working together.

Take, for example, the Carlyle Group, a Washington "merchant bank" founded in 1988 by former Jimmy Carter White House staffer David Rubenstein. For a fee and sometimes a piece of the action, Carlyle matches investors (often impressionable foreigners) with needy American companies (often ones that do business with the government). The firm, which employs former Defense Secretary Frank Carlucci and former Secretary of State James Baker, gets input from a cross section of onetime political foes who have since become allies in commerce. Bush's CIA Director Bill Gates, Clinton consigliere Vernon Jordan, and Nixon aide Fred V. Malek are all in the company's Rolodex of friends and advisers.

Malek is also a friend of Coelho's. The former White House political director, the subject of by reports that he once ordered a head count of Jews working in the Nixon Labor Department, sought out Coelho's counsel on repairing his damaged reputation. The two discovered they had a lot in common, and according to Coelho, Malek, president of another big investment firm, became "a mentor of sorts."

In a way Coelho has become a mentor himself. With members of Congress leaving their political careers in record numbers, Coelho's success story is an inspiration to former lawmakers and to many others facing the imminent prospect of early retirement.

He said he knows what it's like to be an outcast, and not just because he had to give up his job in the House. A victim of epilepsy, he credited the condition with being indirectly responsible for getting him into politics.

When his disability was first diagnosed in 1964, the Los Angeles seminary he was attending promptly dismissed him. In those days, he pointed out, the Catholic Church regarded the disease as a sign of possession by the devil. When they heard the news, his Portuguese parents, who owned a farm in Northern California, didn't take it much better. They thought the family had been cursed and threw Coelho out of the house.

"I became suicidal and almost drank myself to death," he said, tilting back in his chair and staring at the ceiling. "I was down about as low as you can get. I know what it's like to think there's nothing to live for."

But his epilepsy and its unhappy side effects turned out to be an important political asset. One of the reasons he's so good at asking people for money, he said, is that he isn't afraid they'll say no. "After being through what I have, getting the door slammed in your face means nothing."

Fate can be full of pleasant surprises. In a change of fortune that could only happen in Hollywood, a priest introduced young Coelho to comedian Bob Hope. He was invited to move in with the Hopes and stayed for seven months, helping out around the entertainer's estate. When Hope suggested that he go into politics, Coelho wrote to former Rep. Bernie Sisk, a Democrat who represented the district where he grew up. Sisk gave him a job in Washington, and Coelho took it from there.

Not long after he resigned his seat in Congress, Coelho called Hope to ask him what he should do. "He said, 'Try investment banking.' So I did. He gives good advice."

Coelho doesn't think that striking it rich since leaving the Hill has changed his commitment to those in need, a commitment officials at Wertheim Schroder say gives the company a valuable image for caring, a quality not normally associated with Wall

Street. When the late homeless advocate Mitch Synder invited members of Congress to spend a cold winter night with him on a Washington steam grate, Coelho was among the few who accepted. After he left office, Coelho lobbied his former colleagues on behalf of the Americans with Disabilities Act, which he had co-sponsored.

"Tony's still a priest," offered an acquaintance.

His soft spot for the downtrodden also led to his defense of John Mack, an influential Hill staff director before a series of newspaper stories in 1989 detailed his savage attack on a woman fifteen years before. Coelho, who knew of Mack's background, had been an investment partner with him in several real estate ventures. After news of Mack's past came out, Coelho and Wright both tried to help, but with problems of their own to contend with, there wasn't much either could do. Mack eventually resigned his job, and now works as a Washington lobbyist.

The story, which Coelho preferred not to talk about, illustrates the kind of closed and protected society the Congress of the United States really is. The Hill's network of political contacts functions like an elaborate buddy system, protecting members and favored staffers as long as their jobs last and giving them every tool needed to capitalize on business opportunities when their political careers come to an end.

Tony Coelho's last day in office happened to coincide with his forty-seventh birthday. Colleagues held a going-away party, and it was clear by the overflow turnout that his drawing power was as strong as ever. People came to honor a man they regarded as a martyr to the cause that concerns every member of Congress— raising money.

No one in the crowd blamed Coelho for cutting corners or bending the rules. In the cash-intensive 1980s, his contributions to his party were greater than his faults. If it hadn't been for Coelho's perseverance, some suggested, the Reagan-era GOP would have spent the Democrats into oblivion. But to those looking down the road, Coelho was and still is a postpolitical role model. Several lawmakers have let him know they, too, are considering a move to investment banking. "I'm not going to name names," Coelho said. "But sure, I've been approached by guys who are thinking about leaving."

If the idea of congressional term limits is to eliminate careerism from politics, the outcome, Coelho predicted, will be just the opposite.

"The moment somebody gets elected the clock starts ticking down. . . . That's when the job hunt starts. In California, you can go down the list of people in the legislature who found the jobs they wanted and quit before their terms were up."

Coelho knows the feeling. "You reach a point in your life," he said, "where you want to be paid a decent wage for what you do."

He reached that point, and he's not looking back with any regrets. Actually, he's looking back with a the idea of making money. Coelho is part of a group of Democrats and Republicans who recently bought a Washington consulting firm that keeps track of legislation for corporate clients. For a man with "politics in his blood," the purchase is a perfect match of old and new talents.

Coelho's skills could take him only so far on the Hill. "A very important politician, a name you'd recognize, called up the other day and asked me what they think of us on Wall Street," he said, pronouncing "us" like someone who's put a lot of psychic distance between him and his old career. "And you know what I told him? They don't."

It's not that Coelho has forgotten where he came from. He's just moved past politics to the next logical phase in his financial development. Few of his former colleagues could do the same, he snapped in a terse comment on government efficiency. "They don't produce."

Coelho, on the other hand, has always produced, even when federal restrictions imposed an unnatural ceiling on his production levels. He raked in millions during his days in Congress, and now he's doing the same thing with even better results in the private sector.

Building relationships and increasing contacts, he said, "that's what I've always been good at. That's what I know how to do."

He may have honed his talents on Capitol Hill, but after an eleven-year career of supporting other people's spending habits, it was time to heed the call of the profit motive himself.

Some ex-lawmakers never get congressional politics out of their systems. For Coelho it was easy. And it wasn't because a special prosecutor was breathing down his neck. It was in a sense a matter of principle.

"What is government?" he asked. "It's a money game. But everybody in Congress is embarrassed to talk about it. . . . They're embarrassed by the money they give out, embarrassed by the money they raise, embarrassed to vote for their own salaries. . . . To me, it was a big facade. Everybody knew what they were doing. They just pretended they were doing something else, that the game they were playing was about public policy when in reality it's all about money."

And that, he said, is the difference between Wall Street and Capitol Hill.

"Here you're supposed to put runs on the scoreboard. On the Hill you have to make believe the scoreboard doesn't exist."

He's happy, he said, to be retired from Washington, with its campaign reforms, outside-income caps, and other barriers to the free flow of cash, happy to be someplace at last where no one pretends that "money" is a bad word.

BOMBS AWAY

If House Minority Leader Bob Michel is not Capitol Hill's last gentleman, he certainly has to be its last Rotarian. When the ever-affable Michel announced his retirement from Congress in 1993 after nearly four decades in office, the event not only marked the end of a long career but the end of a political era.

There would be a big difference, he told a Washington news conference, between his accommodating style of leadership and the more confrontational approach favored by most of his younger colleagues. The old guard was "giving way to a new generation," Michel said, adding, he "was really much more comfortable operating [the way] we did when I first came to Congress."

That was back in the late 1950s, an age of comparative innocence on Capitol Hill. Of course, lawmaking could be mean and nasty then too, but mean and nasty in those days was a far cry from what goes on now.

Michel, who comes from Peoria, Illinois, the spiritual epicenter of Middle America, asked his GOP "troops" to avoid "fratricidal" bitterness and to be "careful about how you wage your campaigns . . . Please, please don't let [them] interfere with what we ought to be doing as a party."

The combat metaphors were no coincidence. Michel may be an advocate of peaceful coexistence; however, the same can't be said of others in Congress. For Republicans and Democrats in both houses, the Hill has become a theater of almost constant conflict. Bipartisan alliances occasionally form around such issues as free trade or health care, but these are only brief time-outs from the ongoing hostilities.

"I'm frustrated by the . . . culture of this town and by the way it reverberates out into negativism around the country," Bill Clinton said in an interview with *Rolling Stone* magazine at the end of his first year in office.

"I just have to keep working on it. Eventually the results will pile up and pile up and pile up, consequences will ensue, things will change and people will begin to grow more sunny."

Despite his rosy rhetoric, the president was showing telltale signs of combat fatigue.

"I have fought more damn battles here for more things than any president has in twenty years, and not gotten one damn bit of credit," Clinton said, as the interview touched the raw nerve of congressional relations. "I have fought and fought and fought and fought. . . ."

In what could be the city's first suicide memo, White House lawyer Vincent Foster wrestled with the same dilemma. Washington, he wrote, is a place where "ruining people is considered a sport." But the poor guy got it all wrong. The kind of personal attacks by political foes that apparently pushed Foster over the edge aren't sport. They're serious business, and most of the credit for making it that way belongs to Michel's successor: Minority Whip Newt Gingrich.

The foremost practitioner of creative destruction in the House, Gingrich turned the rivalry between Republicans and Democrats into guerrilla warfare. His campaign of liberal cleansing, first conceived in the late 1970s, called for launching a nonstop assault on Democrats in Congress—and on Congress itself. Let voters know what a mess members of the majority party had made of things, the strategy went, and they would soon elect Republicans to take their place.

That's not exactly what happened. Nevertheless, Gingrich's crusade had an impact. By targeting Democratic leaders, Republicans shifted the focus of congressional politics from issues to individuals.

The speeches Gingrich made were such a hit with GOP office seekers that his private PAC sent out lists of key words and phrases so aspiring lawmakers could sound "just like Newt."

"Read them. Memorize as many as possible," said the accompanying instructions. "Apply these words to your opponents, their record, proposals, and their party: 'them' . . . 'sick' . . . 'liberal' . . . 'traitors' . . . 'taxes' . . . 'spend' . . . 'lie' . . . 'cheat' . . . 'corrupt' . . . 'radical' . . . 'incompetent' . . . 'waste.'

"Use these words to define your campaign and your vision of public service: 'us' . . . 'truth' . . . 'courage' . . . 'children' . . . 'family' . . . 'liberty' . . . 'light' . . . 'reform' . . . 'strength' . . . 'help' . . . 'pride' . . . 'dream' . . . 'freedom.'"

When the Democrats retaliated with a counterattack on the GOP-controlled White House, all ideological hell broke loose. One party bashed Congress, while one bashed the presidency. The resulting state of war put both branches on ready alert. Special investigations, cabinet appointments, nominations to the Supreme Court—any false move, any policy disagreement on or off the Hill is an opportunity for each side to lay waste to the other. Add to the congressional power to make laws, the power to make life miserable for whatever public official lawmakers in either party dislike, and Congress isn't an impediment to good government. It's a legislative doomsday machine.

Washington didn't always work this way. The federal system of checks and balances is based on a cooperative division of powers. As strange as it seems, there was actually a time when party politics helped to facilitate the process. The party running the White House usually ran Congress too, and when voters decided it was time for a change, they gave the opposition its turn. Things haven't operated that efficiently in years.

Since 1953, except for a two-year period during the Reagan

administration when Republicans had a majority in the Senate, Congress has been the Democrats' stronghold. The White House for more than half that time has been occupied by Republicans. Bill Clinton was the first Democratic president elected in sixteen years, but that was no guarantee he would get along any better with a Democratic Congress than his GOP predecessors had. During most of Clinton's first year in office, he did noticeably worse, as portions of his own party turned against him on issue after issue from taxes and trade to defense.

Confronted with the same dilemma on a somewhat different scale, Russia's President Boris Yeltsin simply declared his country's parliament out of business. When that didn't work, Yeltsin removed obstinate lawmakers from office by blowing up their headquarters. That's one way to eliminate gridlock.

Although Clinton was quick to support Yeltsin's decision, there's a less than fifty-fifty chance that bombarding the U.S. Capitol would have the same effect. For more than half the year—thanks to vacations, foreign junkets, and golf tournaments—our legislators aren't even in the building.

People's current disdain for politicians is a reflection of politicians' obvious dislike for one another. It's hard to respect a profession that gives itself so much bad publicity.

If the 1992 elections were a referendum on reform, the elections of 1994 will be a referendum on "the reformers." And should the one-quarter turnover trend continue, states won't need to pass term-limit laws.

At this point, though, the grassroots momentum could be hard to stop. A revival of populism, has given rise to movements across the country intent on cleaning up Congress by force. But no form of congressional improvement will drive out every type of abuse, and the kind of extermination project now in progress may only succeed in driving some of the worst pests deeper into the hidden recesses of the institution.

The problems Congress faces are as much managerial as they are moral. Assuming the goal of reform is getting the government to function more effectively, what's needed, more than changes in the election law, is a structural overhaul of the whole legislative system. The Hill's bloblike accretion of power needs to be contained, committee chairs folded, and the congressional workweek rearranged to be longer than the congressional weekend.

People want to see leaders lead, opponents oppose, and defenders defend. And to that end more of what goes on in the House and Senate needs to be made public. Televising floor proceedings, entertaining as they are, doesn't show what members do all day or explain why it costs so much, something lawmakers themselves only seem willing to divulge in plea bargain agreements.

Unfortunately, Congress alone has the authority to fix itself, and, as history demonstrates, that's one power it will only exercise under the threat of heavy collateral damage if it doesn't.

To listen to elected officials, *they're* the hardest working men and women in America. But when whole careers are spent running for office, what most politicians work hardest at isn't upgrading their job performance it's enhancing their reelection chances. After a few years on the Hill, what incumbents learn to do best is campaign. In campaigns, however, promises to change Congress are cheap and usually forgotten once the votes are counted.

Embarrassed into action by Rep. Jim Inhofe, an Oklahoma Republican, the House in 1993 reluctantly passed a bill that eliminated at least one of the ways members can get away with saying one thing and doing another.

A lawmaker's voting record is like a baseball player's batting average. To know how your representative in Congress voted is to know whether or not you're getting the service pledged at election time. Not all legislation, though, makes it to a floor vote. Politicians like to avoid "unsafe" issues. Which is why questions like a balanced-budget amendment, as one example, are often kept locked up in committee where they can do the greatest number of members the least amount of harm.

In the past, the only way to get a House bill unlocked was

through a "discharge petition," something that needed supporting signatures from more than half the members in order to take
effect. The rule was designed to be difficult. Since it was adopted nearly sixty years ago, it's only worked thirty-one times. As
an added safeguard, names on a discharge petition were only
made public if the petition succeeded. In this way, lawmakers
could say they favored a particular piece of legislation that
might be stalled in committee, but no one would ever know if
they had signed up to help free it. Inhofe's bill threatened to end
the secrecy.

Predictably, the measure was kept in committee, so Inhofe circulated a discharge petition to have it released. Prevented by law
from revealing the names of those who had signed the petition, he
instead gave the names of all those who hadn't to the *Wall Street
Journal*, which published them on its editorial page. Inhofe's petition soon had the 218 backers needed to bring the discharge bill
to a vote on the floor, where it passed by a wide margin.

Traditionalists, who like the old way the game is played, saw
the win as one more rude assault on Capitol Hill customs. "The
House may become more responsive, but only at the cost of its
deliberativeness," warned *Washington Post* columnist David
Broder, who complained that change would expose members to
more telephone calls, more letter-writing crusades, more pressure to make hard decisions. But isn't that what politicians are
supposed to be exposed to? When things go on behind closed
doors, only the people with access know what's going on. Open
the doors, and the value of access is reduced. It's not hard to see
why some reporters like the old system better.

Most people concerned about the performance of Congress
aren't concerned with how it works, only *that* it works—and
works for them.

When Democratic Rep. Bobby Rush from Illinois was asked
what he thought of long-awaited plans by Congress to revamp
some of its internal procedures, the former Black Panther said
that his Chicago constituents weren't interested. "They want to
see a product," he told reporters. "They're not necessarily inter-

ested in the inner workings of how that product is produced."

They're not alone.

In Washington, the production of anything is less important than funding it. Politicians, who know the accounting system, know there will always be more money to spend on more lame-brain projects. If Congress were a corporation it would have had to declare bankruptcy long ago. But the country didn't go bust after the savings-and-loan bailout. Nobody filed for Chapter Eleven when the plug was pulled on the Superconducting Super Collider. So why should politicians care what product is produced or not produced? Or what it costs? Wasting Washington money not only means never having to say you're sorry, but never having long to wait for more.

Bill Clinton, the man who promised to reinvent government, was soon buying votes in Congress the same way everyone else does. If presidents want to look presidential, it's going to cost them. On the eve of the make-or-break decision on NAFTA that capped his eventful first year as chief executive, Clinton had the checkbook ready.

Citrus subsidies went to Florida. Price supports to the Ohio broom industry. Every bill that makes it to the House or Senate floor is another opportunity to deal. Even Newt Gingrich showed up at the White House during pre-NAFTA negotiations to dispense his wise counsel and carry home a thank-you treat.

Whether a free-trade agreement, or any other measure, will help or hurt the nation is of minor significance in the give-and-take of lawmaking. To get the votes it needed, the administration had to pay, and the only thing that ever matters on Capitol Hill is how much.

"Yes, there are members of Congress who came and asked me for things," said Clinton, stressing that he never for a minute considered the payoffs to be bribes. "These are people concerned about the problems in their districts."

When the final tally was in, passage of the trade bill ended up costing U.S. taxpayers $3 billion, or roughly $15 million a vote.

On the Hill, they call that a *very* good day at the office.

INDEX